AF559998

ECO-TOXICOLOGY AND ECO-TECHNOLOGY

Edited by
Dr. Pawan Kumar 'Bharti'
Centre for Agro-Rural Technologies (CART-India)
20, Jamaalpur Maan, Raja Ka Tajpur
District: Bijnore – 246 735 (U.P.)
(India)
&
Prof. (Dr.) Mona Saad Ali Zaki
Department of Hydrobiology
National Research Center, Cairo, (Egypt)

Associate Editors
Dr. Abhishek Swami
Dronacharya College of Engineering
Greater Noida - 201 306 (India)
&
Mr. Jaswant Ray
Institute for Industrial Research & Toxicology
Ghaziabad (U.P.) (India)

DISCOVERY PUBLISHING HOUSE PVT. LTD.
NEW DELHI-110 002

Published by:
Tilak Wasan
DISCOVERY PUBLISHING HOUSE PVT. LTD.
4383/4B, Ansari Road, Darya Ganj
New Delhi-110 002 (India)
Phone : +91-11-23279245, 43596064-65
Fax : +91-11-23253475
E-mail : parul.wasan@gmail.com
discoverypublishinghouse@gmail.com
web : www.discoverypublishinggroup.com

***First Edition:* 2013**

ISBN: 978-93-5056-313-7

Eco-Toxicology and Eco-Technology

Printed at:
Aditi Fine Art Press
Delhi

Preface

Eco-toxicology or Ecological toxicology is the study of the effects of manufactured chemicals and other anthropogenic and natural materials and activities on organisms at various levels of organization, from sub-cellular through individual organisms to communities and ecosystems. Generally, fish and invertebrates can often be used to indicate the health of an aquatic system because chemicals can accumulate in invertebrates from the water and sediment and in fish from water, sediment, and the food chain. The monitoring of these effects is extremely important to regulate and remediate pollution. To test the toxicity, they can apply biomarkers to detect low-level pollution in aquatic systems.

The effects of pollutants on the whole organism can be considered as neuro-physiological, reproductive and behavioural effects. These effects can often be inter-related: neurological changes can affect behaviour; changes in behaviour can affect reproduction and so on. A compound doesn't always put forth an effect on a target organism or a community. It always depends on the concentration of that compound and the time of exposure to it. These effects eventually can be either acute or chronic. Acute toxicity occurs rapidly, are clearly defined, often fatal and rarely reversible. Chronic effects develop after long exposure to low doses or long after exposure and may ultimately cause death. The harmful effects that chemicals have upon individual organisms depend on many different factors. Not only the difference between the freshwater species, but also the form in which pollutants occur, and if the pollutant shows up in lotic or lentic systems. To measure the toxicity there has to get done some toxicity tests. Then there is clarity what the dose is of a chemical that a type of specie will die, which will be expressed in a LC50 or LD50.

The effects of pollution on freshwater species are registered in the loss of some species, with maybe some profits for some of them. There normally is a reduction in diversity but not necessarily numbers of individual species, and a change in the balance of such processes as predation, competition and materials cycling. Because of the complexity of pollution, the effects of take-up in the aquatic life are also depended on the pollutants characteristic feature. If two or more poisons are present together in an effluent they may exert a combined effect to an organism, which can be additive, antagonistic or synergistic.

Eco-technology or Environmental biotechnology is the multidisciplinary integration of sciences and engineering in order to utilize the huge biochemical potential of microorganisms, plants and parts thereof for the restoration and preservation of the environment and for the sustainable use of available resources. Environmental biotechnology is defined as the development, use and regulation of biological system e.g. cells, cell compartments, enzymes, for remediation of contaminated environments (air, water, soil and sediments), and for environment-friendly processes. The primary role of eco-technology is to develop better approaches for sustainable development and for understanding the basic processes in the natural environment.

The present book mainly deals with ecological toxicology, eco-technology, aquatic pollution, environmental toxicology, biotechnological applications and updates the subject matter, illustrations and problems to incorporate new concepts and issues related to aquatic ecosystem, environmental toxicology and eco-technology. The approach to presenting this book is traditional covering of environmental pollution, aquatic ecosystem, environmental toxicology and biotechnology.

The book includes 13 chapters contributed by outstanding experts and scientists from Egypt and different parts of India. This book provides comprehensive coverage of the fundamental principles and current practices and trends in the field of aquatic environment, eco-toxicology and eco-technology.

Particularly thanks are due to all contributors from Egypt, India; and publisher also for their contribution and assistance.

I hope this book will be of benefit to both present and future colleagues, who teach, study and working in the field of limnology, freshwater ecology, aquatic ecosystem, environmental pollution, fisheries, aquatic toxicology and eco-technology.

Dr. Pawan Kumar 'Bharti'

(E-mail: gurupawanbharti@gmail.com)

Contents

List of Contributors

Amir Khan, Department of Biotechnology & Biochemistry, Division of Life Science, Sardar Bhagwan Singh Post Graduate Institute of Biomedical Sciences & Research Balawala, Dehradun, (Uttarakhand), (India).

Anubhuti Sharma, Department of Bioscience & Biotechnology, Banasthali University, Banasthali - 304022, (Rajasthan), (India).

Ashish Kumar, Scientist, JNKVV College of Agriculture RIWA, (India).

Attia A. Abou Zaid, Animal Health Research Institute Kafrelsheikh, Kafrelsheikh, Egypt.

Abdel Razek Y. Desouky, Fac. of Vet. Medicine Kafrelsheikh University, Kafrelsheikh, Egypt.

A. Bohra, Faculty of Sciences, J.N.V. Mahila (P.G.) Mahavidyalaya, Jodhpur - 342 008 (Rajasthan), (India).

B.N. Johri, Department of Biotechnology, Barkatullah University, Bhopal, (Madhya Pradesh) (India).

Eglal, A. Omar, Department of Animal and Fish production, Fac. of Agriculture, Alexandria, University, Alexandria, Egypt.

Fatma M. Salman, Animal Production Department, National Research Center, Dokki, Giza, Egypt.

Gajra Garg, Department of Bioscience & Biotechnology, Banasthali University, Banasthali -304 022, (Rajasthan) (India).

Hamed A.A. Omer, Animal Production Department, National Research Center, Dokki, Giza, Egypt.

Hossam H. Abbas, Hydrobiology Department, National Research Center, Cairo, Egypt.

Ibrahim M. Awadalla, Animal Production Department, National Research Center, Dokki, Giza, Egypt.

Jaswant Roy, Institute for Industrial Research & Toxicology, Ghaziabad (Uttar Pradesh) (India).

K.K. Sharma, Vivekanand Parvatiya Krishi Anusandhan Sansthan, Almora - 263 601, (Uttarakhand), (India).

K.K. Mishra, Senior Scientist, VPKAS, Almora - 263 601, (Uttarakhand) (India).

K.K. Sharma, Department of Plant Pathology, College of Agriculture, G.B.P.U.A. & T., Pantnagar- 263 145, (Uttarakhand) (India).

Lalan Sharma, Scientist, NBAIM, Mau (Uttar Pradesh) (India).

Mansour, T.A, Department of Animal and Fish production, Fac. of Agriculture, Alexandria, University, Alexandria, Egypt.

Mahmoud A. El-Seify, Fac. of Vet. Medicine Kafrelsheikh University, Kafrelsheikh, Egypt.

Mamdouh I. Mohamed, Animal Production Department, National Research Center, Dokki, Giza, Egypt.

Mahendra Singh, Department of Soil Science, College of Agriculture, G.B.P.U.A. &T., Pantnagar - 263 145, (Uttarakhand) (India).

Mona S. Zaki, Department of Hydrobiology, National Research Center, Cairo, Egypt.

Nabila El-Batrawy, Department of Microbiology, Veterinary, Zagazig University, Zagazig, Egypt.

Nadia M. Taha, Department of Physiology, Faculty of Veterinary, Cairo University, Cairo, Egypt.

Narendra Kumar, Department of Soil Science, College of Agriculture, G.B.P.U.A. &T., Pantnagar - 263 145, (Uttarakhand (India).

Osman K. Abdel Hady, Hydrobiology Department, National Research Center, Cairo, Egypt.

Pawan Kumar Bharti*

1. Centre for Agro-Rural Technologies (CART), 20, Jamaalpur Maan, Raja Ka Tajpur, Dist.- Bijnore - 246 735 (Uttar Pradesh) (India).
2. Shriram Institute for Industrial Research, Delhi, (India).

Pankaj Sharma, Assistant Plant pathologist, PAU, Ludhiana, (Punjab) (India).

Rashmi Yadav, 412, Yadav Sadan, New Ramnagar, Near Tehsil, Jwalapur, Haridwar (Uttarakhand) (India).

Renu Bisht, Department of Bioscience & Biotechnology, Banasthali University, Banasthali - 304 022, (Rajasthan) (India).

Ruchi tyagi, Department of Bioscience & Biotechnology, Banasthali University, Banasthali - 304 022, (Rajasthan) (India).

R.P.Mali, Associate professor and Head P.G. Department of Zoology, Yeshwant Mahavidyalaya. Nanded - 431605 (Maharashtra) (India).

Safinaz, G.Mohamed, National Institute of Oceanography and Fisheries, Alexandria Branch, Alexandria, Egypt.

Seema Rawat, Department of Biotechnology and Biomedical Science, Dolphin (PG) Institute of Biomedical & Natural Sciences, Dehradun - 248 007, (Uttarakhand) (India).

Shaikh Afsar, Sr. Lecturer, P.G. Department of Zoology, Vivek Vardhini Day College, Jambagh, Hyderabad - 500 095 (Andhra Pradesh) (India).

Shailesh Joshi, Dept. of Biotechnology, Dolphin (P.G.) Institute of Biomedical and Natural Sciences, Dehradun 248 008, (Uttarakhand) (India).

Shahinaz, M.H. Hassan, Animal Research Institute, Alexandria Lab. Alexandria, Egypt.

Soliman, M.K., Department of Poultry and Fish Diseases, Fac. of Veterinary Medicine, Damanhour University, ElBostan, Egypt.

Soha S. Abdel-Magid, Animal Production Department, National Research Center, Dokki, Giza, Egypt.

Sawsan M. Ahmed, Animal Production Department, National Research Center, Dokki, Giza, Egypt.

Srour, T.M., Department of Animal and Fish Production, Fac. of Agriculture, Alexandria, University, Alexandria, Egypt.

Tarun Kumar Sharma, Department of Biotechnology Indian Institute of Technology Roorkee - 247 667 (Uttarakhand) (India).

U.S. Singh, IRRI -India Office, 1st Floor, NASC Complex, New Delhi-110 012, (India).

1

Study on Clinopathological and Biochemical Changes in Some Freshwater Fishes Infected With External Parasites and Subjected to Heavy Metals Pollution in Egypt

Mahmoud A. El-Seify, *Egypt*
Mona S. Zaki, *Egypt*
Abdel Razek Y. Desouky, *Egypt*
Hossam H. Abbas, *Egypt*
Osman K. Abdel Hady, *Egypt*
Attia A. Abou Zaid, *Egypt*

ABSTRACT

The present investigation was carried out to study the impact of external parasites and heavy metals pollution on some liver function tests of some freshwater fishes. 470 Fish species (330 Oreochromis niloticus and 140 Clarias gariepinus) were collected alive from three different ecosystems in Kafr-Elshiekh province, Egypt. The obtained results revealed that aspartate aminotransferase (AST), alanine aminotransferase (ALT) enzymes activities as well as creatinine and urea values were elevated in the external parasites infected fish as well as in the fish exposed pollutants. While fishes exposed to both external parasites infection and heavy metal pollution led to more drastic increase in serum AST and ALT enzymes activities as well as creatinine and urea values. In addition; heavy metals pollution increased the susceptibility of fish to protozoa infection while decrease prevalence of monogenea and crustacean infection. On conclusion; infection with external parasites in fishes exposed to heavy metals had the highest effect on liver and kidney functions in the studied fishes.

Keywords: External parasites, Heavy metals, *Oreochromus niloticus, Clarias gariepinus*, AST, ALT.

Introduction

Most of fish diseases might be occurred as a result of parasitic infection or environmental pollution (Hussain *et al.*, 2003) Knowledge of fish parasites is of particular interest in relation not only to fish health but also to understand ecological problems (Mahfous, 1997).

Aquatic pollution is still a problem in many freshwater and marine environments; it causes negative effects for the health of the respective organisms (Fent, 2007). The number of studies investigating effects of pollutants and concurrently occurring parasites is still relatively low (Sures, 2007). However the effect of environmental pollutants on fish parasites varies depending on the particular parasite and pollutant that interact (Lafferty and Kuris, 1999). Pollutants may affect the immune system of the fish either directly or by change water quality; that in turn may reduce the fish immunity to parasites (Poulin, 1992) also, water pollution may accelerate the life cycle of the external parasites and promote their spread (Noor El-Din, 1997).

It is well known that certain blood parameters serve as reliable indicators of fish health as many parasites can live in a host, sometimes causing damage to it (Bond, 1979). Therefore, the changes associated with hematological parameters due to various parasites establish a database, which could be used in diseases diagnosis and in guiding the implementation of the treatment or preventive measures. These measures are essential in fish farming and fish industry (Roberts, 1981).

Analysis of blood constituents is considered physiological indicators of the whole body and therefore they are important in diagnosis the structural and functional status of fish exposed to pollutants (Adhikari and Betal, 2004). In this respect; Ranzani-Paiva *et al.*, (2000) demonstrated alterations in blood composition related to parasitism in fish from the Parana River, indicating that, determination of blood parameters of fishes is of great importance in evaluation of disturbance that caused by parasitism. Therefore, this study was aimed to investigate the impact of external parasites on some physiological parameters related to both liver and kidney functions of some freshwater fish (*Oreochromis niloticus* and *Clarias gariepinus*), as well as to determine the relation between heavy metal pollution and the infection with external parasites.

Materials and Methods Fish Samples

A total number of 470 (330 *Tilapia species* and 140 *Clarias gariepinus*) freshwater fish were collected a live from three different ecosystems at Kafr El-Shiekh governorate, North Egypt as follow. (River Nile Branch, Drainage canal and Fish farm) by the aid of fisherman and then transported a live to the laboratory where they examined immediately.

Parasitological Examination

Parasitological examination was carried out for the detection and identification of the external parasites on the skin, gills and the accessory respiratory organs of the samples.

Collection and Preparation of the Detected Ectoparasites

Monogenea

Monogenea were collected under binocular dissecting microscopic by means of small pipette in small Petri-dish and cleared several times with water to remove the attached mucous and debris. The worms were then left in refrigerator at 4°C till complete relaxation. Then, they were fixed in 5 per cent formalin for permanent preparation, worms were washed carefully in water to get red of formalin traces and stained with Semichon's acetocarmine stain for about 5-10 minutes till reaching staining, the specimens were passed through ascending grades of ethyl alcohol (30, 50, 70, 90 per cent and absolute) for dehydration. Then, cleared in clove oil, xylene and mounted in Canada balsam (Pritchard and kruse, 1982), while the unstained Monogeneas were mounted in glycerin jelly (Abdel-Hady, 1998).

Protozoa

Some of the positive slides were stained according to Klein's dry silver impregnation method in which the slides were air -dried, covered with 2 per cent aqueous solution of silver nitrate (Ag NO3) for 8 minutes, rinse thoroughly in distilled water and exposed to UV light for 20-30 minutes or to direct sun light for 1-2 hr. The slides were allowed to dry and mounted with neutral Canada balsam. This method is indispensable technique for staining *Trichodina*. Other positive slides were also air-dried, fixed with absolute methanol and stained with 10 per cent Giemsa stain for 20-30 minutes to detect the other protozoa (Ali, 1992).

Crustacea

The detected crustacean parasites were carefully collected by a fine brush and special needle, and transferred into Petri-dish for cleaning by using preserved and cleared in lacto phenol then mounting with polyvol (Raef *et al.*, 2000).

Heavy Metals Detection

Three samples of water from the same sources of fish collection were taken in the fore mentioned flask one liter volume capacity after its rinsing several times with distilled water and sterilized in hot air oven at 180 °C/ hour. The collected water sample bottles were labeled with the locality, date, and time of collection. Chemical examinations of these samples were done to estimate some heavy metals including (copper, zinc, iron, lead, cadmium, selenium, mercury, manganese and nickel) according to Chapman and pratt, (1978).

Blood Samples

Fresh blood samples were collected without anticoagulant from the caudal artery. The needle is run, quite deep, as much as possible through a middle line just behind the anal fin in a dorso-cranial direction till striking the vertebrate. By drawing the needle gently backward, blood is usually sucked into the syringe.

The collected blood was centrifuged post collection at 3000 rpm for 10 minutes to separate serum for biochemical analysis.

Biochemical Analysis

Aspartate aminotransferase (AST) and alanine aminotransferase (ALT) activities in serum were determined according to Reitman and Frankel, (1975). Creatinine value was determined according to Rock *et al*., (1987). Urea concentration was measured according to Pathson and Nauch, (1977).

All these biochemical analyses were measured calorimetrically using spectrophotometer and purchased kits.

Results

The effect of heavy metals pollution on the prevalence of ectoparasites on examined fish spp. are shown in Table 1.1 which indicate that the percentage of ectoparsites infection was 71.8 per cent from the examined *Tilapia spp* in the River Nile branch where the pollution of water with copper (Cu), nickel (Ni), cadmium (Cd), selenium (Se) and mercury (Hg) were higher than the other localities where the degree of pollutants were 2.190, 0.102, 0.260, 3.630 and 1.90 respectively, In this degree of pollution, the present study revealed that ectoprotozoa infection of *Tilapia spp*. were the highest percentage of infection where 65 per cent of examined Tilapia fish were infected and it was followed by Monogenea and Crustaceans where they reached 23 per cent and 13.7 per cent respectively.

In Drainage canal, where the heavy metals pollution were lower than that in river Nile branch, 69 per cent of examined *Tilapia* were infected with ectoparasites, where the protozoa parasite decreased than in river Nile branch 48 per cent. While monogenea and Crustaceans increased (41%, 38% respectively).

In Fish farms; the percentage of infection reached 64.9 per cent from the examined fishes. Parasitic protozoa decreased than in River Nile branch 46.9 per cent, while monogenea and Crustaceans increased (38.0%, 34.5% respectively).

Table 1.1: Effect of Heavy Metals on Parasitic Infection Among Examined Fish spp. in Different Localities

Locality	Parasitic Infection	% of Infection		Heavy Metal Pollutants in ppm								
				Zinc	Lead	Manganes	Copper	Nicke	Cadmium	Selenium	Mercury	Iron
		Tilapia spp	*C. gariepinus*	*1	*_	*1.5	*1	*_	*0.01	*_	*_	*1
Locality 1 (River Nile Branch)	Monogenea	23	28.7	0.2	0	0.08	2.19	0.102	0.26	3.63	1.9	0.12
	Protozoa	65	36.3									
	Crustacea	13.7	0									
	Total	71.8	53.7									
Locality 2 (Drainage Canal)	Monogenea	41	60	0.06	0.5	0.12	0.07	0.102	0.04	0.26	0.25	0.06
	Protozoa	48	20									
	Crustacea	36	0									
	Total	69	65									
Locality 3 (Fish farm)	Monogenea	38	Not examined	0.07	0.5	0.42	0.11	0.068	0.07	0.52	0.15	0.81
	Protozoa	46.9										
	Crustacea	34.5										
	Total	64.6										

– * Permissible limits of trace elements detected in ppm. According to Egyptian Law.

– No available guide line.

In addition; the effect of polluted water on the ectoparasitic infection of *Clarias gariepinus*, it was recorded that, in river Nile branch the fish infected with monogenea (28.7%) and protozoa (36.3%), while in Drainage canal (less polluted with heavy metals) monogenea increased 60 per cent while parasitic protozoa decreased 20 per cent than in River Nile branch. With no infection obtained with Crustacean parasites in the examined areas.

As shown in Table 1.2; Alanine aminotransferase (ALT), Aspartate aminotransferase (AST), Urea and Creatinene were higher in infected *O. niloticus* taken from River Nile branch than infected *O. niloticus* taken from other localities as they were (78.6 U/l), (115 U/l), (52 mg/dl) and (1.9 mg/dl) respectively while in non infected *O. niloticus* were (69 U/l), (101.5 U/l), (41 mg/dl) and (1.54 mg/d/) respectively. In Drainage canal, Alanine aminotransferase (ALT), Aspartate aminotransferase (AST), Urea and Creatinene were (61.3 U/l), (96.7U/l), (37.3 mg/dl) and (1.4 mg/dl) respectively in the infected O. niloticus while in non infected were (51.5 U/l), (85U/l), (26.5 mg/dl) and (1.18 mg/dl) respectively. In Fish farm, Alanine aminotransferase (ALT), Aspartate aminotransferase (AST), Urea and Creatinene were (67 U/l), (97.3 U /l), (36.3 mg/dl) and (1.6 mg/dl) respectively in the infected O. niloticus while in non-infected were (55 U/l), (81 U/l), (31.5 mg/dl) and (1.3 mg/dl) respectively.

Table 1.3 showed that in River Nile Branch, Alanine aminotransferase (ALT), Aspartate aminotransferase (AST), Urea and Creatinene were higher in infected *Clarias garipinus* (101.7 u/l), (177.7 u/l), (69 mg/dl) and (2.17 mg/dl) respectively . Than non infected *Clarias garipinus* as they were (85 u/l), (130 u/l), (50mg/dl) and (1.6 mg/d/) respectively. While in Drainage canal, Alanine aminotransferase (ALT), Aspartate aminotransferase (AST), Urea and Creatinene were (73.3 u/l), (94u/l), (38.7 mg/dl) and (1.63 mg/dl) respectively in the infected *Clarias garipinus* while in non-infected were (54 u/l), (76u/l), (28.5 mg/dl) and (1. mg/dl) respectively.

Discussion

A negative relationship was detected between heavy metals pollution and prevalence of monogenic infection in River Nile drainage canal branch as well as fish farm during this study. This result agreed with Blanar *et al.*, (2009) which may be attributed to the toxic effect of the heavy metal on the parasite itself Gheorghiu *et al.*, (2006).

The present study denoted that the incidence of external protozoa among examined fish was higher percentage in River Nile Branch which it is more polluted with heavy metals than other localities this may be attributed to that the heavy metals decrease the immune system of the exposed fish which become more susceptible to protozoa infection Khan and Thulin, (1991).

Table 1.2: Liver and Kidney Function Tests of *O. niloticus* Infected with Ecto-parasites in Different Localities

Locality	River Nile Branch		Drainage Canal		Fish Farm	
Parameter	Non-infected	Infected	Non-infected	Infected	Non-infected	Infected
ALT (U/L)	69.00	78.60	51.50	61.30	55.00	67.0
AST (U/L)	101.50	115.00	85.00	96.70	81.00	97.30
Urea (Mg/dl)	41.00	52.00	26.50	37.30	31.50	36.30
Creatinene (Mg/dl)	1.54	1.90	1.18	1.40	1.30	1.60

Table 1.3: Mean Liver and Kidney Function Tests of *Clarias gariepinus* Infected with Ecto-parasites in Different Localities

Locality	River Nile Branch		Drainage Canal	
Parameter	Non-infected	Infected	Non-infected	Infected
ALT (U/L)	85.00	101.70	54.00	73.30
AST (U/L)	130.00	177.70	76.00	94.00
Urea (Mg/dl)	50.00	69.00	28.50	38.70
Creatinene (Mg/dl)	1.60	2.17	1.10	1.63

Table 1.4: Mean Liver and Kidney Function Tests of Fish Spp. Infected with Ectoparasites in Different Localities

Locality	River Nile Branch				Drainage Canal				Fish Farm	
	O.niloticus		*C. gariepinus*		*O. niloticus*		*C. gariepinus*		*O. niloticus*	
Parameter	Non-infected	Infected	Non-infected	Infected	Non-infected	Infected	Non infected	Infected	Non infected	Infected
ALT (U/L)	69.00	78.60	85.00	101.70	51.50	61.30	54.00	73.30	55.00	67.00
AST (U/L)	101.50	115.00	130.00	177.70	85.00	96.70	76.00	94.00	81.00	97.30
Urea (Mg/dl)	41.00	52.00	50.00	69.00	26.50	37.30	28.50	38.70	31.50	36.30
Creatinene (Mg/dl)	1.54	1.90	1.60	2.17	1.18	1.40	1.10	1.63	1.30	1.60

The lowest rate of infection with parasitic crustacean was recorded in River Nile Branch, where the heavy metals pollution increased, this result agree with Galli *et al*., (2001) who recorded that the distribution of *Lamproglena pulchella* was limited to the unpolluted and slightly polluted river sectors. This negative relation may be attributed to the toxic effect of the heavy metals on the crustaceans which may cut its life cycle Ruben et al., (2006).

The blood serum Aspartate aminotransferase (AST), Alanine aminotransferase (ALT) enzymes activities, Creatinine and Urea values were elevated in the infected fish species (*Oreochromus niloticus* and *Clarias gariepinus*) with external parasites than the non infected fishes in different localities, this indicate that the external parasites stimulated the activities of ALT and AST enzymes as well as both Urea and Creatinine. This result was agreed with Younis, (1999) recorded that aspartate aminotransferase (AST), alanine aminotransferase (ALT) and urea showed significant increase in *O. niloticus* infected with external protozoa and monogenetic trematodes. Osman *et al*., (2009) reported that blood serum Aspartate aminotransferase (AST), Alanine aminotransferase (ALT) enzymes activities, Creatinine and Urea values were increased in Trichodina infected *Clarias gariepinus*.

Concerning the effect of parasitic infection on biochemical parameters of examined fish in the presence of heavy metal pollution, the present study indicated that the blood serum Aspartate aminotransferase (AST), Alanine aminotransferase (ALT) enzymes activities, Creatinine and Urea values were more higher in both *Oreochromis niloticus* and *Clarias gariepinus* that examined from river Nile branch (more polluted locality with heavy metals) than infected fish spp. taken from drainage canal and fish farm (less polluted with heavy metals). This indicated that exposure of fish to parasitic infection in the presence of heavy metals is more powerful in stimulating the activities of ALT and AST enzymes (Adams, 2002). This may be due to hepatic cells injury or increased synthesis of the enzymes by the liver (Yang and Chen, 2003). The elevation in the urea level in the infected fish may be due to gill dysfunctions as the urea excreted mainly through the gills (Murray *et al*., 1990). Also these findings may be attributed to the inflammatory reactions and intoxications produced by the parasite in the affected fish.

REFERENCES

Abd EL- Hady. O. K (1998): Comparative Studies on Some Parasitic Infection of Fishes in Fresh and Polluted Water Sources. Ph.D. Thesis (Parasitalogy), Fac. Vet. Med., Cairo University.

Adham, K. G. (2002): Sub Lethal Effects of Aquatic Pollution in Lake Maryût on the African Sharptooth Catfish, *Clarias Gariepinus* (Burchell, 1822). Journal of Applied Ichthyology, 18: 87-94.

Adhikari, S. and Betal, S. (2004): Effects of Cypermehrin and Carbofuran on Certain Haematological Parameters and Prediction of Their Recovery in Fresh Water Teleost, *Labeo rohita* (Ham). Ecotoxicol. Environ. Safety 58: 220-226.

Ali, M.A. (1992): Biological and Ecological Studies on Protozoan Parasites Infecting Cultured Tilapia in Serow Fish Farm. M.Sc. Thesis, Fac. Science, Cairo University, Egypt.

Blanar, A.C.; Munkittrick, R.K.; Houlahan, G.; Maclatchy, L.D.

Bond, C.E. (1979): Biology of Fishes. Saunders College Publishing, Philadelphia, Pennsylvania, USA.

Chapman, H.D. and Pratt, P.F. (1978): Methods of Analysis for Soils, Plants and Waters. Univ. California Div. Agric. Sci. Priced. 4034.

Fent, K. (2007): Ökotoxikologie. Georg Thieme Verlag, Stuttgart, 2007.

Galli, P.G.; Crosa, G.; Mariniello. L.M.; Ortis, M. and D'Amelio, S. (2001): Water Quality As a Determinant of the Composition of Fish Parasite Communities. Journal of Hydrobiologia, 452: 173-179.

Gheorghiu, C.; Cable, J.; Marcogliese, D.J and Scott, M.E. (2006): Effects of Waterborne Zinc on Reproduction, Survival and Morphometrics of *Gyrodactylus turnbulli* (Monogenea) on Guppies (*Poecilia reticulate*). Int. J. Parasitology, 37: 375-381.

Hussain, S.; Hassan, M.Z.; Mukhtar, Y. and Saddiqui, B.N. (2003): Impact of Environmental Pollution in Human Behaviour and Up-left of Awareness Level Through Mass Media Among the People of Faisalabad City. Int.J.Agric.Biol., 5: 660-661.

Khan R.A., Thulin J. (1991): Influence of Pollution on Parasites of Aquatic Animals. Advances in Parasitology, 30: 201-238.

Lafferty, K.D. and Kuris, A.M. (1999): How Environmental Stress Affects the Impacts of Parasites. Limnol. Oceanogr., 44: 925-931.

Mahfouz, N.B.M. (1997). Effect of Parasitism on Immunity of Cultured Freshwater Fish. Ph D. Thesis, Faculty of Veterinary Medicine, Tanta University, Egypt.

Murray, R.K.D.K.; Rranne, P.A.M. and Rodwell, V.W. (1990): Harper's Biochemistry Publisher, Norwalk, Connecticut/ Los Altos, California.

Noor El-Din, A.N. (1997): Studies on the Effect of Water Pollution Along Different Sites of the River Nile on the Survival and Production of some Freshwater Fishes. Ph.D. Thesis, Zoology Dep, Fac. Science, Cairo Univ., Egypt.

Osman H. A. M.; Ismaiel, M.M.; Abbas, T.W and Ibrahim, T.B. (2009): An Approach to the Interaction Between Trichodiniasis and Pollution with Benzo-a- pyrene in Catfish (*Clarias gariepinus*). World Journal of Fish and Marine Sciences 1(4): 283-289.

Pathson, C.J. and Nauch, S. R. (1977): Determination of Serum Urea. Anal. Chem., 49: 464-469.

Poulin, R. (1992): Toxic Pollution and Parasitism of Freshwater Fish.

Pritchard, M.H. and Kruse, G.O.W. (1982): The Collection and Preservation of Animal Parasites. University Nebraska, Lincoln, London, p. 141.

Raef, A.M.; El-Ashram, A.M. and El-Sayed, N.M. (2000): Crustacean Parasites of some Cultured Freshwater Fish and Their Control in Sharkia. Egypt. Vet. J., 28(2): 180-191.

Ranzani-paviva, M.J.T.; Silva-souza, A.T.; Pavanelli, G.C. and Takemoto, R.M. (2000): Hematological Characteristics and Relative Condition Factor (Kn) Associated with Parasitism in *Schizodon Borellii* (Osteichthyes, Anostomidae) and *Prochilodus Lineatus* (Osteichthyes, Prochilodontidae) of the Paraná River, Porto Rico region, Paraná, Brazil. Acta Scientiarum, Maringá, 22(2): 515-521.

Reitman, S. and Frankel, S. (1957): Colorimetric Composition of Glutamic Oxaloacetic and Glutamic Pyruvic Transaminases, Am. J. Clin. Pathol., 28: 53-56.

Roberts, R.S.(1981) Patologia de los peces. Madrid, Mundi-prensa, p. 336.

Rock, R.C.; Walker, W.G. and Jennings, C.D. (1987): Nitrogen Metabolites and Renal Function. In: Tietz, N.W., ed. Fundamentals of Clinical Chemistry, 3rd Ed Philadelphia: W.B. Saunders, pp: 669-704.

Ruben, A.P.; Asbjorn, L.V.; Lars, E.W.F. and Antonio, B.S.P (2006): Effects of Aqueous Aluminum on Four Fish Ectoparasites. Biology Journal of the Linnean Society 90(3): 525-538.

SURES, B. (2007): Host-parasite Interactions from an Ecotoxicological Perspective. *Parassitologia*, 49, 173-176.

Yang, J. and Chen, H. (2003): Serum metabolic enzyme activities and hepatocyte ultra structure of common carp after gallium exposure. Zoological studies, 42(3): 455-461.

Younis, A. A. E. (1999): Effect of Some Ectoparasites on the Blood and Serum Constituents of *Oreochromis niloticus* Fish with Referring to Treatment. Beni Suif. Vet. Med. J., 9(3): 341- 351.

2

Alteration and Recovery of Some Physiological Aspects from Lead Intoxicated Freshwater Fish Anabas Testudineus

Shaikh Afsar, ***India***
R.P. Mali, ***India***

ABSTRACT

Lactic acid, Pyruvate, Glycogen phosphorylase "a" and Glycogen phosphorylase "ab" content are important amongst the several molecules available in the cells, Carbohydrates play an important role in the cellular process Under extreme stress conditions, carbohydrate metabolite and enzymes have been known to act as the energy supplier in metabolic pathways and biochemical reactions. In the present investigation fish treated with an equitoxic dose of 10 ppm of lead nitrate and lead acetate intoxicated fish After a period of 15 days of exposure a batch from lead nitrate exposed fish and a batch from lead acetate exposed fish were transferred to lead-free water. Fishes were scarified on 1, 4, 8, 12 and 15 days for the analysis of recovery pattern in tissues viz. liver, muscle, kidney, gill and brain. It is found that lead toxicated fishes were recovered after 15 days depends upon physical condition of the fish.

Key words: Carbohydrate metabolism, lead,anabas.

Introduction

The modern industries are making use of various heavy metals such as iron, steel, copper, nickel, platinum and lead. Because of the industrial, agricultural and zoo technique developments, following industrial revolution, various chemical substances have been diffused into the environment causing pollution of rivers, lakes, seas and coasts, soil and atmosphere.

The pollution explosion witnessed in this century through the various beneficial uses of toxic substances in the agriculture, industry and treatment of diseases which are essential to the very existence of mankind, have led civilization to the edge of environmental disaster. The increasing awareness of the problem of pollution began with the rapid increase in the occurrence of industrial health hazards.

Among the different types of pollutions, chemical pollution appears to be the major type which threatens the living systems very extensively. Pesticides and the metals head the list of chemical pollutants at this moment, posing a greater potential risk than the organic wastes and eutrophicating nutrients. Metals are the intrinsic components of the earth crust, and the first materials available in the nature to the prehistoric man.

The heavy metal exists in variety of state, the toxicity of metal depends on its nature and chemical form weather it is ionic form or in an oxidized or reduced state in combination with organic substances and other metals (Mali, 2002).

Among the environmental contaminants heavy metals have been recognized as strong biological poisons because of their persistent nature and cumulative action. Metals are concerned not only from the point of view of toxicity but also by their property of carcinogenicity. A first property of metals of which we must be aware when dealing with them as environmental contaminants, is that they are immutable. They can neither be created nor be destroyed nor can one metal be transformed into another; this means that once a metal is mobilized in the environment its total amount there remains the same.

The metals in general whether they are toxic metals or essential trace metals, when administered in excess doses interact with the living system through their ligand binding property. These interactions bring about interference with the bio-chemical functioning of the living system and can cause either short term or long term abnormalities.

A characteristic feature of metal pollution is its persistence and biomagnifications through the food chain causing significant biological concern even at very low concentrations.

Heavy metals interfere with the metabolism of the organisms. Biochemical and physiological alterations beyond a point in the animals after heavy metal intoxication may cause mortality or decrease the capability of survival and reproduction. Toxicity may be acute & kill the organism relatively quickly or chronic showing gradual effect on activity, feeding, development, reproduction & general physiology (Mali, 2002).

The most potent sources of lead pollution as far as toxicity to humans concerned are; auto exhaust, lead in metal type, particularly in the newspaper industry, the use of lead based paints, exposure of lead loaded dust and fumes from lead smelters and radio active fallout from atomic explosion etc. Tetraethyl lead is a potential pollutant of the air as well as the soil near highways and roads with heavy traffic.

Lead also released from factories where storage batteries manufactured or where heavy metals was used as raw material. In dry cell batteries manufacturing factories or those engaged in lead smelting, lead soldering and persons who routinely handle lead arsenate containing insecticide sprays are also subjected to serious lead toxicity (Kanwar & Sharma, 1987).

Lead in its different forms has been known and used by man from ancient times and its toxic properties were recognized as far back as second century B.C. Lead is relatively easily refined from natural ores. It was mined in considerable quantities by Greeks and Romans and has continued to be of commercial significance throughout modern history. Lead rarely occurs in the elemental state, but exists widely throughout the world in a number of ores, the most common of which is the Sulphide.Lead exists in organic form as a divalent plumbous salt in water and as a tetravalent plumbic compound in the organic form. It is one of the heaviest and the softest of the common metals available.

It has been known for many years that concentration of heavy metals is significantly higher in aquatic biosphere (Waldichuk , 1974). Lead is a common heavy metal found in the environment and is derivable from urban waste water, industrial discharges and agricultural runoff. Its inclusion in gasoline as anti-knock contribute to its occurrence in the air, which is transported to the streams and rivers by runoffs where fish and other aquatic organisms take it up and incorporate it in their body (Olojo et.al., 2005) Heavy metals have a tendency to accumulate in living organisms.

In aquatic environment, heavy metals accumulate in all levels of a food chain including phytoplankton from the concentrations available in surrounding waters (Yigit and Altindag, 2007).

Presence of potentially hazardous heavy metals in water should be considered abnormal and its concentration causes hazardous effects on aquatic biota. Higher concentrations of these pollutants can cause damage to the physiological system by affecting the organism either at organ, cellular or even at molecular level (Mali et.al., 2010). Fish can accumulate heavy metals more than any other aquatic organisms either directly from water or indirectly through the food chain (Bryan, 1976).

Freshwater fishes act as indicators of heavy metal pollution (Karthikeyan et. al., 2005).The absorption of soluble lead salts such as lead acetate or lead nitrate is more than that of insoluble lead salts, such as lead sulphide and lead chromate. Most of the lead ultimately pervades into water course during rainy season.

There have been a number of reports on the accumulation and bioconcentration of Lead. A level not exceeding 0.03 mg/l at any time or place has been considered safe to aquatic life (water quality criteria, 1972).

Amongst the soft tissues liver and kidney were found to accumulate more lead in comparison to other tissues. Survey of literature reveals quite a good number of responses of various fish models to lead toxicity. The responses mainly include the uptake and concentration of the toxicant and alterations in the biochemical and physiological organization of the tissues.

Recent times researchers have been focusing their attention on the prevention of toxicity of heavy metals on aquatic biota. Survey of literature reveals few attempts on recovery patterns of fish exposed to heavy metal toxicants. The recovery also varies according to the species (Spehar et.al., 1981).

Information documented on the impact of lead in fresh water fish is less in comparision to the other heavy metals. Hence in the present investigation an attempt is made to know the alteration in enzymes and metabolite profiles related to carbohydrate metabolism in the various tissues of *Anabas testudineus* exposed to sublethal dose of lead nitrate and lead acetate sampled at predetermined days of exposure, 1, 4, 8, 12 and 15. The investigation is also aimed to understand the differences in the responses in inorganic versus organo metallic lead forms. It is also further aimed to know the functional recoveries of the above mentioned parameters by withdrawing the toxicant from the ambient medium.

Material and Methods

Anabas testudineus which is selected as test species in the typical representative of Anabantoid fishes in South India. It is fresh water, euryhaline and eurythermal teleost. Biochemical assays were made in different tissues from both experimental and Normal fishes. Stock solutions of Lead nitrate and Lead acetate was prepared. From these stock solutions, eight different concentrations were prepared in distilled water with required dilutions.

Fishes in batches of 20 each were taken in glass aquarium was exposed for 15 days to the selected concentrations. The mortality of fish at each concentration was recorded at regular intervals. LC50 was determined by graphical plot of percent mortality versus log concentrations and probit mortality versus log concentrations by Probit Analysis (Finney, 1971) . The median lethal concentration (LC_{50}) for Lead nitrate was found to be 40 ppm and for Lead acetate 30 ppm (Fig., 2.a, 2.b, 2.c, 2.d). The 1/3 of LC_{50} value is a sub lethal value for a particular duration (Konar, 1969). But in the present investigation an equitoxic dose of 10 ppm was selected in order to examine the relative toxic potentialities of both inorganic and organic-metallic form of lead.

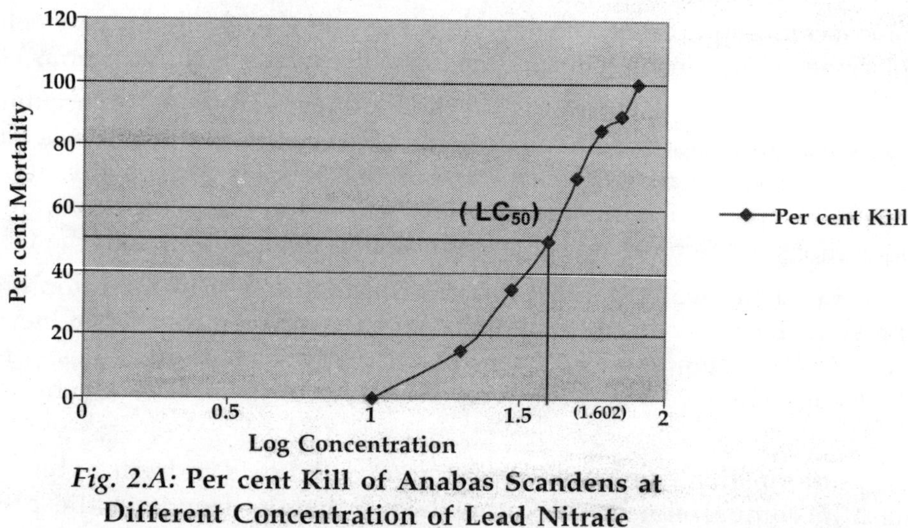

Fig. 2.A: **Per cent Kill of Anabas Scandens at Different Concentration of Lead Nitrate**

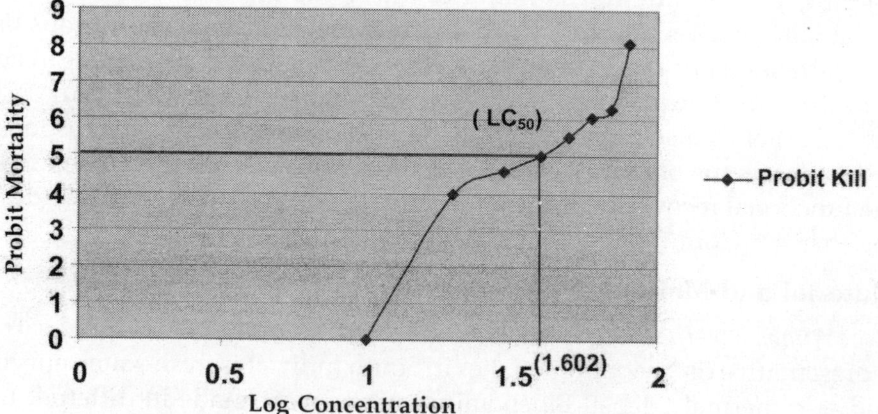

Fig. 2.B: **Probit kill of Anabas Scandens at Different Concentration of Lead Nitrate**

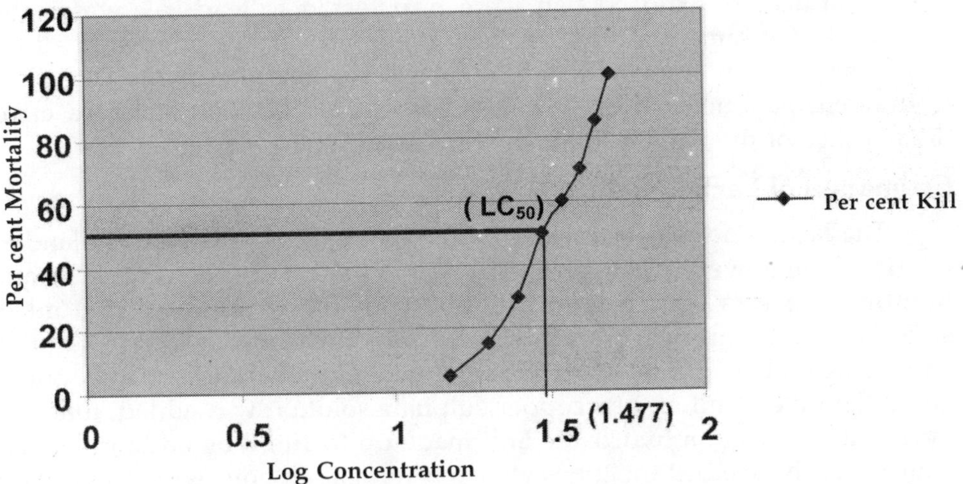

Fig. 2.C: **Per cent Kill of Anabas Scandens at Different Concentration of Lead Acetate**

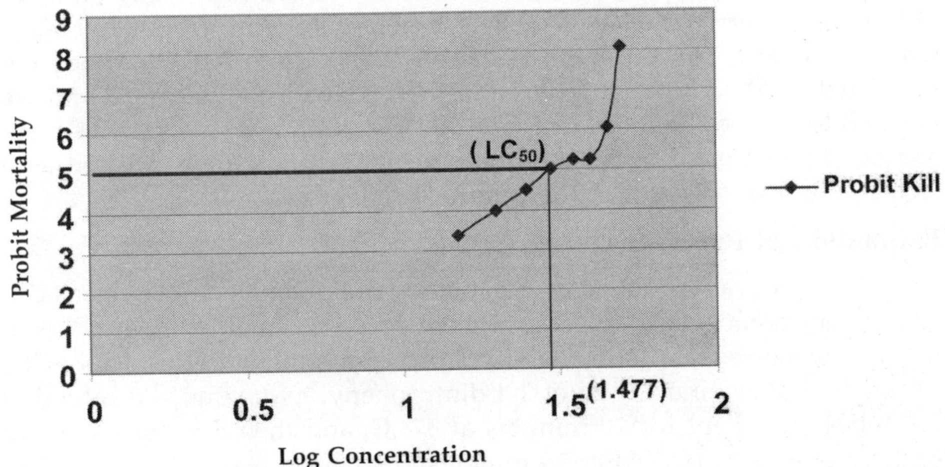

Fig. 2.D: **Probit Kill of Anabas Scandens at Different Concentration of Lead Acetate**

Fish approximately of same size and weight were selected and grouped into 6 batches. 2 batch of fish served as controls, 2 batches of fish were exposed to lead nitrate and the remaining two batches were exposed to lead acetate for a period of 15 days. Control and treated fishes were scarified on 1, 4, 8, 12 and 15 days of exposure for the analysis of various biochemical parameters in tissues viz. liver, muscle, kidney, gill and brain. After a period of 15 days of exposure a batch from lead nitrate exposed fish and a batch from lead acetate exposed fish were transferred to lead-free water and scarified at the same intervals to observe the recovery responses. In all the experiments, a minimum of six individual observations were made.The values of different parameters were expressed as mean with their standard error. Significance of the values obtained were tested using student 't' test.

Estimation of Lactic Acid

The lactic acid was estimated by the method, modified by Hollanders (1961). Tissues were homogenized (10% W/V) in 10 per cent TCA and homogenate was centrifuged at 2,000 rpm for 15 minutes. 1.0 ml of supernatant, 1.0 ml of freshly prepared standard sodium lactate solution and a reagent blank (2 ml of water) were taken in separate centrifuge tubes. To all the tubes 1 ml of 20% copper sulphate solution was added, followed by 1 gram of calcium hydroxide and made up to 10 ml by adding distilled water to each tube. All the tubes were left for half an hour with intermittent shaking. After this, the tubes were centrifuged at 1500 rpm for 15 minutes. 1 ml of supernatant was taken into another test tube from each centrifuge tube and 0.1 ml of 4 per cent copper sulphate solution and 6 ml of chilled analar sulfuric acid were added. All the tubes were boiled in a water bath for 5 minutes and were cooled at 20° C. to 0.1 ml of parahydroxybiphenyl reagent was added and contents were shaken thoroughly. All the tubes were incubated at 30° C for 30 minutes and then boiled for 90 seconds, and were allowed to cool to the room temperature. The colour developed was read at 560 nm against blank in spectrophotometer. Values were expressed as mg lactate/gram wet weight of the tissue.

Estimation of Pyruvate

Pyruvate was estimated by the method of Friedman and Hangen (1942). 10 per cent homogenates of tissues were prepared in 10 per cent TCA and the homogenates were centrifuged at 2,500 rpm for 15 minutes. 1 ml of TCA filtrate was taken and 1.0 ml of 2-4 dintrophenyl hydrazine was added and the tubes were kept for 10 minutes at 37° C, and then 5 ml of 4N sodium hydroxide was added. After 10 minutes, the colour was read at 540 nm in spectrophotometer against a reagent blank.

A standard graph was prepared by taking sodium pyuvate. The pyuvate level was expressed as mg pyruvate/gram wet weight of the tissue.

Glycogen Phosphorylase 1-4 D-Glucon: Orthophosphate glucosyl transferase, E.C.2.4.1.1

Glycogen phosphorylase activity was assayed by the method of Cori et al., (1955) in the direction of glycogen synthesis by the determination of the amount of inorganic phosphate released from glucose-1-phosphate.

10 per cent (W/V) homogenate of liver, kidney, gills, muscle and brain were prepared in cold aqueous medium containing 0.1 M sodium fluoride (pH 6.5) and 0.037 M ethylene diamine tetraacetic acid (EDTA) of pH 6.5 as recommended by Guillory and Mommarets (1962) to avoid enzymatic interconversion of two phosphorylases. The homogenate was centrifuged for 15 minutes at 2,500 rpm and supernatant was diluted to four times (1:3) with cystein hydrochloride (0.03 M) Na β glycerophosphate (0.015 M) buffer of pH 6.5. the incubation mixture for active phosphorylase 'a' in 0.8 ml contained: 0.4 ml enzyme, 0.2 ml of 2 per cent glycogen and 0.2 ml glucose 1-phosphate (0.016 M) and for the total phosphorylase 'ab': 0.4 ml enzyme, 0.2 ml of 2 per cent glycogen and 0.2 ml glucose-1-phosphate (0.016 M), containing adenosine-5-monophosphate (0.004 M).

Active phosphorylase 'a' and total phosphorylase 'ab' enzyme assay mixtures were incubated at 37° C for 30 minutes and 15 minutes respectively. Reaction was stopped by the addition of 5 ml dilute sulfuric acid (10 ml of 5N H_2SO_4 was diluted by 690 ml distilled water). After stopping the reaction, inorganic phosphate was estimated by the method of Taussaky and Shorr (1953). 2 ml of freshly prepared ferrous ammonium molybdate reagent was added to 3 ml of the above supernatant. The blue colour developed was read at 720 nm against the zero controls. The values of enzymes activity are expressed as μ moles Pi/mg protein/hour.

Results and Discussions

1. Lactic Acid

Lactate was found accumulated in all the tissues of the fish exposed to lead salts. Accumulation of lactate was found progressive throughout the exposure period. On the 1st day of exposure the lactic acid was found accumulated in all the tissues at various levels of significance ($P < 0.001$; 0.05).However the values of the brain remain insignificant. Maximum amount of lactic acid was found accumulated in liver (+6.83% for lead nitrate, +8.15% for lead acetate) followed by kidney (+6.47%) for lead nitrate, +7.19 per cent for lead acetate), gill (+4.76% for lead nitrate; +6.19% for lead acetate) muscle (3.48% for lead nitrate, +4.33 per cent for lead acetate). Though brain recorded the measurable percent variation, the values remain insignificant.

On the 4th day exposure all the tissues recorded the accumulation of lactic acid, the maximum accumulation was found in muscle (+22.22% for lead nitrate +25.12% for lead acetate) followed by liver, kidney, gill and brain. All the values were found significant at $P < 0.001$ in liver, muscle, kidney and gill. However brain recorded an enhancement at $P < 0.01$ for lead acetate. On 12th day the per cent enhancement varied from +21.08 per cent to +35.74 per cent for lead nitrate and +27.5 per cent to +46.73 per cent for lead acetate.

On 15th day of exposure liver showed maximum accumulation (+48.67% for lead nitrate, +57.98 per cent for lead acetate, $P < 0.001$) followed by gill (+41.31% lead nitrate, +52.58% lead acetate $P < 0.001$) kidney (+40.21% for lead nitrate, +48.45% lead acetate, $P < 0.001$), muscle (+30.99% for lead nitrate, +34.73% for lead acetate, $P < 0.001$) and brain (+24.22% for lead nitrate, 26.56% for lead acetate 0.01).

During recovery period there was gradual decrease in the enhanced lactate levels in all the tissues. Brain recovered and reached the control levels at the end of 8th day with statistically insignificant variation from controls. Gill and muscle recovered on 12th day, whereas liver and kidney reached normal levels on 15th day of recovery period, with insignificant variation from controls (Fig. 2.1).

2. Pyruvic Acid

Pyruvic acid levels were found decreased in the initial exposure periods, later on there was an enhancement in the pyruvate content. Almost all tissues exhibited similar response to lead toxicity.

On 1st day of exposure the pyruvate content was found significantly decreased in all the tissue at $P < 0.01$ and < 0.05. Maximum depletion was found in kidney (-17.44% for lead nitrate, -18.60% for lead acetate) followed by brain (-15.09% for lead nitrate, -16.98% for lead acetate), liver (-15.49% for lead nitrate, -14.79% for lead acetate), muscle (-12.5% for lead nitrate, -16.67% for lead acetate), and gill (-10.42% for lead nitrate, -12.5% for lead acetate).

On the 4th day of exposure a further depletion in pyruvate content was recorded in all the tissues. The values were found statistically significant at ($P < 0.001$, $P < 0.01$ and $P < 0.05$). The maximum depletion was recorded in kidney followed by brain, liver, gill and muscle. The depletion ranges from -14.67 to -20.73 per cent for lead nitrate and -17.33 per cent to -23.17 per cent for lead acetate.

On the 8th day of exposure an exactly opposite response was witnessed in comparision to its early exposure periods. Accumulatory values were found significant at $P < 0.001$; $P < 0.01$; $P < 0.05$. The accumulation was found to be tissue-specific and in general the accumulation was more in the tissues of fish intoxicated with lead acetate. The order of accumulation for lead nitrate: Brain < gill < muscle < kidney < liver and for lead acetate brain < liver < muscle < gill < kidney.

On 12th day of exposure maximum enhancement in pyruvate content was noticed in kidney (+23.33% for lead nitrate, +26.67% for lead acetate $P < 0.001$) followed by liver (+22.29% for lead nitrate, +24.00% for lead acetate $P < 0.001$); muscle (+22.06% for lead nitrate $P < 0.001$; +23.53% for lead acetate

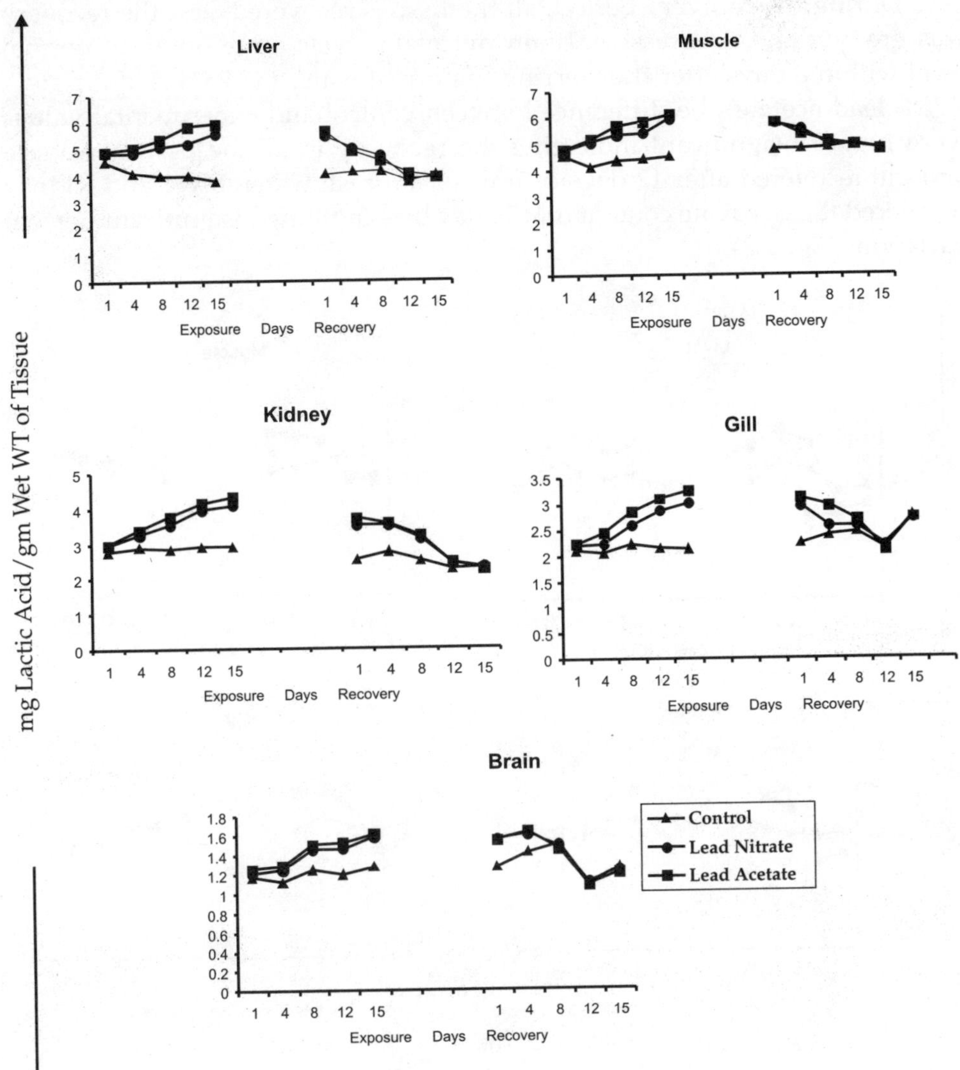

Fig. 2.1: **Lactic Acid Content in the Tissues of *Anabas testudineus* during Exposed and Recovery Days After Lead Intoxication**

P < 0.01); brain (+20.83% for lead nitrate P < 0.05; +22.92% lead acetate P < 0.01); and gill (+18.00% for lead nitrate, +22.00% for lead acetate P < 0.05).

On 15th day of exposure enhancement in the pyruvate was found increased in all the tissues. Kidney accumulated more pyruvate (+31.96% lead nitrate +34.02% lead acetate P < 0.001) followed by liver (+30.41% lead nitrate, +33.78% lead acetate, P < 0.001). Muscle (+29.38% lead nitrate, +32.31% lead acetate, P < 0.01) Gill (+26.09% lead nitrate, +28.26% lead acetate, P ,< 0.05) and Brain (+26.92% lead nitrate P < 0.05, +30.77% lead acetate P < 0.01).

During the recovery period, all the tissues recovered, and the recovery was gradual and progressive. Brain pyruvate levels came down to normal level within 8 days after transferring to normal water (+1.75% lead nitrate, -1.75% lead acetate) the difference between control and experimental values were found insignificant indicating the recovery in all the tissues. Muscle and gill recovered after 12 days of transfer to fresh water. Liver and Kidney recovered the pyruvate content on 15th day by exhibiting insignificant percent variation (Fig. 2.2).

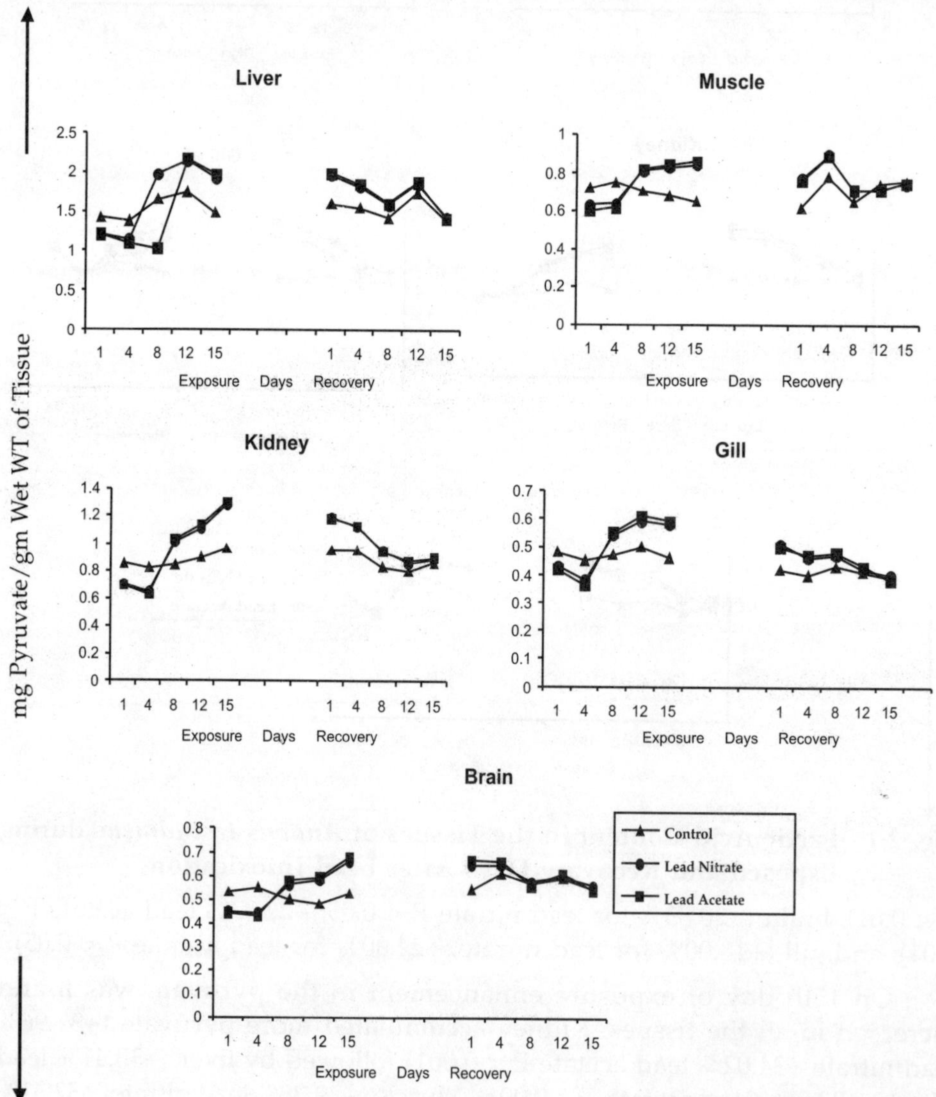

Fig. 2.2: **Pyruvate Content in the Tissues of *Anabas testudineus* during Exposed and Recovery Days After Lead Intoxication**

3. Glycogen Phosphorylase 'a'

The activity of glycogen phosphorylase 'a' was found elevated throughout the exposure period and maximum increase in activity was observed on 15th day of exposure. Liver and muscle exhibited maximum elevation, in comparison to other tissues. The activity patterns of glycogen phosphorylase 'a' are clearly reflected in the levels of glycogen. The activity of this enzyme was tissue-specific and time-dependent.

On 1st day of exposure maximum activity was recorded in kidney (+7.97% for lead nitrate, +7.25% for lead acetate, $P < 0.05$), followed by muscle (+3.92% for lead nitrate and +6.45% for lead acetate, $P < 0.01$ and $P < 0.001$ respectively and liver (+3.35% for lead nitrate $P < 0.05$ and +7.48% for lead acetate $P < 0.001$). Gill and brain exhibited insignificant rise in phosphorylase 'a' activity.

On 4th day of exposure maximum activity was recorded in gill (+13.64% for lead nitrate, +16.23% for lead acetate; $P < 0.05$) followed by liver (+11.90% for lead nitrate, +14.59 for lead acetate $P < 0.001$), kidney (+8.23% for lead nitrate, $P < 0.05$ and +17.35% for lead acetate $P < 0.001$), brain (+11.59% for lead nitrate, $P < 0.01$; +16.91% for lead acetate $P < 0.001$), and muscle (+8.07% for lead nitrate +11.04% for lead acetate, $P < 0.01$).

On 8th day of exposure maximum elevation was found in liver (+25.53% for lead nitrate, +24.38% for lead acetate $P < 0.001$) followed by kidney (+22.53% for lead nitrate, +29.94% for lead acetate, $P < 0.001$), muscle (+21.75% for lead nitrate, +23.58% for lead acetate; $P < 0.001$); gill (24.14% for lead nitrate, +22.41% lead acetate $P < 0.05$) and brain (+14.91% for lead nitrate $P < 0.01$; +27.63% acetate $P < 0.001$).

On 12th day of exposure kidney exhibited more enhancement in the activity of phosphorylase 'a' (+35.02% for lead nitrate, +43.43% for lead acetate $P < 0.001$) and brain exhibited minimum enhancement (+18.67% for lead nitrate, +33.61% for lead acetate, $P < 0.001$). The percent enchancement ranged between + 18.67% to +39.53% for lead nitrate and +30.23% to +43.43% for lead acetate. In the remaining tissues also the percentage varation was significant at $P < 0.001$

On 15th day of exposure maximum enhancement was observed in all the tissues and percent enhancement over control was statistically significant at $P < 0.001$ in all the tissues. Liver and muscle exhibited maximum enhancement, followed by Kidney, Gill and Brain. The present enhancement ranged from +31.16 per cent to 42.78 per cent for lead acetate

On transferring fish to toxicant free water the present enhancement in glycogen phosphorylase 'a' was gradually reduced in all the tissues. The values between experimental and control exhibited statistically insignificant variation indicating the maximum recoveries in the tissues. The recoveries were found more in the lead nitrate intoxicated fish in comparison to lead acetate intoxicated fish. tissues. Early recovery was witnessed in the brain on 8th day of recovery period in the lead nitrate intoxicated fishes, and on 12th day in lead acetate intoxicated fishes (Fig. 2.3).

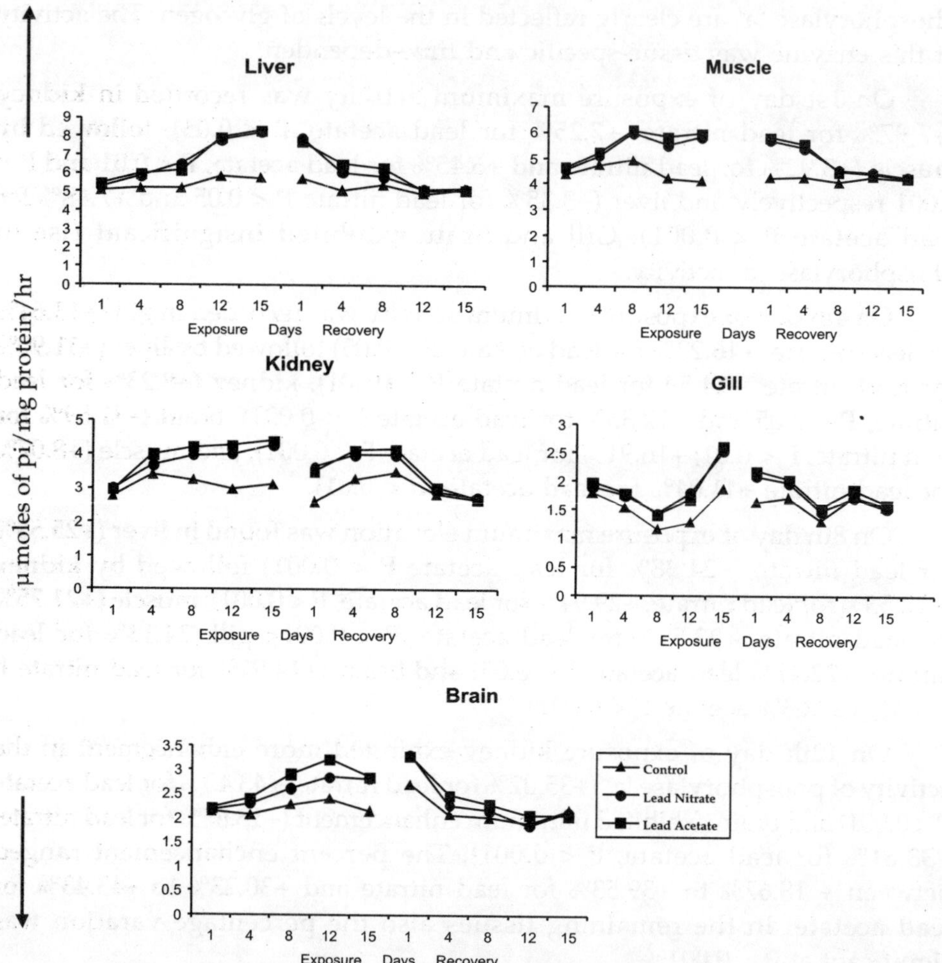

Fig. 2.3: **Activity of Glycogen Phosphorylase "a" in the tissues of *Anabas testudineus* during exposed and recovery days after Lead intoxication**

4. Glycogen Phosporylase "ab"

The total glycogen phosphorylase activity was found enhanced throughout the exposure period in all the tissues. The enhancement was tissue-specific and time-dependent. However maximum activity was noticed on 15th day of exposure period.

On 1st day of exposure maximum enhancement was witnessed in liver (+6.06% for lead nitrate, + 6.53 per cent for lead acetate $P < 0.001$) followed by muscle (+4.27% for lead nitrate., +6.28% for lead acetate; $P < 0.01$ and $P < 0.001$ respectively) and kidney (+4.27% for lead nitrate, +5.19% for lead acetate, $P < 0.01$) gill and brain exhibited an insignificant elevation over controls.

On 4th day of exposure significant elevation was noticed in all the tissues ($P < 0.001$). The percent enhancement ranged from +9.09 to +13.45% for lead nitrate and +11.78 to +17.39 per cent for lead acetate. Maximum activity was witnessed in muscle (+13.45% for lead nitrate, +17.39% for lead acetate) follwed by liver (+13.21% for lead nitrate, +14.18% for lead acetate), kidney (+10.80% for lead nitrate, +11.78% for lead acetate), brain (+10.25%) for lead nitrate and + 12.53 per cent for lead acetate) and gill (+9.09% for lead nitrate, +13.90% for lead acetate).

On 8th day of exposure the elevation in activity was significant at $P < 0.001$ in all the tissues. Maximum activity was observed in liver (+28.75% for lead nitrate, +29.98% for lead acetate). Minimum enhancement was noticed in gill (+14.48% lead nitrate, +17.27% lead acetate). The percent enhancement ranged between +14.48% to +28.75% for lead nitrate and +17.27 per cent to + 29.98 per cent for lead acetate.

On the 12th day of exposure all the tissues recorded significant enhancement in total phosphorylase activity at $P < 0.001$. The magnitude of response was more in lead acetate in comparison to lead nitrate. The highest amount of activity was recorded in the liver (+34.75% for lead nitrate +40.98% for lead acetate) followed by kidney (+30.18% for lead nitrate, +28.25% for lead acetate), brain (+23.05% for lead nitrate, +24.28% lead acetate) and gill (+18.59% for lead nitrate, +23.37% for lead acetate).

On the 15th day of exposure maximum enhancement was observed over all exposure periods. Liver witnessed high enhancement (+40.34% for lead nitrate, +42.74% for lead acetate), followed by kidney (+37.35% lead nitrate, +41.83% lead acetate) , muscle (+33.84% lead nitrate +39.50% lead acetate) brain (+35.20% lead nitrate, +37.36% lead acetate) and gill (+35.20% for lead nitrate and +37.36% lead acetate). The present enhancement was significant at $P < 0.001$ in al the tissues.

During recovery period all the tissues recovered progressively. Brain and Gill recovered rapidly than muscle, kidney and liver. At the end of 15th day the difference between control and experimental values were statistically insignificant indicating recovery of this enzyme in all the tissues. However the brain and gill exhibited an early recovery in comparison to other tissue (Fig. 2.4).

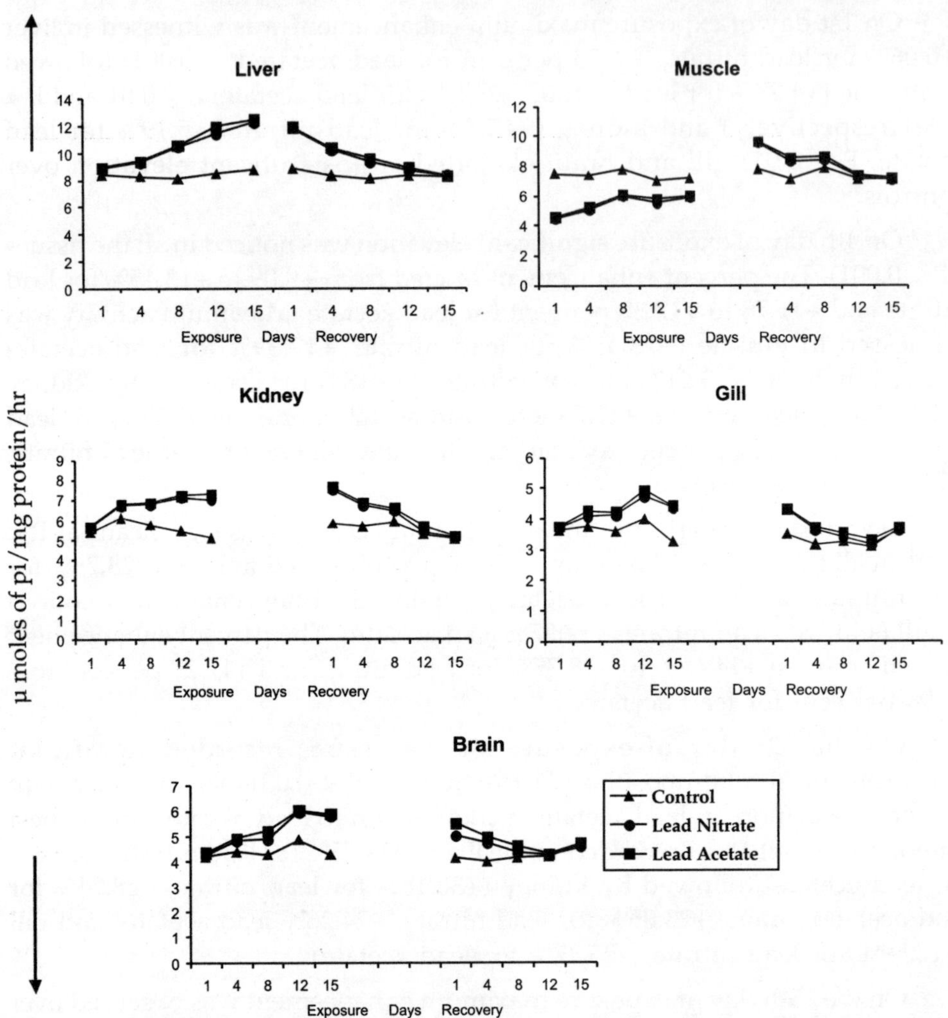

Fig. 2.4: **Activity of Glycogen Phosphorylase "ab" in the tissues of *Anabas testudineus* during exposed and recovery days after Lead intoxication**

Discussion

The present investigation is aimed to understand the alterations in various metabolites and enzymes of carbohydrate and energy metabolism during exposure and recovery periods after lead nitrate and lead acetate intoxication. Two salts of lead i.e. lead nitrate and lead acetate were selected in order to understand the relative toxicities of these salts. The alterations observed in various metabolites and enzymes appear to be tissue-specific and time-dependent. The differential responses of tissues during exposure to lead salts can be attributed to absorption, distribution and elimination kinetics of lead nitrate and lead acetate and also on the characteristics of tissues like vascularity, perfusion and residual blood volume (Villarreal and Villegas, 1987).

Lactic acid was found accumulated in all the tissues throughout the exposure period. The accumulation was progressive and tissue-specific. Maximum accumulation was recorded in liver followed kidney, muscle, gill and brain. The lactic acid accumulation was more in the fishes treated with lead acetate in comparison to the lead nitrate. Accumulation of lactic acid indicates the operation of glycolysis. Similar observations were recorded in fresh water field carb *Barytelphusa guerini* exposed to mercuric chloride and cadmium chloride (Reddy et al., 1989) and in fishes: *Heteropneustes fossils* (Sastry & Subhadra 1985) ; *Cyprinus carpio* (Sastry & Anuradha 2004) after copper and cadmium intoxication) *Cyprinus carpio* (Kamlaveni et.al., 2002). Amongst the organs the maximum responses were recorded in the liver and kidney, this may be due to the more accessibility of the toxicant to these tissues. Liver is known to retain more amount of toxicant (Villerreal and Villegas, 1987) may be due to enterohepatic circulation phenomenon and similarly the kidney is known to receive these metals in the process of its elimination. Thus these concentration factors may be responsible for the pronounced elevation of lactic acid in these tissues.

The maximum responses in the liver and kidney suggest the hepatotoxic and nephrotoxic nature of lead ions. Amongst the organs brain recorded less amount of lactate accumulation. This may due to the less accumulation of lead ions in this tissue due to the presence of blood brain barrier. However, methylated metals are known to cross blood brain barrier and induce toxic manifestations.

The pyruvate levels exhibited a tissue specific and time-dependent changes in the tissues. The pyruvate content was found depleted upto 4th day of exposure in all the tissues, however, an enhancement in the pyruvate levels were recorded from 8th day onwards. The depletion of pyruvate suggests its utilization during early stages of toxic manifestation, while the accumulation suggests an impairment of its utilization. The maximum responses in liver and kidney indicates the hepatotoxic and nephrotoxic nature of the lead ions.

The magnitude of responses was found more in the organic form of lead comparison to the inorganic form. The differences in the responses between these two lead forms may be due to the differences in the rate of absorption, elimination and retention of these two salts of lead in the tissues. The tissues-specific variation in responses could be attributed to concentration factors of the lead in the tissues.

The decrease in the pyruvate content during early stages of exposure could be attributed to its oxidative decarboxylation (Tokaski et al., 1978) by pyruvate dehydrogenase (PDH) to yield an acetyl Co A essential for the commencement of the krebs cycle. Pyruvic acid is important metabolite in the metabolic pathway of carbohydrate. It is convertible in to lactic acid or acetyl Co A depending upon the absence or presence of molecular oxygen in the tissues and also NAD (Raj kumar et.al, 2008). Decrease in pyruvate level in the organs of mussel and fish exposed to cadmium could be due to the speedy reduction of pyruvate to lactate(Venkata chandrudu et.al, 2008).

An increase in the PDH activity in muscle of *Channa punctatus* during chromium toxicity (Sastry & Sunitha, 1982a) lends support for the depletion of pyruvate content. Accumulation of pyruvic acid in the tissues during the subsequent exposures to lead may be due to the impairment of PDH. Inpairment of PDH in tissues of *Channa punctatus* during chronic exposure to chromium (Sastry & Sunitha, 1983b) suggests that, the duration of exposure plays an important role in the pyruvate accumulation in the tissues.

The pyruvate utilization depends on the aerobic and anaerobic state of an animal. Under aerobic situations the pyruvate may be oxidized by PDH to acetyl CoA to meet the excess of energy demands posed by toxic manifestations of lead. The accumulation of pyruvate during the later stages of exposure suggests the arrival of anoxic or hypoxic conditions in the fishes due to the less availability of oxygen.

The depletion in the pyruvate levels could also be attributed to its utilization in the biosynthesis of amino acid like alanine , through transamination reactio. The studies on glutamate pyruvic transaminase would present a correct picture of pyruvate utilization. Further, the chances of pyruvate utilization in the gluconeogenic pathway through oxaloacetate to provide excess of glucose during metal induced anaerobic situations cannot be ruled out in the present study.

Studies on the pyruvate carboxylase would confirm the pyruvate utilization in gluconeogenisis. Accumulation of pyruvate levels may be due to decrease oxidative decarboxylation of the pyruvate. (Tokarski et al., 1978) or may be due to the transamination of alanine amino acid. In evidence to this ALAT activity in all the tissues of the present study was found elevated. The level of pyruvic acid was found to be depleted after exposure to phosalone toxicity in the tissue of freshwater fish *Channa punctatus* (Raj kumar et.al, 2008).

The activity patterns of glycogen phosphorylase a & ab in all the tissues are clearly reflected in the glycogen levels throughout the exposure. The maximum enhancement in the activity of glycogen phosphorylase with the consequential depletion in the glycogen levels in the liver and kidney, indicate the hepatotoxic and nephrotoxic nature of lead ions.

The differences between active and total phosphorylases could be attributed to the variation in the a/ab ratios during toxic manifestations. Enhancement in the glycogen pohosphorylase activity in the tissues of the present model was in agreement with the observations recorded in prawn (Sujay Kumar et.al, 2001) in fishes, *Anabas Scandens* (Sadath 1990) . The activity patterns of glycogen phosphorylase 'a' and 'ab' in all the tissues are clearly reflected in the glycogen levels throughout the exposure period.

The maximum enhancement in the activity of phosphorylase with consequential depletion in the glycogen levels in the liver and kidney indicate the hepatotoxic and nephrotoxic nature of lead. Another possible reason for glycogen depletion may be due to impairment of aerobic respiration .Under such conditions energy is derived from anaerobic respiration resulting in rapid glycogen utilization leading to its depletion. Arrival of anoxic or hypoxic conditions in the fish during lead toxicity may also be one of the factors responsible for the observed glycogen depletion. Impairment of hormonal release and accumulation of biogenic amines may also cause the glycogen depletion in the tissues.

REFERENCES

Bryan, G.W. (1976). Some Aspects of Heavy Metal Tolerance in Aquatic Organism In: Effects of Pollution on Aquatic Organisms *A.D.M. Lock Wood (Ed) Cambridge University Press. U.K.* pp. 7-34.

Cori, G.T. Illingworth, B., and Keller, P.J. (1955) in: "Methods in Enzymology" (S.P. Colowick and N.O. Kaplan eds.), Vol. 1, p. 200, Academic Press. N.Y.

Friedman, T.E. and Hangen, G.E. (1942). Pyruvic Acid 1. Collection of Blood for the Determination of Pyruvic Acid and Lactic Acid. J. Biol Chem. 144(1) 67-74.

Finney, D.J. (1971) Probit Analysis, 3rd Ed. Cambridge University Press, London p. 333.

Hollanders, F.D. (1968) The Production of Lactic Acid by the Perfused Rat Diagphram Comp. Biochem. Physiol. 26(3) pp. 907-916.

Karthikeyen, S, P.R. Palaniappan and S. Sabanayakam (2005). Bioaccumulation of Nickel in Various Organs of Freshwater Fish Cirrhinus Mrigala Exposed to Sub-lethal Concentrations. I.J. Env. Prot., Vol. 25(7): 629-634.

Kanwar, K.C. and Shakti Sharma (1986). Fluctuations in Serum Proteinsand Enzymes in Mouse Following Oral Lead Administration. Res. Bull. Punjab. Univ. Sci., 37 (3/4) 99-104.

Konar, S.K. (1969). Laboratory Studies on the Organophosphorus Insecticides, DDVP and Phosphamidon, As Selective Toxicants *Trans. Am. Fish. Soc.* 98(3) 430-437.

Mathis, B.J. and Chevron, N.R. (1975). Distribution of Mercury, Cadmium, Lead and Thallium in a Eutropic Lake. Hydrobiologia 46: pp. 207-221.

Mali, R.P., (2002). Studies on Some Aspects of Physiology of Freshwater Female Crab Brytelphusa Guerini With Special Reference to Inorganic Pollutants. Ph.D. Thesis Submitted to Swami Ramanand Teerth Marathwada, University, Nanded, Maharashtra.

Mali R.P and Shaikh Afsar (2010). Protien Content Variation in Some Body Component of Barytelphusa Guerini After Exposure to Zinc Sulphate. Journal of Ecology and Fisheries Vol. 3 (2): 57-60.

Olojo, E.A.A., Olurin, K.B., Mbaka, G. and Oluwemimo, A.D. (2005). Histopathology of the Gill and Liver Tissues of the African Catfish Clarias Gariepinus Exposed to Lead. African Journal of Biotechnology Vol. 4 (1) 117-122.

Raj kumar. T, rangappa. a and m. Srinivasulu reddy (2008). Evaluation of Changes in Intermediary Metabolites of Carbohydrates in Tissues of Fresh Water Fish Channa Punctatus during Exposure to Phosalone Toxicity. J.Aqua.Biol., Vol. 23 (2) 147-149.

Reddy, S.L.N., Venugopal, N.B.R.K. and Ramana Rao, J.V. (1989). In Vivo Effects of Cadmium Chloride on Certain Aspects of Carbohydrate Metabolism in the Tissues of a Freshwater Female Crab Barytelphusa guerini. Bul. Environ. Contam. Toxicol. 42(6) 847-857.

Spehar, R.L., Carlson, R.W., Lemke, A.E., Mount, D.L., Pickering, Q.H. and Snarski, V.M. (1981a) "Effects of Pollution on Freshwater Fish". Journal WPCF 52(6) 1703-1767.

Sastry K. V.and KM. Subhadra (1985). In Vivo Effects of Cadmium on some Enzyme Activities in Tissues of the Freshwater Catfish, Heteropneustes fossilis. Environ. Res. Volume 36(1) 32-45.

This Article is not Included in your Organization's Subscription. However, you may be Able to Access this Article Under your Organization's Agreement with Elsevier.

Sastry, K.V., & Anuradha (2004). Effect of Cadmium and Copper on some Biochemical and Enzymological Parameters in the Fresh Water Fish Cyprinus Carpio. National Symposium on Biodiversity, Biotechnology and Environmental Toxicology in the New Millennium held at Mumbai, India on 22nd to 24th November. p. 85.

Sadath Sulthana (1990). "Physiological Responses of Freshwater Fish Anabas Testudineus (Cuvier) during Exposure and Recovery Periods after CdCl2 Intoxication. Doctoral Dissertation Submitted to Osmania University.

Sastry, K.V. and Sunita K. (1982a) Effects of Cadmium and Chromium on the Intestinal Absorption of Glucose in the Snake Head Fish Channa Punctatus. Toxicol Lett. 10 (2-3) 293-296.

Sastry, K.V. and Sunita, K. (1983b). Enzymological and Biochemical Chanes Produced by Chronic Chromium Exposure in a Teleost Fish Channa Punctatus. Toxicol. Lett. 16(1-2) 9-15.

Sreenivasa Reddy , A , M.Venkata Reddy and K.Radhakrishnaiah (2006). Impact of Lead on the Energetics of Common Carp Cyprinus Carpio (Linnaeus) J.Aqua.Biol., Vol. 21(2): 234-238.

Sujay Kumar, G, M.Hanuma Reddy and M.Srinivasulu Reddy (2001). Phosphamidon Induced Changes in the Glycolytic Potentials of Penaeid Prawn Metapenaeus Monoceros J.aqua.biol. Vol.16 (1) 71-76.

Tokarski, Elisabeth and Lembitu Reio (1978). Effect of Lead on the Thiamine Status and Function in Liver and Blood of Rats. Acta. Chem Scand Ser B Org Chem. Biochem 32(5) 375-379.

Villarrel-trevino, C.M., A. Vilegas-Navorro (1987)" Dfferentia acc of Lead by Soft Tissues of Rabbit" Bull. Environ. Contam. Toxicol 1987. 39: 334-342.

Yigit, S. and A. Altindag (2007). Concentration of Heavy Metals in the Food Web of Lake Egirdir, Turkey. J. Environ. Biol. 27(3): 475-478.

Waldichuk, M. 1974. Some Biological Concerns in Heavy Metal Pollution. In: Pollution and Physiology of Marine Organism. *F.J. Vernberg and W.B.Vernberg (Eds) Academic Press New York 1-57.*

Water Quality Criteria, 1972: A Report of the Committee on Water Quality Criteria, Environmental Studies Board, National Academy of Sciences, National Academy of Engineering, Washington, D.C., 1972, pp. 1-594.

3

Ameliorate the Drastic Effect of Ochratoxin A by Using Yeast and Whey in Cultured Oreochromus Niloticus in Egypt

Mansour, T.A, ***Egypt***
Safinaz, G.Mohamed, ***Egypt***
Soliman, M.K., ***Egypt***
Eglal, A. Omar, ***Egypt***
Srour, T.M., ***Egypt***
Mona S. Zaki, ***Egypt***
Shahinaz, M. H. Hassan, ***Egypt***

ABSTRACT

Ochratoxin A is one of the most important mycotoxins in fish feed. In the present study the effects of OTA on cultured Oreochromus niloticus were evaluated. Trials for ameliorate the drastic effect of OTA were done by using active life yeast and whey. The results indicted that significant ($p<0.05$) decrease in RBCS, WBCS, phagocytic activity and phagocytic index were occurred in both levels of OTA. Hypoalbuminemia, hypoproteinemia, decrease of globulin, and antibody titer as well as increase of liver enzymes, creatinine and uric acid were noticed. The histopathological examination showed that OTA caused diffuse hydropic degeneration and advanced fatty changes in liver. Tubular necrosis and hydropic degeneration of the kidneys were observed .The activation of melano macrophage centers (MMCs) were recorded. The results proved that OTA produce serious physiological, immunological and pathological effects on, O.niloticus. Morovere active life yeast and whey were succeed to neutralize the drastic toxic effects of OTA.

Keywords: Ameliorate; Drastic Effect; Ochratoxin; Oreochromus niloticus; Egypt.

Introduction

Ochratoxin is a group of secondary metabolites produced by fungi of two genera: *Penicillium* and *Aspergillus*, this group include Ochratoxin A; Ochratoxin B; Ochratoxin C; Ochratoxin á, and the most toxic member is Ochratoxin A (OTA))Ringot *et al.*, 2006).

Manning *et al.*, (2005) indicated that juvenile channel catfish fed OTA had greater mortality when challenged with *Edwardsiella ictaluri* compared with control group. Saad (2002) reported that OTA has immunosuppressive effect on *O. niloticus* and Common carp in acute (50 μg/kg fish) and chronic toxicity (10 μg/kg fish).

The role of microorganisms on detoxification of OTA has a lot of concern because they promote the hydrolysis of OTA to its nontoxic form (Ochratoxin α (OTα)) in case of ruminant (Sreemannarayana *et al.*, 1988) and non ruminant (Madhyastha *et al.*, 1992).

In many studies on OTA detoxification by yeast showed antagonistic effect on the production of OTA by fungi. Petersson *et al.*, (1998) showed that *Saccharomyces cerevisiae* inhibit production of toxin from *Penicillium verrucosum*. Péteri et al. (2007) found that yeast strain, *Phaffia rhodozyma*, degraded more than 90 per cent of OTA in 15 days at 20°C where hydrolysis it to OTα.

Moreover, yeast enhanced immune response of treated fish (Elkafoury, 2006; Reyes-Becerril *et. al.*, 2008). Useful microflora in the intestine such as Lactobacillus and Bifidobacterial can utilize the lactose for proliferation (Naghton *et al.*, 2001).

The proliferation of this species causes increase in the acidity of intestine by producing lactic acid and short-chain fatty acids formed unsuitable environment to pathogen bacteria like *Salmonida* and *Escherichia coli* (Juven *et al.*, 1991). This competition leads to excluding harmful bacteria out of the gut (Nurmi and Rantal, 1973). Consequently digestion and absorption increased and feed utilization improved (Tellez *et al.*, 1993). No available studies conducted to investigate the effect of whey on fish.

Moreover, whey protein concentrates enhanced ex-vivo lymphoid cell proliferative responses and increased in vivo antibody production (Knowles and Gill, 2002).

The aim of the present study is to investigate the effects of OTA on cultured *O. niloticus* and attempt to ameliorate the drastic effect of OTA by using yeast and whey as diet supplementations.

Materials and Methods

Apparently healthy 210 *O. niloticus* with an average body weight of 40 ±5 g/fish were used. Fish was obtained from private fish farm in Alexandria governorate and kept for 21 days in circular fiberglass tanks (800L) for acclimatization and fed on a diet contained 30 per cent crude protein.

Water temperature was ranged 25-27C. Continuous aeration was maintained in each tank using an electric air pumping compressor.

The 210 *O. niloticus* fish were randomly allotted in fourteen fiberglass tanks (two tanks/treatment) with fifteen fish per tank. The fish treated by Ochratoxin A (OTA) in two doses according to Saad (2002), 80 µg/kg fish as low dose (LOTA) and 160 µg/kg fish as high dose (HOTA). The OTA doses performed by stomach intubations once in day zero of the experiment in all fish groups by dissolving OTA in chloroform according to Trucksess and Pohland (2001) then dissolved in corn oil (Abdel-Wahhab *et al.*, 2005) and left to evaporate the chloroform before using. The individual stomach) intubations performed by using syringe attached with butterfly cannula to get the doses through the stomach of the fish (Abdel-Wahhab *et al.*, 2005). Fish in control group which fed basal diet received 0.5 ml corn oil.

Yeast (Tonilisat®): Active live yeast (China Way Corporation, Taiwan kindly supplied by EL Zahra Vetrinary), *Saccharomyces cerevisiae*, (8 X 10^9 cells/ gram) was used. The yeast added in the ration by incorporating 0.5 kg/ton ration after coating it with oil according to (Elkafoury, 2006). Fish were kept under daily observation for 8 weeks.

Whey: Whey powder (Dairy Farmers Company of America New Wilmington, PA 16142 U.S.A) free fats were used in the experiment. The whey incorporated into the diet at 14 per cent. The whey contained 11, 62, 0.5 and 11 per cent of Protein, Lactose, Fiber and Ash, respectively.

Seven experimental treatments were designed as follows: the basal diet (BD), BD with LOTA dose (80 µg OTA/kg fish), BD with HOTA dose (160 µg OTA/ kg fish), AY diet (0.5 g/kg diet) and LOTA dose,AY diet (0.5 g/kg diet) and HOTA dose, W diet (14% of diets) and LOTA dose and W diet (14% of diets) and HOTA dose.

Every two weeks, blood samples were taken from the caudal vasculature of - fish after anesthetized with MS222 (ten fish/treatment) for hematological assay and serum separation. Total red blood cell (RBCs), white blood cell (WBCs) were performed according to the methods of Anderson and Siwicki (1995) and Hesser (1960) respectively.

Determination of phagocytic activity and phagocytic index:

Phagocytic activity was determined according to Kawahara *et al.* (1991) and Safinaz, (2001). Phagocytosis was estimated by determining the proportion of macrophages which contained intracellular yeast cells in a random count of 300 phagocytes and expressed as percentage of phagocytic activity (PA). The number of phagocytized organisms was counted in the phagocytic cells and called phagocytic index.

Clinico-biochemical determination was used to examine total protein, albumin, globulin and albumin/globulin ratio, alkaline phosphatase, glutamic-oxaloacetic transaminase, uric acid and creatinine were done according to Saad (2002) and Safinaz (2001) by using commercial kits (Biodiagnostic, Cairo, Egypt).

Evaluation of immune response of *O. niloticus* against *Aeromona. hydrophila* bacterin.

Aeromonus hydrophila isolate was used in the bacterin preparation according to the method described by (Sakai *et al.*, 1984)

The preparation of bacterin for injection was carried out according to the method of Badran (1990). The formalin inactivated bacterin cells were mixed with an equal volume of 0.85 per cent sterile saline. Bacterial number was adjusted to Fit MacFarlan's No. 2.

At the 4th week one hundred and five *O. niloticus* fish exposed to both dose of OTA and control were inoculated intraperitoneally (IP) with 0.2 ml/fish of formalin inactivated bacterin. One hundred and five *O. niloticus* fish were similarly injected IP with 0.2 ml/fish sterile saline. After 2 weeks, the injected fish received booster dose from bacterin. After 1, 2, 3 and 4 weeks post-injection with inactivated bacterin blood collection was carried out from the caudal vasculature of inoculated fish after anesthetized with MS222 for antibody determination by microagglutination test according to the method described by Badran (1990).

Histopathological Studies

At the end of experiment specimen from kidneys, spleens and livers were removed from fish of the experimental groups and rapidly placed in adequate amount of 10 per cent neutral buffered formalin for at least 24 hrs and used for histopathological studies according to Culling (1983).

Statistical Analysis

Statistical analysis of the experimental results was conducted according to SPSS (version 16.00). Duncan's (1955) multiple range test was carried out to test the significance levels among means of treatments.

Results

The effects of OTA, yeast and whey on red blood cells (RBCs), white blood cells (WBCs) count PA and PI are demonstrated in (Table 3.1). The red blood cells count differ significantly (***P***> 0.05) all over experimental period, where OTA presented severe decrease of RBCs especially with HOTA dose and showed anemia. Meanwhile, addition of yeast and whey with both OTA doses increased RBCs count and improved the body health condition.

Table 3.1: Effect of Ochratoxin A (OTA), Yeast and Whey on Red Blood Cells (RBCs), White Blood Cells (WBCs) Phagocytic Activity (PA) and Phagocytic Index (PI) of Blood of *O. niloticus* Through out Experimental Period ($\overline{X} \pm SE$)

Items	Treatments	Week 2	Week 4	Week 6	Week 8	Total Mean
1	2	3	4	5	6	7
Total protein (g/dl)	Control	4.39±0.21	4.37±0.10	4.39±0.12^{a}	4.46±0.06^{a}	4.40±0.06^{a}
	LOTA dose	4.14±0.31	4.05±0.22	3.73±0.08^{cd}	3.55±0.09^{bc}	3.87±0.11^{BC}
	HOTA dose	3.91±0.10	3.69±0.17	3.42±0.04^{d}	3.06±0.06^{d}	3.52±0.09^{D}
	LOTA dose + yeast	4.34±0.17	4.29±0.12	4.12±0.13^{ab}	3.84±0.14^{b}	4.15±0.08^{AB}
	HOTA dose + yeast	4.31±0.32	4.14±0.06	3.88±0.14^{bc}	3.44±0.08^{bcd}	3.94±0.12^{BC}
	LOTA dose + whey	4.22±0.18	4.20±0.18	4.02±0.20^{bc}	3.65±0.25^{bc}	4.02±0.11^{BC}
	HOTA dose + whey	4.18±0.12	3.98±0.25	3.70±0.03^{cd}	3.42±0.10^{cd}	3.82±0.10^{C}
	Total Mean	**4.21±0.08^{A}**	**4.10±0.07^{AB}**	**3.90±0.07^{B}**	**3.63±0.09^{C}**	**3.96**
Albumin (g/dl)	Control	3.10±0.11	3.16±0.21	3.06±0.10^{a}	3.13±0.08^{a}	3.11±0.06^{A}
	LOTA dose	3.03±0.23	2.87±0.03	2.73±0.06^{b}	2.52±0.04^{c}	2.79±0.07^{B}
	HOTA dose	2.95±0.04	2.76±0.14	2.65±0.08^{b}	2.47±0.05^{c}	2.71±0.06^{B}
	LOTA dose + yeast	3.09±0.25	2.97±0.13	2.81±0.14^{b}	2.73±0.05^{b}	2.90±0.08^{B}
	HOTA dose + yeast	3.04±0.33	2.87±0.09	2.75±0.06^{b}	2.76±0.07^{b}	2.84±0.09^{B}
	LOTA dose + whey	3.06±0.12	2.92±0.09	2.79±0.07^{b}	2.73±0.06^{b}	2.87±0.05^{B}
	HOTA dose + whey	3.00±0.04	2.81±0.06	2.67±0.04^{b}	2.52±0.06^{c}	2.75±0.05^{B}
	Total Mean	**3.04±0.06^{A}**	**2.91±0.05^{AB}**	**2.78±0.04^{BC}**	**2.69±0.04^{B}**	**2.85**

(Contd…)

1	2	3	4	5	6	7
Globulin (g/dl)	Control	1.29±0.17	1.21±0.22	1.34±0.11	1.33±0.11^{a}	1.29±0.07^{A}
	LOTA dose	1.11±0.38	1.18±0.22	0.99±0.12	1.03±0.12^{ab}	1.08±0.11^{A}
	HOTA dose	0.96±0.10	0.92±0.26	0.77±0.11	0.59±0.07^{b}	0.81±0.08^{B}
	LOTA dose + yeast	1.25±0.22	1.33±0.23	1.31±0.07	1.11±0.17^{ab}	1.25±0.09^{A}
	HOTA dose + yeast	1.27±0.07	1.27±0.12	1.12±0.12	0.73±0.13^{b}	1.10±0.08^{A}
	LOTA dose + whey	1.16±0.24	1.29±0.27	1.24±0.26	0.92±0.31^{ab}	1.15±0.13^{A}
	HOTA dose + whey	1.18±0.15	1.17±0.21	1.03±0.03	0.89±0.10^{ab}	1.07±0.07^{A}
	Total Mean	**1.17±0.07^{A}**	**1.19±0.08^{A}**	**1.12±0.06^{AB}**	**0.94±0.07^{B}**	**1.11**
A/G Ratio	Control	2.55±0.36	3.01±0.74	2.33±0.20	2.42±0.26	2.58±0.21
	LOTA dose	4.00±1.54	2.68±0.46	2.87±0.34	2.60±0.44	3.04±0.41
	HOTA dose	3.17±0.34	4.18±1.47	3.84±0.87	4.48±0.71	3.92±0.44
	LOTA dose + yeast	2.75±0.55	2.53±0.57	2.16±0.17	2.66±0.48	2.53±0.22
	HOTA dose + yeast	2.43±0.33	2.36±0.35	2.55±0.31	4.46±1.34	2.95±0.40
	LOTA dose + whey	3.00±0.58	2.63±0.62	2.67±0.68	4.50±1.54	3.20±0.47
	HOTA dose + whey	2.69±0.36	2.74±0.62	2.59±0.11	2.95±0.39	2.74±0.19

Values in the same item with different letters are significantly different.
LOTA dose (80 µg OTA/ kg fish). HOTA dose (160 µg OTA/ kg fish).

Significant (***P*** >0.05) differences were observed after two weeks of treatment and showed decrease of WBCs count with LOTA and HOTA doses significantly than control group and reduced insignificantly than yeast and whey treatments all over the experimental period.

The significant (***P***>0.05) differences of PA were observed at week four until the end of the experiment. The PA of HOTA dose reduced significantly than other treatments. Meanwhile, insignificant (***P***<0.05) differences were observed among LOTA dose and detoxification treatments.

The phagocytic index differ significantly from the second week of treatment, where HOTA dose recorded the lowest significant (***P***>0.05) PI and showed insignificant (***P*** <0.05) differences with LOTA dose and HOTA dose plus whey all over the experiment. The addition of yeast ameliorate the drastic effect of OTA significant (***P***>0.05) on PI especially with LOTA dose. Meanwhile, slightly improve of PI observed with HOTA dose plus yeast and LOTA dose plus whey.

The significant effects of OTA, yeast and whey on total protein (Table 3.2) observed at week six to eight and showed significant (***P***<0.05) decrease of total protein with both LOTA and HOTA doses treatments. Meanwhile, the addition of yeast increased total protein values with both LOTA (significant ***P***<0.05) and HOTA doses. Whey addition increased total protein but not significantly (***P*** <0.05) with both LOTA and HOTA doses.

Regarding to albumin level, significant effects was observed at week six where each OTA treatments and detoxification treatments showed significant (***P*** <0.05) decrease of albumin value (hypoalbuminemia) than control group although yeast and whey improved albumin levels insignificantly (***P***<0.05) than LOTA and HOTA doses.

Insignificant (***P*** <0.05) decrease of globulin with LOTA and HOTA doses and increased in case of yeast and whey until sixth week were found. Meanwhile, at eighth week globulin decrease significant (***P***<0.05) with LOTA dose and HOTA dose.

The results of antibody titer of *O. niloticus* after vaccination with *A. hydrphila* and exposed to OTA and detoxification agents (yeast and whey) were 4, 2.67±0.33, 2±0.00, 3.33±0.33, 3±0.00, 3.67±0.33 and 3.00±0.00 in case of control, LOTA, HOTA, LOTA plus yeast, HOTA plus yeast, LOTA plus whey and HOTA plus whey respectively. The results indicated that significant (***P*** <0.05) differences were observed among other treatments and control group. However, the addition of yeast and whey to the diet increased significantly antibody titare.

Table 3.2: Effect of Ochratoxin A (OTA), Yeast and Whey on the Total Protein, Albumin, Globulin and Albumin/ Globulin Ratio (A/G Ratio) in Serum of *O. niloticus* Through Out Experiment

Items	Treatments	Week 2	Week 4	Week 6	Week 8	Total Mean
1	2	3	4	5	6	7
Total protein (g/dl)	Control	4.39±0.21	4.37±0.10	4.39±0.12^{a}	4.46±0.06^{a}	4.40±0.06^{a}
	LOTA dose	4.14±0.31	4.05±0.22	3.73±0.08^{cd}	3.55±0.09^{bc}	3.87±0.11^{BC}
	HOTA dose	3.91±0.10	3.69±0.17	3.42±0.04^{d}	3.06±0.06^{d}	3.52±0.09^{D}
	LOTA dose + yeast	4.34±0.17	4.29±0.12	4.12±0.13^{ab}	3.84±0.14^{b}	4.15±0.08^{AB}
	HOTA dose + yeast	4.31±0.32	4.14±0.06	3.88±0.14^{bc}	3.44±0.08b^{cd}	3.94±0.12^{BC}
	LOTA dose + whey	4.22±0.18	4.20±0.18	4.02±0.20^{bc}	3.65±0.25^{bc}	4.02±0.11^{BC}
	HOTA dose + whey	4.18±0.12	3.98±0.25	3.70±0.03^{cd}	3.42±0.10^{cd}	3.82±0.10^{C}
	Total Mean	**4.21±0.08^{A}**	**4.10±0.07^{AB}**	**3.90±0.07^{B}**	**3.63±0.09^{C}**	**3.96**
Albumin (g/dl)	Control	3.10±0.11	3.16±0.21	3.06±0.10^{a}	3.13±0.08^{a}	3.11±0.06^{A}
	LOTA dose	3.03±0.23	2.87±0.03	2.73±0.06^{b}	2.52±0.04^{c}	2.79±0.07^{B}
	HOTA dose	2.95±0.04	2.76±0.14	2.65±0.08^{b}	2.47±0.05^{c}	2.71±0.06^{B}
	LOTA dose + yeast	3.09±0.25	2.97±0.13	2.81±0.14^{b}	2.73±0.05^{b}	2.90±0.08^{B}
	HOTA dose + yeast	3.04±0.33	2.87±0.09	2.75±0.06^{b}	2.76±0.07^{b}	2.84±0.09^{B}
	LOTA dose + whey	3.06±0.12	2.92±0.09	2.79±0.07^{b}	2.73±0.06^{b}	2.87±0.05^{B}
	HOTA dose + whey	3.00±0.04	2.81±0.06	2.67±0.04^{b}	2.52±0.06^{c}	2.75±0.05^{B}
	Total Mean	**3.04±0.06A**	**2.91±0.05AB**	**2.78±0.04^{BC}**	**2.69±0.04B**	**2.85**

(Contd...)

1	2	3	4	5	6	7
Globulin (g/dl)	Control	1.29±0.17	1.21±0.22	1.34±0.11	1.33±0.11^{a}	1.29±0.07^{A}
	LOTA dose	1.11±0.38	1.18±0.22	0.99±0.12	1.03±0.12^{ab}	1.08±0.11^{A}
	HOTA dose	0.96±0.10	0.92±0.26	0.77±0.11	0.59±0.07^{b}	0.81±0.08^{B}
	LOTA dose + yeast	1.25±0.22	1.33±0.23	1.31±0.07	1.11±0.17^{ab}	1.25±0.09^{A}
	HOTA dose + yeast	1.27±0.07	1.27±0.12	1.12±0.12	0.73±0.13^{b}	1.10±0.08^{A}
	LOTA dose + whey	1.16±0.24	1.29±0.27	1.24±0.26	0.92±0.31^{ab}	1.15±0.13^{A}
	HOTA dose + whey	1.18±0.15	1.17±0.21	1.03±0.03	0.89±0.10^{ab}	1.07±0.07^{A}
	Total Mean	**1.17±0.07A**	**1.19±0.08A**	**1.12±0.06^{AB}**	**0.94±0.07^{B}**	**1.11**
A/G Ratio	Control	2.55±0.36	3.01±0.74	2.33±0.20	2.42±0.26	2.58±0.21
	LOTA dose	4.00±1.54	2.68±0.46	2.87±0.34	2.60±0.44	3.04±0.41
	HOTA dose	3.17±0.34	4.18±1.47	3.84±0.87	4.48±0.71	3.92±0.44
	LOTA dose + yeast	2.75±0.55	2.53±0.57	2.16±0.17	2.66±0.48	2.53±0.22
	HOTA dose + yeast	2.43±0.33	2.36±0.35	2.55±0.31	4.46±1.34	2.95±0.40
	LOTA dose + whey	3.00±0.58	2.63±0.62	2.67±0.68	4.50±1.54	3.20±0.47
	HOTA dose + whey	2.69±0.36	2.74±0.62	2.59±0.11	2.95±0.39	2.74±0.19

Values in the same item with different letters are significantly different.

LOTA dose (80 µg OTA/kg fish). HOTA dose (160 µg OTA/kg fish).

Yeast (0.5 g/kg diet). Whey (14% of diets).

Data presented in (Table 3.3) showed the effect of OTA, yeast and whey on the liver and kidneys function. Significant differences of GOT were observed at the sixth week of treatment where GOT values with LOTA and HOTA doses increased significantly than control and yeast supplementation treatments.

Table 3.3: Effect of Ochratoxin A (OTA), Yeast and Whey on the Glutamic-oxaloacetic Transaminase (GOT), Alkaline Phosphatase (ALP), Creatinine and Uric Acid of *O. niloticus* Through Out Experimental Period ($\overline{X} \pm SE$)

Items	Treatments	Week 2	Week 4	Week 6	Week 8	Total Mean
1	2	3	4	5	6	7
GOT (units/ml)	Control	24.67±4.06	28.33±5.07	29.67±2.51^{b}	36.00±3.46^{c}	29.67± .07
	LOTA dose	26.33±5.49	30.83±4.80	33.33±0.29^{ab}	44.83±2.13^{ab}	33.33±2.39
	HOTA dose	28.00±1.15	34.33±2.67	35.78±1.61^{a}	49.00±2.08^{a}	35.78±2.06
	LOTA dose + yeast	21.50±3.62	26.33±4.70	29.61±0.46^{b}	38.67±2.40^{bc}	29.61±2.64
	HOTA dose + yeast	24.50±1.04	27.00±2.75	31.05±1.01^{b}	41.00±1.53^{bc}	31.06±2.13
	LOTA dose + whey	23.67±0.73	30.83±4.64	32.11±0.86^{ab}	41.83±1.92^{abc}	32.11±2.24
	HOTA dose + whey	24.67±4.42	30.33±0.88	32.78±0.24^{ab}	45.33±2.60^{ab}	32.78±2.44
	Total Mean	**24.76±1.16^{C}**	**29.71±1.36B**	**32.05±0.60^{B}**	**41.67±1.11^{A}**	**32.05**
ALP (IU/L)	Control	21.60±2.18	17.62±2.14	18.58±1.49^{b}	18.06±1.48^{c}	18.97±0.92
	LOTA dose	20.43±0.75	19.52±3.42	21.98±0.40^{ab}	23.32±1.33^{ab}	21.31±0.92
	HOTA dose	23.19±0.60	20.54±1.44	23.63±0.54^{a}	25.10±1.58^{a}	22.32±0.89
	LOTA dose + yeast	20.48±0.44	18.49±0.49	21.79±0.88^{ab}	20.40±0.74^{bc}	20.29±0.45
	HOTA dose + yeast	22.13±3.22	18.14±3.26	21.51±1.58^{ab}	22.32±1.13^{ab}	21.02±1.18
	LOTA dose + whey	20.00±1.86	18.70±3.24	20.38±0.79^{ab}	20.45±1.14^{bc}	20.68±0.90
	HOTA dose + whey	21.86±2.64	19.62±0.97	23.07±1.95^{a}	23.47±1.29^{ab}	22.00±0.90
	Total Mean	**21.38±0.66^{A}**	**18.95±0.79^{B}**	**21.56±0.52^{A}**	**21.87±0.63^{A}**	**20.94**

(Contd...)

1	2	3	4	5	6	7
Creatinine (mg/dl)	Control	0.78±0.03	0.62±0.11	1.59±0.14[c]	1.76±0.33	1.31±0.21
	LOTA dose	1.10±0.25	1.61±0.62	2.10±0.04[bc]	3.06±0.31	1.97±0.27
	HOTA dose	1.32±0.46	1.83±0.32	3.63±0.32[a]	3.50±0.28	2.57±0.34
	LOTA dose + yeast	1.10±0.09	1.34±0.47	1.66±0.30[c]	2.72±0.52	1.71±0.25
	HOTA dose + yeast	1.07±0.21	1.36±0.17	2.43±0.37[bc]	3.02±0.14	1.97±0.26
	LOTA dose + whey	1.08±0.30	0.64±0.35	1.84±0.46[c]	2.57±0.97	1.53±0.33
	HOTA dose + whey	0.92±0.39	1.10±0.27	2.80±0.08[ab]	3.17±1.10	2.00±0.40
	Total Mean	**1.05±0.10[C]**	**1.22±0.15[C]**	**2.29±0.18[B]**	**2.90±0.22[A]**	**1.87**
Uric acid (mg/dl)	Control	0.83±0.26	1.26±0.26	2.25±0.45	2.19±0.31[c]	1.63±0.23
	LOTA dose	0.86±0.34	1.56±0.27	3.00±0.42	3.86±0.62[ab]	2.32±0.40
	HOTA dose	2.05±0.47	2.45±0.53	3.55±0.59	4.14±0.43[a]	3.05±0.33
	LOTA dose + yeast	0.93±0.23	1.29±0.27	3.04±0.41	2.98±0.17[abc]	2.06±0.31
	HOTA dose + yeast	0.83±0.35	1.62±0.37	2.65±0.17	3.02±0.37[abc]	2.03±0.29
	LOTA dose + whey	1.12±0.09	2.24±0.33	2.88±0.18	2.25±0.52[c]	2.13±0.24
	HOTA dose + whey	1.51±0.41	2.13±0.48	2.73±0.21	2.51±0.33[bc]	2.22±0.21
	Total Mean	**1.16±0.14[C]**	**1.79±0.15[B]**	**2.87±0.15[A]**	**2. 99±0.21[A]**	**2.20**

Values in the same item having different letters are significantly different. LOTA dose (80 µg OTA/kg fish). HOTA dose (160 µg OTA/kg fish). Yeast (0.5 g/kg diet). Whey (14% of diets).

In the same time the levels of liver enzymes in case of OTA plus yeast were less than OTA only.

The results of creatinine and uric acid showed increase especially with HOTA dose than other treatments. Moreover, the addition of yeast and whey decreased creatinine and uric acid levels especially with LOTA dose.

The histopathological examination in the present study showed that LOTA dose after 8 weeks from treatment caused diffuse hydropic degeneration of hepatic cells, congestion of hepatic sinusoids and mild incidence of melanomacrophage centers (MMCs). Moreover, the posterior kidney showed mild acute cellular swelling and MMCs activationwere observed in kidney and spleen (Figs. 3.1, 3.2 and 3.3).

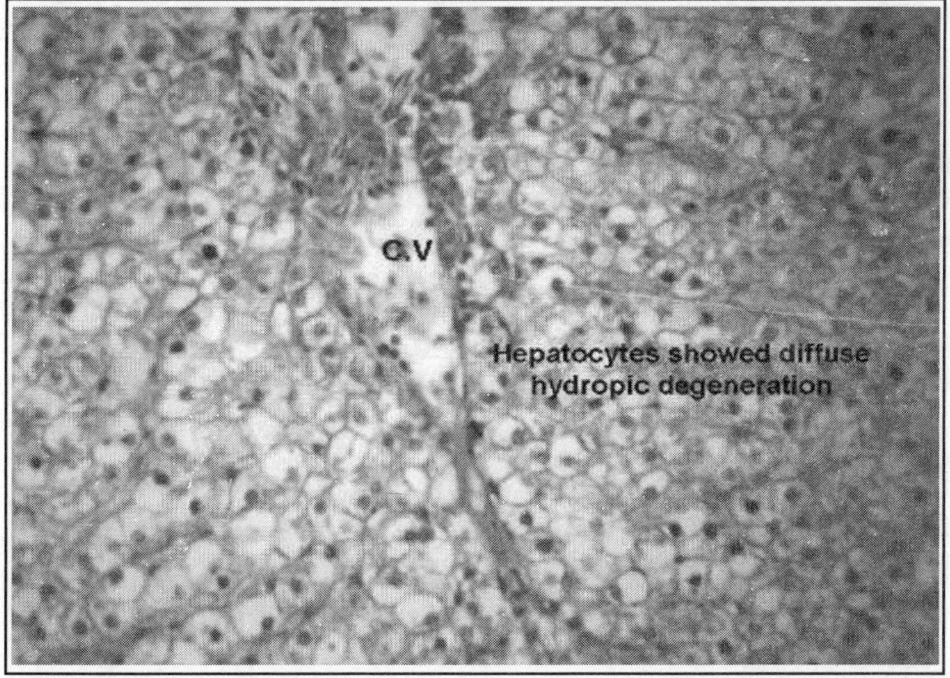

Fig. 3.1: **Liver of *O. niloticus* exposed to LOTA dose showing diffuse hydropic degeneration of hepatic cells. H&E. (X 250)**

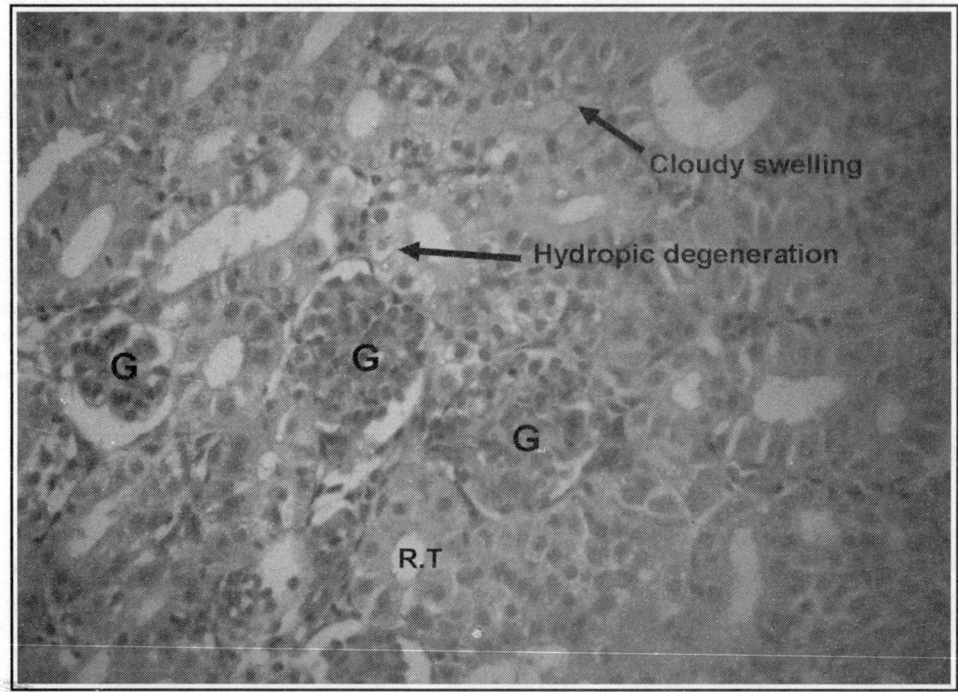

Fig. 3.2: Kidney of *O. niloticus* exposed to LOTA dose showing mild acute cellular swelling. H&E. (X 250)

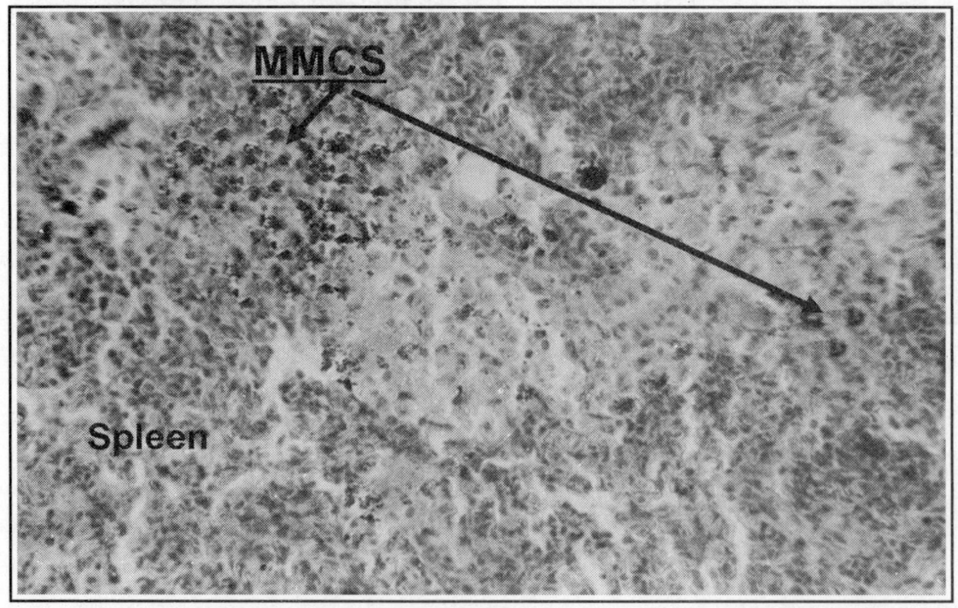

Fig. 3.3: Spleen of *O. niloticus* exposed to LOTA dose showing activation of MMCS. H&E. (X 250)

In case of HOTA dose diffuse advanced fatty changes appeared as Signet ring, atrophied of hepatic cells and activation of MMCs in pancreatic islets were recorded. In kidney, infiltration and activation of MMCs and acute tubular necrosis were recorded. Severe infiltration of MMCs to extent that total replaced of the splenic tissues were also noticed (Figs. 3.4, 3.5 and 3.6).

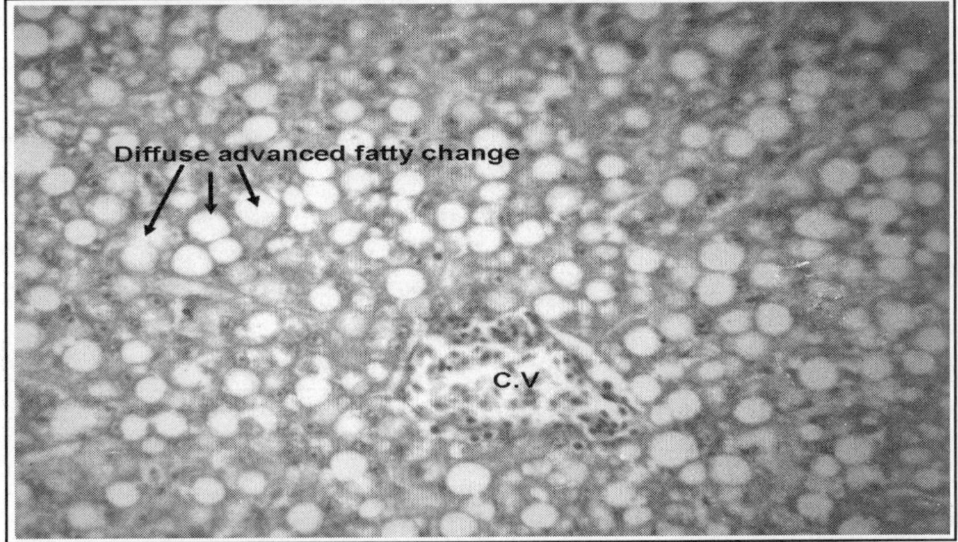

Fig. 3.4: **Liver of *O. niloticus* exposed to HOTA dose showing diffuse advanced fatty changes characterized by hepatic cells appear as signet ring. H&E. (X 250)**

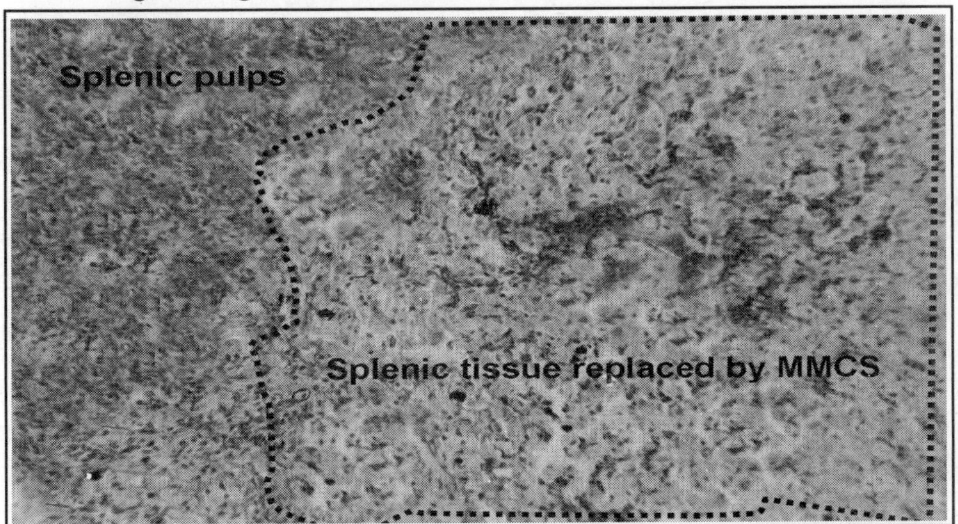

Fig. 3.5: **Spleen of *O. niloticus* exposed to HOTA dose showing severe infiltration of the splenic pulps with MMCS to extent that total replacement of the splenic tissues. H&E. (X 160)**

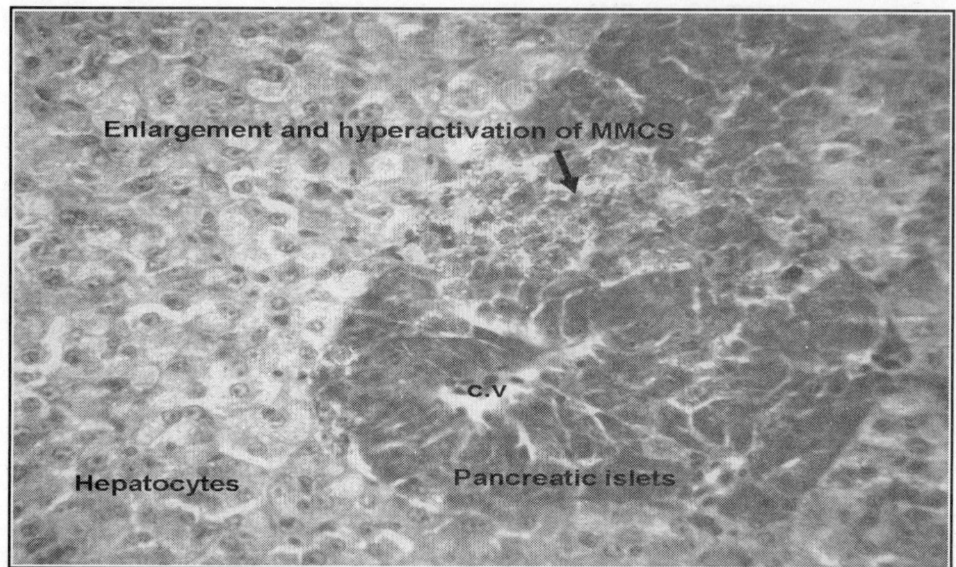

Fig. 3.6: **Liver of *O. niloticus* exposed to HOTA dose showing severe infiltration of MMCS in pancreatic islets. H&E. (X 250)**

Regarding to addition of yeast to diets the drastic effects of OTA on hepatopancreas and kidneys in LOTA treatment were similar as control.

HOTA dose showed acute cloudy swelling, tubular necrosis and mild activation of MMCs. Also spleen in LOTA dose didn't affected but in HOTA dose spleen showed mild activation of MMCs (Figs. 3.7, 3.8 and 3.9).

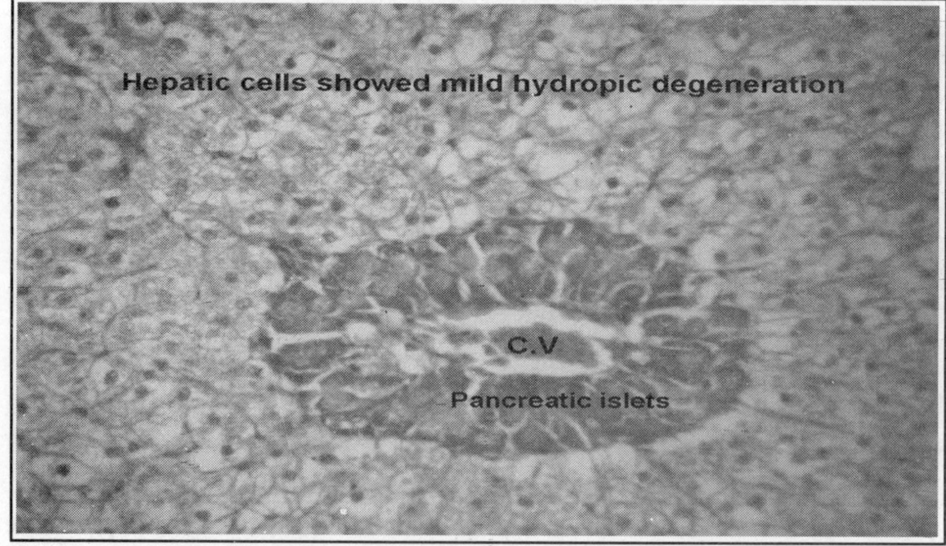

Fig. 3.7: **Liver of *O. niloticus* exposed to HOTA dose plus yeast showing mild hydropic degeneration of the hepatic cells. H&E. (X 250)**

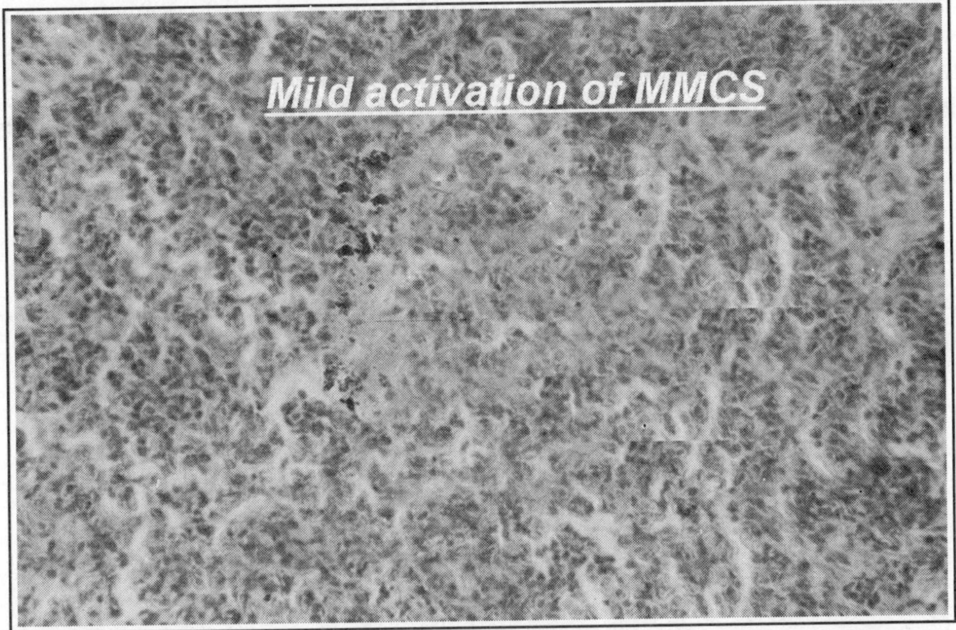

Fig. 3.8: Spleen of *O. niloticus* exposed to HOTA dose plus yeast showing mild activation ofMMCS. H&E. (X 160)

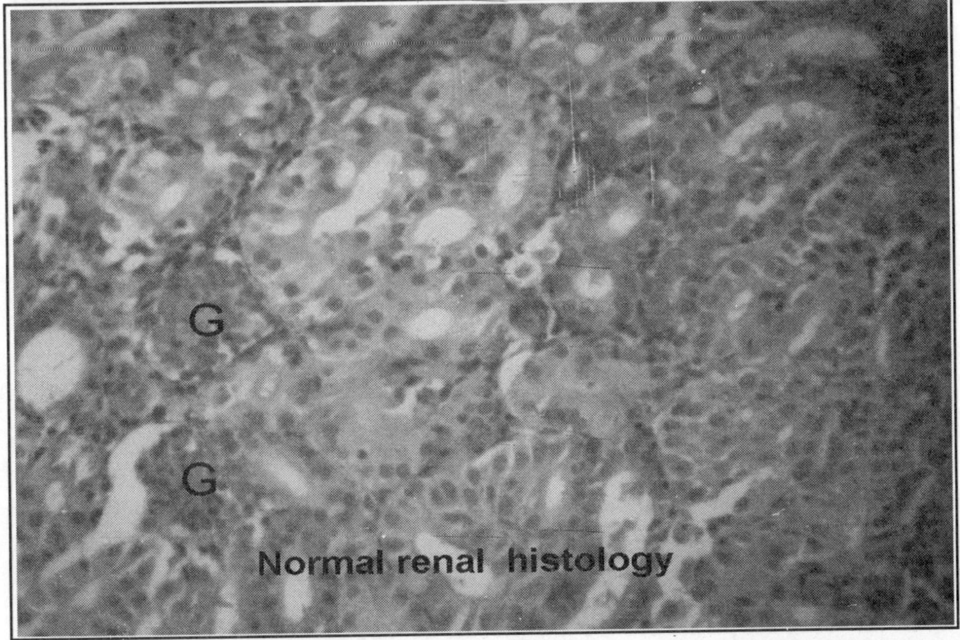

Fig. 3.9: Kidney of *O. niloticus* exposed to LOTA dose plus yeast showing normal renal architecture and histology. H&E. (X 250)

Addition of whey to fish diets with OTA showed mild congestion and hydropic degeneration of liver cells in case of LOTA. Meanwhile, with HOTA dose the alteration appeared as mild fatty changes, focal lymphocytic aggregation, enlargement and hyper activation of MMCs. Kidney in LOTA dose showed slight acute cellular swelling of tubular epithelial lining with mild MMCs infiltration. The effect of HOTA dose with whey on posterior kidney appeared as focal tubular necrosis replaced by inflammatory cells. In spleen the alteration is activation of MMCs in both OTA doses but the severity increased with HOTA dose (Fig. 3.10, 3.11 and 3.12).

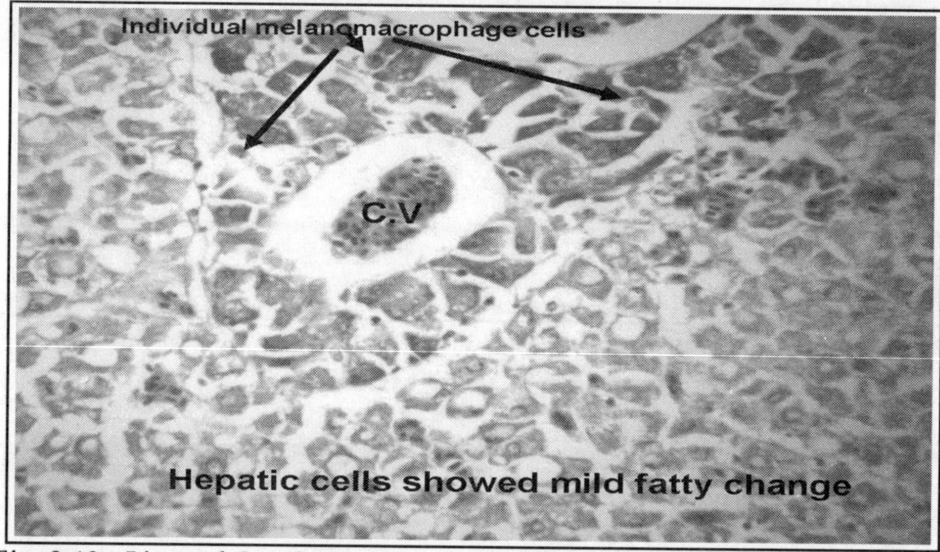

Fig. 3.10: **Liver of *O. niloticus* exposed to HOTA dose plus whey showing mild fatty change of hepatic cells beside individual infiltration of MMC plus in pancreatic islets. H&E. (X 250)**

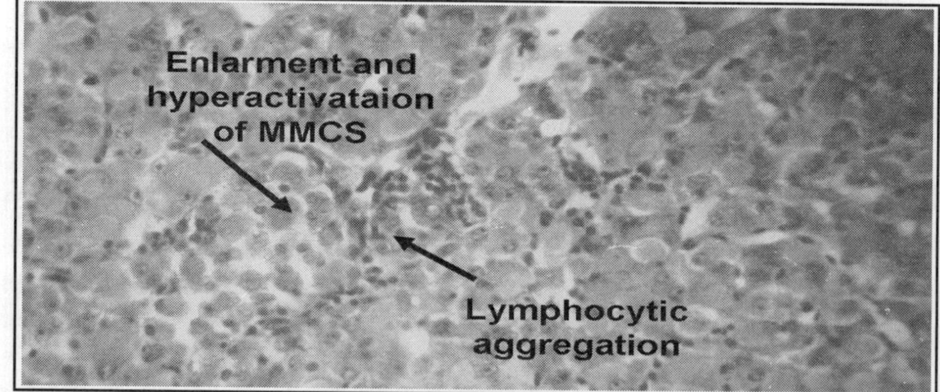

Fig. 3.11: **Hepatopancreas of *O. niloticus* exposed to HOTA dose plus whey showing focal lymphocytic aggregation and enlargement and hyperactivation of MMCS. H&E. (X 250)**

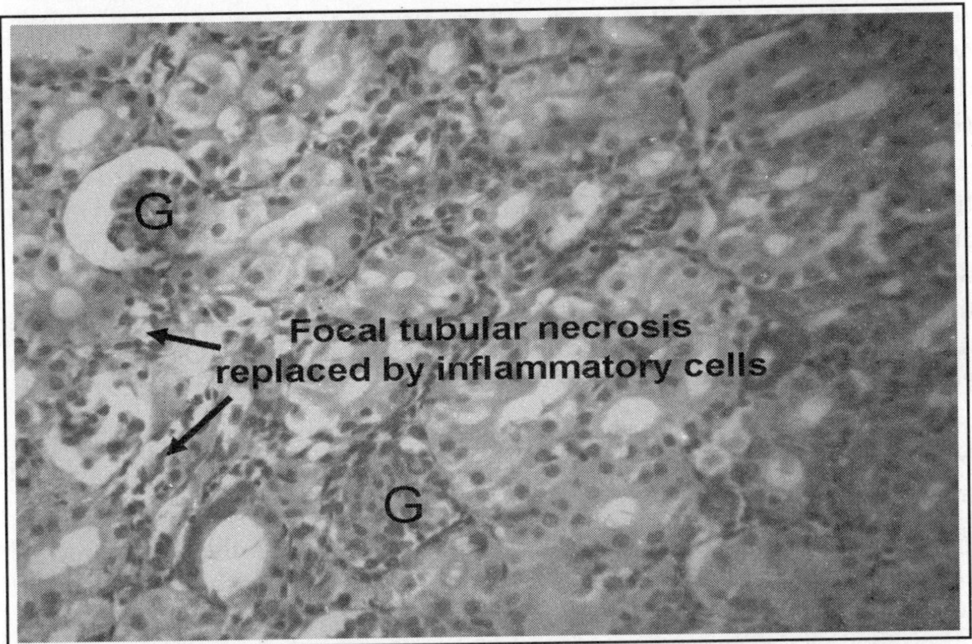

Fig. 3.12: **Posterior kidney of *O. niloticus* exposed to HOTA dose plus whey showing focal tubular necrosis replaced by inflammatory cells. H&E. (X 160)**

Discussion

The reduction of RBCs count which observed in the present study may be due to destruction of mature RBCs and inhibition of erythrocyte production due to reduction of haeme synthesis by ochratoxicosis. Also, the decrease in the RBCs may related to the elimination of RBCs from circulation as a result of ochratoxin – induced extravasations of the blood (Jordan *et al.*, 1977).

Moreover, Shalaby (2004) found a significant reduction in RBCs of *O. niloticus* feed contaminated diet with OTA.

Decrease of WBCs count with LOTA and HOTA doses significantly than control group and reduced insignificantly than yeast and whey treatments all over the experimental period were noticed. The decrease of WBCs may be due to the immunosuppressive effects of OTA. Saad (2002) reported lymphopenia in case of acute and chronic exposure of *O. niloticus* to OTA.

This change usually associated with acute stage of haemolytic anemia (Chang *et al.*, 1979) and destructive effects of OTA on spleen, kidney and liver (Smith and Hamilton, 1970). Moreover, Easa (1997) confirmed these results by recording depletion of hematopiotic elements due to the effects of OTA.

The PA of HOTA dose reduced significantly than other treatments. Meanwhile, insignificant (*P* <0.05) differences were observed among LOTA dose and detoxification treatments. Control showed the highest significant (*P*>0.05) PA value.

The phagocytic index differ significantly from the second week of treatment, where HOTA dose recorded the lowest significant (*P*>0.05) PI and showed insignificant (*P* <0.05) differences with LOTA dose and HOTA dose plus whey all over the experiment. The addition of yeast ameliorate the drastic effect of OTA significant (*P*>0.05) on PI especially with LOTA dose. Meanwhile, slightly improve of PI observed with HOTA dose plus yeast and LOTA dose plus whey.

Saad (2002) who found that OTA (10,000 ng/kg fish) decreased phagocytic activity and phagocytic index in *O. niloticus* after eight weeks of treatments.

The decrease of PA and PI by OTA may be due to the stress effect of OTA on *O. niloticus* (Pickering, 1981). This lead to increase level of serum cortisol which leads to suppression of phagocytosis process (Khalil, 1998).

The increase of Phagocytic activity by addition of yeast may be attributed to enhancing the phagocytic and oxidative activities of kidney phagocytic cells Sakai et,al (2001).

The significant effects of OTA, yeast and whey on total protein observed at week six to eight and showed significant (*P*<0.05) decrease of total protein with both LOTA and HOTA doses treatments. Meanwhile, the addition of yeast increased total protein values with both LOTA (significant *P*<0.05) and HOTA doses. Whey addition increased total protein but not significantly (*P* <0.05) with both LOTA and HOTA doses.

In general, OTA disruptive total protein level in *O. niloticus* and addition of yeast and whey improved total protein level especially with HOTA dose. Moreover, total protein levels decreased significant (*P*<0.05) with term of exposure.

OTA and detoxification treatments showed significant (*P* <0.05) decrease of albumin value (hypoalbuminemia) than control group. Although LOTA and HOTA doses decreased albumin level significant (*P*<0.05) than control, yeast treatments and whey with LOTA dose.

The results showed insignificant (*P* <0.05) decrease of globulin with LOTA and HOTA doses and significant (*P* <0.05) increase with yeast and whey until sixth week. Meanwhile, at eighth week globulin decrease significant (*P* <0.05) with LOTA and HOTA dose.

The reduction of plasma total protein may be due to liver damage caused by OTA where all plasma protein synthesis usually occurs in liver except gamma globulins which are produced by lymphocytes (Coles, 1986 and Khalil, 1998). This reduction may be interpreted to the inhibitory effect of OTA to protein synthesis (Ringot *et al.*, 2006).

The hypoproteinemia and hypoalbuminemia my be attributed to three main causes: hepatic insufficiency, renal loss (protein-losing nephropathy), and gastrointestinal loss (protein-losing enteropathy) Carlye-Rose, (2002). Moreover, OTA found to be hepatotoxic (Gagliano *et al.* 2006), nephrotoxic (Saad, 2002), and increase the permeability of gastrointestinal tract (McLaughlin *et al.*, 2004) which interpreted the decrease of total protein and albumin with OTA treatments in the present study.

Globulin is the building source of antibody where called immunoglobulin (White, 1986). So globulin used as immune indicator and the decrease of its level in the present study with OTA treatments revealed the immunosuppressive effects of OTA. Elkafory (2006) reported increase in fish serum proteins (total protein, albumin, globulin and A/G ratio) received yeast with diet.

Antibody titer reduced significantly with HOTA dose than control group. Insignificant (P <0.05) differences were observed among other treatments and control group. In eighth week (the forth week after vaccination) a significantly (P >0.05) decreased of antibody titration was observed with LOTA and HOTA doses compared to other treatments. However, the addition of yeast and whey to the diet increase significantly antibody titration especially with HOTA dose.

Regarding to the overcome of detoxification agents to OTA on antibody titer where significantly increase of antibody titer was observed with yeast supplementation. Yoshida *et al.* (1995) showed that *Saccharomyces cerevisiae* was a source of nucleic acids and â-1,3-glucans which have been recognized to effectively enhance immune functions of African catfish. Also, Anderson *et al.* (1995) reported that Baker's yeast, *S. cerevisiae*, contains various immunostimulating compounds such as â-glucans, nucleic acids and mannan oligosaccharides. Moreover, Glucan treatment in fish enhanced the expression of interleukin 1 and complement activity Engstad *et al.* (1992).

In case of whey, which increase antibody titer may be due to whey act as source of biologically active molecules. Several of which are known to impact on the immune system (Knowles and Gill 2002). The biological components of whey protein, including lactoferrin, beta-lactoglobulin, alpha-lactalbumin, glycomacropeptide, and immunoglobulins, demonstrate a range of immune-enhancing properties (Horton, 1997).

Also, whey protein concentrates found to be enhanced humoral immunity, with significantly elevated serum and intestinal tract antibody responses to orally administered antigens (Rutherfurd-Markwick, *et al.*, 2005).

The significant differences of GOT observed at the sixth week of treatment where GOT values with LOTA and HOTA doses increased significantly than control and yeast supplementation treatments. Alkaline phosphatase showed significantly ($P<0.05$) different at sixth week where control group decreased significantly than other treatments.

The increase of serum transaminases may reflect myocardial and hepatic toxicity leading to extensive liberation of the enzymes in to blood circulation (Fuchs *et al.*, 1986). These results agreed with Saad (2002) who found significant increase of serum aspartat aminotransferase and alkaline phosphatase with OTA treatment on *O. niloticus*.

The increase of liver function enzymes in case of LOTA and HOTA doses may be due to the toxic effect of toxin in liver cells. Moreover the liver used to be the site of detoxification of the OTA to 4(*R*)-and 4(*S*) - hydroxyochratoxin A (Stormer and Pederson, 1980). In the same time the level of liver enzymes in case of OTA plus yeast were less than OTA only. This may be indicated that yeast decreased the toxic effect of OTA on liver and in the same time increase liver function.

The increase of creatinine and uric acid in serum of ochratoxicosis fish my be attributed to renal disturbance associated with damage of proximal tubules and thickening of the glomerular basement membrane caused by OTA which lead to reduce the ability of kidney to produce concentrated urine (Marquadret, 1996). Moreover, kidney is the main target organ of OTA genotoxicity, where induced DNA single-strand breaks and DNA adducts in kidney (Pfohl-Leszkowicz,et.al, 1993).

Saad (2002) found that in case of OTA on acute and chronic toxicity in *O. niloticus* causes severe destruction of the proximal tubules of the posterior kidney and hydropic degeneration of the tubular epithelium.

Creatinine is a protein produced by muscle and released into the blood hence removed by the kidney and the increase of creatinine levels indicated to decrease of kidney function (Zotti *et al.*, 2008).

The histopathological alteration which confirmed in case of LOTA and HOTA in the form of activation of melanomacrophage centers in liver and spleen atrophied of hepatic cells, severe fatty changes, and cellular degeneration of kidneys could be attributed to the toxic effects of OTA (Saad 2006).

Similar results obtained by Manning *et al.*, (2003) in case of catfish fed dietary concentrations of 2.00 to 8.00 mg OTA/kg which revealed increase incidence and activation of MMCs centers in hepatopancreatic tissue and posterior kidney.

Orrenius and Bellomo (1986) demonstrated that lipid perox idation which caused by OTA may be an early event in hepatotoxicity, which results in structural changes in the cell membrane and allow an influx of cellular calcium to cause changes in metabolic activity within the cell and ultimately cause cell necrosis.

Also the activation of the MMCs considered as indicative on the degree of the tissue damage (Roberts, 2001).

Regarding to addition of yeast to diets of ochratoxicosis fish elimenate the drastic effects of OTA on hepatopancreas. Also spleen in LOTA dose didn't affected but in HOTA dose spleen showed mild activation of MMCs .

Addition of whey to toxicated fish diets affects the histological findings as follow; Hepatopancreas in LOTA dose are congestion and hydropic degeneration. Meanwhile, with HOTA dose the alteration appeared as mild fatty changes, focal lymphocytic aggregation, enlargement and hyper activation MMCs. Posterior kidney in LOTA dose showed acute cellular swelling of tubular epithelial lining with mild MMCs infeltiration. The effect of HOTA dose on posterior kidney appeared as focal tubular necrosis replaced by inflammatory cells. In spleen the alteration is activation of MMCs in both OTA doses but severity increased with HOTA dose.

The histopathological examination results concluded that yeast more effective than whey in minimize the destructive effect of ochratoxin in the most affected organs (hepatopancreas, kidney and spleen) especially at the LOTA dose.

Moreover, yeast reduce the presence of potentially pathogenic bacteria by competitive exclusion and causes intestinal microbial balance of the host organism and confer various beneficial effects include immunostimulation and enhance disease resistance (Gatlin *et al.*, 2006).

The detoxification effect of yeast on OTA may be revealed to the ability of yeasts to secrete an enzyme related to carboxypeptidases which convert OTA to OTá (non toxic form) (Péteri *et al.*, 2007) by the cleavage of the peptide bond between isocoumarin and phenylalanine in OTA moiety (Marquardt, 1996). Furthermore, yeast cell wall was an effective adsorbent for OTA (Ringot *et al.*, 2007) which may reduce OTA absorption from the fish gastro intestinal tract and excluded with feces.

Molnar *et al.* (2004) found that yeast strain of the genus *Trichosporon* from the hindgut of the termite, refers to important characteristics to detoxify mycotoxins such as OTA. Since, fish gastric microorganisms able to transform mycotoxin to non toxic form in various environmental conditions (Guan *et al.*, 2009). Moreover, yeast showed antagonistic effects to OTA production and growth of OTA producing fungi (Petersson *et al.*, 1998 and Masoud & Kaltoft, 2006).

In conclusion, OTA proved to produce drastic effects on physiological and pathological levels of *O. niloticus*. Meanwhile, active yeast and Sweet whey were successed to neutralize the drastic toxic effects of OTA.

REFERENCES

Abdel-Tawwab, M., Abdel-Rahman, A.M. and Ismael N.E.M. (2008a). Evaluation of Commercial Live Bakers' Yeast, *Saccharomyces cerevisiae* As a Growth and Immunity Promoter for Fry Nile Tilapia, *Oreochromis niloticus* (L.) Challenged *in situ* with *Aeromonas hydrophila*. Aquaculture, 280: 185-189.

Abdel-Tawwab, M., Mousa, M.A.A. and Mohammed, M.A. (2008b). Effect of Yeast Supplementation on the Growth Performance and Resistance of Galilee Tilapia *Sarotherodon galilaeus* (L.) to Environmental Copper Toxicity. 8th International Symposium on Tilapia in Aquaculture, 459-474.

Abdel-Wahhab, M.A., Hassan, A.M., Aly, S.E. and Mahrous, K.F. (2005). Adsorption of Sterigmatocystin by Montmorillonite and Inhibition of its Genotoxicity in the Nile Tilapia (*Oreochromis niloticus*). Mutation Research, 582: 20-27.

Anderson, D.P. and Siwicki, A.K. (1995). Basic Haematology and Serology for Fish Health Programmes. In: Diseases in Asian Aquaculture II. M. Shariff, J. R. Arthur and R.P. Subasinghe (Eds). Fish Health Section, Asian Fisheries Society, Manila, Philippines, pp. 185-202.

Anderson, D.P., Siwicki, A.K. and Rumsey, G.L. (1995). Injection or Immersion Delivery of Selected Immunostimulants to Trout Demonstrate Enhancement of Non-specific Defense Mechanisms and Protective Immunity. In: Shariff, M., Arthur, J.R., Subasinghe, R.P. (Eds.), Diseasesin Asian Aquaculture: II. Fish Health Section. Asian Fisheries Society, Manila. 413-426.

Badran, A.F. (1990). The Role of Adjuvants in the Immune Response of the Fish. Zagazeg Veterinary Medicine Journal. 18: 126-136.

Carlye-Rose, D.V.M. (2002). Evaluation of Hypoalbuminemia. HCVMA Newsletter, February. 1-2.

Chang, C.F., Huff W.E. and Hamilton. P.B. (1979). Aleucocytopenia Induced in Chickens by Dietary Ochratoxin-A. Poultry Science. 58: 555-558.

Coles, E.H. (1986). Veterinary Clinical Pathology. 2nd Ed. W.B. Saunders Company, Philadelphia and London.

Culling, C.F. (1983). Handbook of Histopathologic and Histochemical Staining. 3rd Ed., Buterworth, London.

Duncan, D. B. (1955). Multible Range and Multible F test. Biometric, 11: 1-42.

Easa, A.A.M. (1997). Effect of *Aspergillus ochraceus* Mould and Its Metabolites on some Cultured Fresh Water Fishes in Egypt. M.V. Sc. Faculty of Veterinary Medicine. Cairo University.

Elaroussi, M.A., Mohamed, F.R., El Barkouky, E.M., Atta, A.M., Abdou, A.M. and Hatab, M.H. (2006). Experimental Ochratoxicosis in Broiler Chickens. Avian Pathology, 35(4): 263-269.

Elkafoury. M.A. (2006). Comparative Studies Between *Oreochromas niloticus* and Monosex Tilapia from Immunological and Pathological Aspect of View. M.V. SC. Faculty of Veterinary Medicine. Alexandria University.

Engstad, R.E., Robertsen, B. and Frivold, E. (1992). Yeast Glucan Induces Increase in Activity of Lysozyme and Complemente Mediated Haemolytic Activity in Atlantic Salmon Blood. Fish Shellfish Immunol, 2: 287-97.

Fuchs, R., Appelgren, L.E. and Hult, K. (1986). Distribution of 14 C-ochratoxin A in the Rainbow Trout (*Salmogaidneri*). Acta pharmacologica et toxicologica, 59: 220-227.

Fuchs, S., Sontag, G., Stidl, R., Ehrlich, V., Kundi, M. and Knasmüller, S. (2008). Detoxification of Patulin and Ochratoxin A, Two Abundant Mycotoxins, by Lactic Acid Bacteria. Food and Chemical Toxicology, 46 (4): 1398-1407.

Gatlin III, D.M., Li, P., Wang, X., Burr, G.S., Castille F. and Lawrence, A.L. (2006). Potencial Application of Prebiotics in Aquaculture. En: Editores: L. Elizabeth Cruz Suarez, Denis Ricque Marie, Mireya Tapia Salazar, Martha G. Neito Lopez, David A. Villarreal Cavazos, Ana C. Puello Cruzy Armando Garcia Ortega. Avances en Nutricion Acuicola VIII. VIII Simposium International de Nutricion Acuicola. 15-17 Noviembre. Universidad Autonoma de Nuevo Leon, Monterrey, Nuevo Leon, Mexico. ISBN 970-694-333-5.

Guan, S., He, J., Young, J.C., Zhu, H., Li, X., Ji, C. and Zhou T. (2009). Transformation of Trichothecene Mycotoxins by Microorganisms from Fish Digesta. Aquaculture, 290: 290-295.

Hesser, E.F. (1960). Methods for Routine Fish Haematology. Progressive Fish Culturist, 22: 164-171.

Hichey, C.R. (1976). Fish Haematology, Its Used and Significance. New York Fish com. J., 33: 170-175.

Horton, B. (1997). The Whey Processing Industry. Into the 21st Century. In: Proceedings of the Second International Whey Conference, Chicago, USA, 27-29 October. International Dairy Federation. pp. 12-25.

Jordan, M., Rzehak, K. and Maryanska, A. (1977). The Effect of Two Pesticides; Miedzian 50 and Gtsagard 50, on the Development of Tadpoles of *Rana Temporaia*. Bulletin of Environmental Contamination, 17: 349-354.

Kawahara, E., Ueda T. and Nomura. S. (1991). In Vitro Phagocytic Activity of White-spotted Shark Cells After Injection with *Aermonas salmonicida* Extracellular Products. Gyobyo Kenkyu, Japan, 26: 213-214.

Kermanshahi, H. and Rostami, H. (2006). Influence of Supplemental Dried Whey on Broiler Performance and Cecal Flora. International of Journal Poultry Science, 5: 538-543.

Khalil, R.H. (1998). Effect of Bayluscide on some Cultured Fresh Water Fish *Oreochromis niloticus*. Ph. D. thesis, Faculty of Veterinary Medicine. Alexandria University.

Knowles, G. and Gill, H.S. (2002). Immune Modulation by Dairy Ingredients: Potential for Improving Health. In: Shortt C, O'Brien J, Editors. Functional Dairy Products. Boca Raton 7 CRC Press; pp. 125-54.

Madhyastha, M.S., Marquardt, R.R. and Frohlich, A.A. (1992). Hydrolysis of Ochratoxin A by the Microbial Activity of Digesta in the Gastrointestinal Tract. Archives of Environmental Contamination and Toxicology, 23: 468-472.

Manning, B.B., Ulloa, R.M., Li, M.H., Robinson, E.H. and Rottinghaus, G.E. (2003). Ochratoxin A Fed to Channel Catfish (*Ictalurus punctatus*) Causes Reduced Growth and Lesions of Hepatopancreatic Tissue. Aquaculture, 219: 739-750.

Manning, B.B., Terhune, J.S., Li, M.H., Robinson, E.H., Wise, D.J. and Rottinghau, G.E. (2005). Exposure to Feedborne Mycotoxins T-2 Toxin or Ochratoxin A Causes Increased Mortality of Channel Catfish Challenged with *Edwardsiella ictaluri*. Journal of Aquatic Animal Health. 17: 147-152.

Marquardt, R.R. (1996). Effects of Molds and Their Toxins on Livestock Performance: A Western Canadian Perspective. Animal Feed Science and Technology, 70: 3968-3988.

Masoud, W. and Kaltoft, C.H. (2006). The Effects of Yeasts Involved in the Fermentation of Coffea Arabica in East Africa on Growth and Ochratoxin A (OTA) Production by *Aspergillus ochraceus*. International Journal of Food Microbiology, 106: 229- 234.

McLaughlin, J., Padfield, P.J., Burt, J.P.H. and O'Neill, C.A. (2004). Ochratoxin A Increases Permeability Through Tight Junctions by Removal of Specific Claudin Isoforms. American Journal of Cell Physiology, 287: C1412-C1417.

Molnar, O., Schatzmayr, G., Fuchs, E. and Prillinger H. (2004). *Trichosporon mycotoxinivorans sp.* nov., A New Yeast Species useful in Biological Detoxification of Various Mycotoxins. Systematic and Applied Microbiology, 27: 661-671.

Naghton, P.J., Mikkelsen, L.L. and Jensen, B.B. (2001). Effects of Non Digestible Oligosaccharides on *Salmonella Typhimuium* and Non Pathogenic Escherichia *in vitro*. Journal of Applied and Environmental Microbiology, August pp. 3391-3395.

Nurmi, E.V. and Rantal (1973). New Aspects of Salmonella Infection in Broiler Production. Nature, 241: 210-211.

Orrenius, S., and Bellomo, G. (1986). Toxicological Implications of Perturbation of Ca2+ Homeostasis in Hepatocytes. In: W.Y. Cheung (Ed.) Calcium and Cell Function. p 185. Academic Press, Orlando, FL.

Péteri, Z., Téren, J., Vágvölgyi, C. and Varga, J. (2007). Ochratoxin Degradation and Adsorption Caused by Astaxanthin-producing Yeasts. Food Microbiology, 24: 205-210.

Petersson, S., Hansen, M.W., Axberg, K., Hult, K. and Schnurer, J. (1998). Ochratoxin A Accumulation in Cultures of *Penicillium Verrucosum* with the Antagonistic Yeast *Pichia Anomala* and *Saccharomyces Cerevisiae*. Mycological Research, 102 (8): 1003-1008.

Pfohl-Leszkowicz, A., Grosse, Y., Kane, A., Creppy, E.E. and Dirheimer, G. (1993b). Differential DNA Adducts Formation and Disappearance in Three Mouse Tissues after Treatment with the Mycotoxin Ochratoxin A. Mutation Research, 289: 265-273.

Pickering, A.D. (1981). Stress and fish. Academic Press, Londo, New York. pp. 149-152.

Reyes-Becerril, M., Tovar-Ramírez, D., Ascencio-Valle, F., Civera-Cerecedo, R., Gracia-López, V. and Barbosa-Solomieu, V. (2008). Effects of Dietary Live Yeast *Debaryomyces Hansenii* on the Immune and Antioxidant System in Juvenile Leopard Grouper Mycteroperca Rosacea Exposed to Stress. Aquaculture, 280: 39-44.

Ringot D., Chango A., Schneider Y. and Larondelle Y. (2006). Toxicokinetics and Toxicodynamics of Ochratoxin A, an Update. Chemico-Biological Interactions 159: 18-46.

Ringot, D., Lerzy, B., Chaplain, K., Bonhoure, J., Auclair, E. and Larondelle, Y. (2007). *In vitro* Biosorption of Ochratoxin A on the Yeast Industry by-products: Comparison of Isotherm Models. Bioresource Technology. 98: 1812-1821.

Roberts, R.J. (2001). Fish Pathology. Third Edition. Harcourt Publishers Limited 2001.

Rutherfurd-Markwick, K.J., Johnson, D., Cross, M.L. and Gill, H.S. (2005). Modified Milk Powder Supplemented with Immunostimulating Whey Protein Concentrate (IMUCARE) Enhances Immune Function in Mice. Nutrition Research. 25: 192-203.

Saad, T.T. (2002). Some Studies on the Effects of Ochratoxin-A on Cultured *Oreochromis Niloticus* and Carp Species. M.V.SC. Faculty of Veterinary Medicine. Alexandria University.

Safinaz, G.M. I. (2001). Effect of Phenol on the Immune Response of Tilapia Fish and Susceptibility to Disease. Ph. D. Thesis Faculty of Veterinary Medicine Suez Canal University, Egypt.

Sakai, M., Yoshida, T., Atsuta, S. and Kobayashi, M. (1984). Enhancement of Resistance to Vibriosis in Rainbow Trout, *Oncorhynchus mykiss* (walaum), by Oral Administration of *Clostridium Butyricum* Bacterin. Journal of Fish Diseases, 18: 187-190.

Sakai, M., Taniguchi, K., Mamoto, K., Ogawa, H. and Tabata, M. (2001). Immunostimulant Effects of Nucleotide Isolated from Yeast RNA on Carp, *Cyprinus Carpio* L. Journal of Fish Disease, 24: 433-438.

Shalaby, A.M.E. (2004). The Opposing Effect of Ascorbic Acid (vitamin C) on Ochratoxin Toxicity in Nile Tilapia (*Oreochromis niloticus*). In: Proceedings of the 6th International Symposium on Tilapia in Aquaculture (R.B. Remedios, G.C. Mair and K. Fitzsimmons, eds), pp. 209-221.

Smith, J.W. and Hamilton, P.B. (1970). Aflatoxicosis in the Broiler Chicken. Poultry Science. 49: 207-215.

Soliman, M.K. (1996). Principals of Fish Disease. Effect of Stress on Immune System of Fish. Faculty of Veterinary Medicine. Alexandria University, pp. 12-23.

Sreemannarayana, O., Frohlich, A.A., Vitti, T.G., Marquardt R.R. and Abramson, D. (1988). Studies of the Tolerence and Disposition of Ochratoxin A in Young Calves. Journal of Animal Science, 88: 1703.

Stormer, F.C. and Pederson, J.I. (1980). Formation of (4R)- and (4S)-hydroxyochratoxin A from Ochratoxin A by Rat Liver Microsomes. Applied and Environmental Microbiology, 39: 971-975.

Tellez, C.E., Dean, C.E., Corrier. D.E., Deloach, J.R., Jaeger, L. and Hargis, B.M. (1993). Effect of Dietary Lactose on Cecal Morphology, pH, Organic Acid and *Salmonella Enteritidis* Organ Invasion in Leghorn Chicks. Poultry Science, 72: 636- 642.

Trucksess, M.W. and Pohland, A. E. (2001). Mycotoxin Protocols, in: J.M. Walker (Ed.), Methods in Molecular Biology, Volume 157, Humana Press, New Jersey.

Wang, G.H., Xue, C.Y., Chen, F., Ma, Y.L., Zhang, X.B., Bi, Y.Z. and Cao, Y.C. (2009). Effects of Combinations of Ochratoxin A and T-2 Toxin on Immune Function of Yellow-feathered Broiler Chickens. Poultry Science, 88: 504-10.

White, D.G. (1986). Evaluation of a Rapid, Specific Test for Detecting Colostral IgG in the Neonatal Calf. Veterinary Record, 118: 68-70.

Yoshida, T., Kruger, R. and Inglis. V. (1995). Augmentation of Non-specific Protection in African Catfish, *Clarias gariepinus* (Burchell) by the Long-term Oral Administration of Immunostimulants. Journal of Fish Disease, 18: 195-198.

Zotti, F.D., Visonà, E., Massignani, D., Abaterusso, C., Lupo, A. and Gambaro, G. (2008). General Practitioners' Serum Creatinine Recording Styles. Journal of Nephrology, 21(1): 106-109.

4

Diversity and Community Dynamics of Thermophilic Fungi in Compost Ecosystem

Seema Rawat, *India*
Amir Khan, *India*
B.N. Johri, *India*

ABSTRACT

Compost is a complex man-made ecosystem, which is of great relevance from microbial ecological point of view as it represents a complete spectrum of microbial diversity. Thermophilic fungi constitute the most important and dominant component which contributes significantly to the quality of compost. This necessitates the monitoring and characterization of the thermophilic mycoflora community composition and succession pattern with the changing physico-chemical characteristics of compost. Compost is not only structurally diverse but also functionally since it harbours a number of guilds. In situ functionality of each thermophilic mycoflora component especially the polysaccharolytic, proteolytic and lipolytic communities plays a decisive role in successful colonization and succession in mushroom compost. The understanding of in situ functionality provides a way to manipulate the compost environment and hasten the process of composting besides improving the quality of compost. The cultivation-dependent approaches provided a limited insight into the ecological relevance of the community structure however applications of phenotypic and genetic tools with culturable and non-culturable components of the microbial diversity define the complexity of this ecosystem.

Key words: Compost, Man-made ecosystem, Thermophilic fungi, Guilds, *In situ* functionality, Cultivation-dependent approaches, Phenotypic tools, Genetic tools.

Introduction

The biotechnological potential of thermophilic fungi has been well-known for years because composting as a mean of providing nutrient-enriched plant material has been in vogue for degradation of agro-residues, mushroom production, solid waste management and for understanding the role of fungi in plant litter ecosystem. Though the first thermophilic fungus, *Mucor pusillus* was discovered by Lindt in 1886 yet the real early beginnings are attributed to Miehe (1905) who made pioneering investigations of self-heating hay and discovered two important thermophilic fungi, *Malbranchea pulchella* var. *sulfurea*, known for production of penicillin and *Thermoascus aurantiacus* with strong hemicellulolytic machinery. His book "Die Selbsterhitzung des Heus" published in 1907 is a distinguished landmark in the development of this subject. However, this monumental work could not draw wide attention of mycologists and as a result a wide lacunae remained till a comprehensive account of the systematic morphology and general biology of thermophilic fungi came into picture with the monograph of Cooney and Emerson (1964) which served as the major understanding of thermophilic fungi (Rawat and Johri, 2002).

The inherent ability of this group to occupy a temperature niche that would preclude most other fungi results in their ubiquitous distribution. The community structure of this small group of Eumycota is very heterogenous exhibiting a wide structural distributional pattern. They occur both in natural and man-made habitats like soil, compost, wood chip piles, coal spoil tips, stored grains and though limited to few species, encompasses various taxonomic groups. The most interesting feature of this group is that they have been recovered not only from hot climatic regions but also from cold and stressed environments (Ellis, 1980a, b; Mouchacca *et al.*, 1995).

Their ubiquitous presence in different temperature zones and habitats raises many question regarding their survival and dispersal. The presence of self-heating masses of organic debris all around the globe lends sustainability to this community. It is therefore imperative to explore out their geographically diverse reservoir in order to have a fair picture of their species spectrum and as well as to understand their functionality in a given habitat as this group is not only structurally diverse but also functionally. The survival and dominance exhibited by thermophilic fungi in a wide array of habitats is attributed to their inherently strong extracellular enzymatic machinery, release of volatile sporostatic and fungistatic compounds and colonization potential (Satyanarayana and Johri, 1981).

The use of molecular tools in recent years has however added considerable information to extend our knowledge of this group. The availability of molecular- and immuno probes have opened up newer possibilities, which would permit retrieval of information concerning the role of thermophilic fungi in colonization, succession and *in situ* functioning in various habitats.

Compost is an important habitat of thermophilic fungi which serves as their rich reservoir. The concentration of thermophilic propagules is approximately 10^6 times higher in compost than in soil and therefore thermophilic fungi are considered primarily as compost fungi. Optimization of compost quality is directly linked to the composition and succession of microbial communities. This means tools are required to monitor and characterize microbial communities during composting and to relate them to compost quality. Although, analysis of the presence and distribution of different operational taxonomic units (OTU) within a population provides insights into the ecological functioning of communities, the analysis of taxonomic structure of communities alone, however, limits insight into the ecological relevance of community structure. The exclusion or addition of different microflora does not necessarily change the resultant function of the community (White and Findlay, 1988). Analysis of phenetic characteristics which directly relate to important processes in the environment under investigation and correlation of such characteristics to environmental parameters allow for greater insight into factors which regulate the community structure (Garland and Mills, 1991). The changes in individual abundances may not equate to meaningful shifts in the community function. Cultivation approaches inevitably favour growth of some community members due to the selective nature of the media and can thus exclude majority of the endogenous microbes (Troussellier and Legendre, 1981) and thus do not give a full description of the microbial diversity. Moreover, the time consuming nature of isolate-based methods severely limits the spatial and temporal intensity to sampling (Garland and Mills, 1991).

Cultivation-independent methods have been in recent use to characterize the microbial community succession and structure. These include assessment of the diversity based on the directly extracted phospholipids (Boggs *et al.*, 1998; Herrmann and Shann, 1997; Klamer and Baath, 1998), measurement of carbon source utilization by substrate extracted microbial cell consortia (Boggs *et al.*, 1998; Insam *et al.*, 1996) and nucleic acid-based techniques (Kowalchuk *et al.*, 1999; Peters *et al.*, 2000)

This chapter deals with the physico-chemical aspects of composting along with microbial community structure and functionality in compost ecosystem. While information on some aspects is still scanty due to only horizontal advancements in that area as compost has a very complex ecology, but an effort to compile all the available information has been made. However, readers may find a bias towards diversity of thermophilic mycoflora in mushroom compost, an intersting ecosystem, due to our active engagement during the past many years with the thermophiles in this habitat.

Composting

Composting represents an astonishing example of solid-state fermentation (SSF) wherein a crude variety of wastes such as sewage sludge, refuse, animal manure, industrial wastes, food wastes, leaves, tree bark, agriculture residues, abattoir residues etc. can be treated through microbial route irrespective of their suitability as feed-stock for compost production (Satyanarayana and Grajek, 1999). Refuse (municipal solid waste) is partly compostable but poses problems due to its extreme heterogeneity as it consists of food scrapes (garbage), paper, glass, plastic, metal, sweepings, yard waste, ash etc. The organic rich fraction after separation can however be composted; the whole municipal solid waste can also be passed through the composting stage (mass composting), possibly with subsequent segregation (Satyanaryana and Grajek, 1999).

The basic aims of composting according to Miller (1994) are:

1. achievement of a suitable bulk density (compost makes a more physically stable landfill and can be easily stored, transported and disposed off than the original material as bulk density of former is higher);
2. modification of complex polysaccharides and plant materials;
3. biological removal of readily available nutrients to avoid overheating;
4. building up of an appropriate biomass and a variety of microbial products;
5. establishment of selectivity;
6. conversion of nitrogen into stable organic form; and
7. sanitation i.e., killing of pathogenic microbes, larvae and weeds.

The various methods of composting are: Sheet composting, Trench composting, In –vessel composting, Bin composting and Aerated static pile composting- It involves air for the operation by placing the heap on holed piping that allows circulation (Hultman, 2009). Composting is done at small scales like decomposition of domestic wastes as well as large scales like decomposition of industrial wastes.

The composting is carried out *via* either batch or a continuous mode. Batch mode is a long process comprising of four sequential phases, the mesophilic phase, thermophilic phase, cooling phase and the curing phase. The initial stage of decomposition of mass of organic matter, initiated by mixing and wetting the substrates, the mesophilic stage is governed by the mesophilic microflora, which uses up the readily available nutrients. The aerobic fermentation (composting) commences as a result of growth and activity of microorganisms resulting in release of heat, ammonia and CO_2 as by products along with other unpleasant smelling compounds. The metabolic activity of the mesophilic microorganisms that results in rise in temperature and paves way for development of thermophilic microflora which initiates the second phase of composting. This phase of composting starts very rapidly and may last days, or weeks or even months. It is the thermophilic stage that results in maximum decomposition of organic matter besides sanitation. During the cooling stage, mesophilic microflora recolonizes the compost and it is during this phase that more resistant organic matter is degraded (Tiquia *et al.*, 2002; Hiraishi *et al.*, 2003). The final phase of composting is called curing, aging or maturing stage, which is long and an important one since it provides a safety net for destruction of the pathogens. Uncured compost can produce phytotoxins, besides depriving soil of oxygen and nitrogen and can contain high levels of organic acids. In the continuous mode of composting, similar phases occur but they are not as apparent as they are in the batch mode and these could occur concurrently rather than sequentially. A well-designed continuous system can eliminate the need for a mesophilic stage and operate continuously at thermophilic temperatures. This mode offers a mean of decomposition of putrescible materials quickly under close process control.

Municipal compost is prepared by batch mode while garden composting is performed in a continuous mode. Mushroom compost and vermicompost, though prepared by batch mode, are significantly different from general municipal compost. Municipal compost is prepared by batch mode while garden composting is performed in a continuous mode. Mushroom compost and Vermicompost, though prepared by batch mode, are significantly different from general municipal compost. Mushroom compost is prepared very rapidly (18-24 d) and does not involve curing stage. It is prepared, either by long method (LMC) or short method (SMC), from various agro-residues viz., wheat straw/ paddy straw/ sugarcane bagasse as a base material along with other additives viz., chicken manure, calcium ammonium nitrate, urea, superphosphate, muriate of potash, wheat bran, gypsum as additives. LMC is the primitive, cheap method involving only one phase (without pasteurization) (Mantel *et al.*, 1972). SMC is a quick method constituting of a general advance in controlled composting (Sinden and Hauser, 1950) and involves two sequential phases: phase I (an uncontrolled self-heating process initiated by mixing and wetting the ingredients as they are stacked in windrows which are periodically turned and watered at approximately two days interval) and Phase II which is the indoor process of pasteurization, carried out in tunnels.

Vermicomposting is a method of decomposing organic materials viz., straw, shredded newspaper saw dust and horse manure using surface feeding worms especially *Eisenia foetida* (redworm). The worms primarily feed on the microbes that are actively involved in the break down of the organic matter.

Physico-chemical Aspects

The quickly changing physico-chemical conditions during composting select for a succession of microbial communities and thus exerts a profound effect on the entire process. Amongst the various parameters, composting is affected mainly by temperature, ammonia, carbon dioxide, moisture and C: N ratio of the substrate. The mass of decomposing organic materials is an exception to most ecosystems as it results in not only intensive heat production due to the metabolic activity of microorganisms but also acts as an effective retention system resulting in a significant rise in temperature. Generally, self-heating occurs when organic materials are assembled provided there is sufficient mass, atleast one ton, for insulation, and that moisture, aeration and nutrition level are adequate (Satyanarayana and Grajek, 1999).

Temperature is directly proportional to the biological activity within the composting system. As the metabolic rate of the microbes accelerates, the temperature within the system increases while with the decrease in the metabolic rate, the system temperature decreases (Namkoong *et al.*, 2002; Antizar-Ladislao *et al.*, 2005). The temperature in the composting stack usually reaches as high as 70°C within 2 or more days (Finstein and Morris, 1975). A peak temperature of 70°C can be attained within 4 days in metro-waste composting system meant for processing 150 tons of general municipal refuse daily (Kane and Mullins, 1973). A maximum temperature of 67°C was observed in wheat straw composting after 8 days, remained above 50°C for about 3 weeks (Chang and Hudson, 1967); on the other hand, composting of grass cuttings can attain 66°C within 16 h, reaching a maximum of 76°C after 48 h before a decline. The difference in temperature recorded is attributed to the type of material and other factors, such as age of the plant material (Satyanarayana and Grajek, 1987). In pig manure and chicken manure compost too, maximum temperature can reach upto 75°C (Kowalchuk *et al.*, 1999).

The size of the compost pile is crucial for not only temperature build up also for maintenance of appropriate microbial equilibrium and successional pattern. In phase I of mushroom compost, a gradient of 20°C (outer region of stack) to 70°C (center) exists while phase II runs at lower temperature of 50 to 60°C (Johri and Rajni, 1999; Peters *et al.*, 2000). The high temperature (75-80°C) of compost pile is necessary to induce Millard reactions i.e., fixing of free ammonia through reactions with carbohydrates and lignatious polymers. Millard reaction transforms carbohydrates into chemical from which is accessible to the mushroom crop but not to competitors, and hence, provides for compost selectivity. High temperature is also necessary for the chemical incorporation of nitrogen into stable form within the compost (Johri and Rajni, 1999).

The initial pH of the compost varies between 6 and 7and rises by 0.9-1.8 units during the first week due to the release of ammonia but later drops off (Chang and Hudson, 1967). During vermicomposting the pH changes from acidic to neutral while in municipal waste (Stutzenberger *et al.*, 1970), poulty manure-saw dust mixtures (Galler and Davey, 1971) and grass composts (Forsyth and Webley, 1948), initial pH of 4.5-6.0, stabilizes within 7 to 9, possibly due to the loss of organic acids through volatilization and microbial decomposition and the release of ammonia through mineralization of organic nitrogen; Peters *et al.* (2000) have reported the decrease in pH from 5.6 to 4.5 within the first two days of mushroom composting followed by an increase to 7.0 (Peters *et al.*, 2000) while Rawat (2004) reported variation in pH from 6.7 to 8.6 (end of phase I) with phase II composting pH stabilizing at 7.8. During the early stages of composting, a rapid growth of microbes reduces the pH value due to the formation of short chain organic acids, mainly lactic acid and acetic acid, and thereafter, the pH value of the composting materials rises gradually due to the increment in the amount of ammonia generated by the biochemical reactions of nitrogen-containing materials (Khiyami *et al.*, 2008).

Moisture content has significant effects on enzyme activities and microbial respiration of the composting process (Horng, 2003; Margesin *et al.*, 2006). A moisture content of 50-60 per cent is ideal for composting and microbial activity (Horng, 2003). The ratio between dry matter, water and air is an important factor in composting because raw materials have different moisture contents. Straw compost has high organic matter and can therefore retain more water. In mushroom compost, the optimum moisture is generally 75 per cent at the time of filling, 69 per cent at the time of spawning and 66 per cent after spawn run (Johri and Rajni, 1999). Rawat (2004) reported a variation of 60 per cent (zero day) to 56 per cent (filling) in moisture content during phase I and 62 per cent to 56 per cent during phase II. An increase in electrical conductivity (8.28 to 33.86 mmhos. cm^{-1}) occurs from zero day to end of phase I of mushroom compost with a sharp decline to 23.11 at peak-heat stage, and slight increase (25.60) at the end of phase II (Rawat, 2004).

The changes in oxygen concentration in the compost atmosphere between turnings represent net result of O_2 utilized by microorganism and that replenished by convection and diffusion through compost. The change in O_2 concentration is related with temperature. In the center of compost pile where the temperature is highest, anaerobic conditions exist. When the stack is turned, heat loss occurs and the resulting temperature of about 50^{0}C stimulates microbial activity and depletes oxygen. Turning of the stack also results in a change in physico environment whereby the existing temperature gradients are disturbed. The loss and recovery of oxygen in the compost atmosphere is thus largely due to combined influence of temperature, which affects microbial activity and changes the ventilation pattern (Johri and Rajni, 1999). The CO_2 evolution on the surface of compost pile shows good correlation with microbial activity compared to the number of propagules, for example it has been shown that whereas the total number of propagules is low during peak heating, CO_2 evolution is high due to higher rate of respiration of the abundant thermophilic microflora (Johri and Satyanarayana, 1984). Respiratory CO_2 of *Scytalidium thermophilum* was documented to be the likely reason for the growth promotory effect of this fungus on mushroom yield (Weigant, 1992).

Johri and Rajni (1999) reported that decomposition during composting was dependent upon carbon, nitrogen, lignin and carbohydrate composition of the organic material and expressed this relationship as:

$$CO_2 \text{ evolved} = \sqrt{\frac{\text{\% carbohydrate}}{\text{C/N residues} \times \text{\% lignin}}}$$

The rate of decomposition in compost pile is maximum during the first few days followed by a decline and ceases after sometime although large quantities of cellulose and hemicellulose are still present. In mushroom compost, about 60-70 per cent polysaccharides are consumed by compost microorganisms, however, only 15-25 per cent of total polysaccharides are used during mushroom production. The absolute amount of lignin remains unaltered though changes occur in the degree and condensation of lignins during composting because general microflora is devoid of basidiomycetes. During spawn running and fruiting about 15 per cent of wall polysaccharides are utilized from compost and thus, considerable amounts (17-31%) remain at the end of mushroom production (Iiyama *et al.*, 1994).

The rate of decomposition is markedly influenced by size as well as C: N ratio of the composting material. The variation in composition (% by dry weight basis) of municipal compost to garden composts ranges from 25.0-80.0 (organic matter), 8.0-50.0 (carbon), 0.4-3.5 (nitrogen); a C: N ratio of 30: 1 is considered ideal for the activity of most microbes (Biddlestone and Garay, 1985).

Microbial Ecology

Compost is an interesting example of man-made ecosystem which harbours a complete spectrum of microbial diversity. The microbial abundance, composition and activity changes substantially during the composting process and is correlated with high microbial diversity and low activity in matured compost.

Microbial community succession during composting is a classical example of how the growth and activity of one group of organisms can create conditions necessary for the growth of others. Several generations of microorganisms succeed each other during composting wherein each crop of microbial form utilizes the available material in the substrate as also the cellular components of its predecessors for growth, spread and sustenance. The study of community structure and diversity by various workers (Bilai, 1984; Beffa *et al.*, 1996; Straatsma *et al.*, 1994 a, b; Peters *et al.*, 2000; Rawat *et al.*, 2005) has been instrumental in manipulating the compost environment in order to quicken the composting process and to improve the compost quality.

(a) Structural diversity

The compost is a rich reservoir of microbial types, comprising of mesophilic and thermophilic bacteria, fungi and actinomycetes. Fungi are the most predominant component. *Aspergillus, Chaetomium, Humicola, Mucor, Penicillium* and *Thermomyces* are the dominant fungi of compost ecosystems. Species of *Aspergillus* and *Mucor* are predominant in composting of biowaste (Ryckeboer *et al.*, 2003). *Aspergillus fumigatus* and *Humicola grisea* var. *thermoidea* have been reported to be the dominant member of the spent mushroom compost. Other fungi reported from spent mushroom compost are, *Aspergillus flavus, Aspergillus nidulans, Aspergillus terreus, Aspergillus versicolor, Chrysosporium luteum, Mucor* spp., *Nigorospora* spp., *Oidiodendron* spp., *Paecilomyces* spp., *Penicillum chromogenum, Penicillum expansum, Trichoderma viride* and *Trichurus* spp. (Kleyn and Wetzler, 1981). The mesophilic microflora forms the pioneer community while thermophiles form the climax community.

In paddy straw compost, *Chaetomium thermophile, Humicola* spp. and *Sporotrichum thermophile* have been reported to be abundantly present in paddy straw compost (Satyanarayana, 1978). Antagonism appears to play a significant role in determining the population structure. The volatiles of *Chaetomium thermophile* and *Sporotrichum thermophile* can inhibit conidial germination of *Humicola lanuginosa* by impairing essential metabolic processes whereas *Chaetomium thermophile* suppresses mycelial growth of *Humicola lanuginosa* and *Torula thermophila*. However, effect of the fungistatic volatile factors in compost ecosystem is only marginal in view of high temperature at which they grow (Johri and Rajni, 1999).

Satyanarayana and Grajek (1999) observed that the colonizing ability of thermophilic fungi on paddy straw was directly proportional to the inoculum concentration. For example, colonization by *Humicola lanuginosa, Sporotrichum thermophile* and *Torula thermophila* increased with higher inoculum dose. During peak heating period, only a few thermophilic fungal propagules were present exhibiting high rate of respiration. However, Johri and Rajni (1999) reported that thermophilic fungi were not present at peak high temperature in wheat and broadbean straw composts. When it cooled down to 51.5^{0}C, *Myriococcum albomyces, Penicillium dupontii* and *Sporotrichum thermophile* were found in abundance.

Chang and Hudson (1967) studied the diversity of mycoflora of wheat straw compost. *Absidia ramosa, Aspergillus fumigatus, Chaetomium thermophile, Humicola grisea* var. *thermoidea, H. insolens, H. lanuginosa, Mlabranchea pulchella* var. *sulfurea, Mucor pusillus* and *Stilbella thermophila* occurred abundantly in the compost. The mesophilic fungi were soon killed off by the high temperature developed during the first few days; *A. fumigatus* and *M. pusillus* were also suppressed by the high temperature. *Mucor pusillus* did not recur even when the temperature of th compost later become suitable presumably due to lack of easily available carbon sources in the later stages. In contrast *A. fumigatus* persisted, with its ability to utilize cellulose and hemicellulose. *Humicola lanuginosa* developed early and persisted throughout composting due to its ability to lead commensal life with other forms (Rawat and Johri, 2002). Besides, this eukaryotic thermophile can tolerate wide temperature fluctuations on either side of optima and elaborates a variety of hydrolytic enzymes that help in continued presence. *Chaetomium thermophile, H. insolens, H. lanuginosa* and *Talaromyces dupontii* develop abundantly in the plateau period and rapidly utilise cellulose and hemicellulose. *Sporotrichum thermophile* alongwith some mesophilic fungi succeed when the temperature of the compost dropped. However, Moubasher *et al.* (1982) reported that thermophilic fungi were not present at peak high temperature in wheat and broadbean straw composts. When it cooled down to 51.5^{0}C, *Myriococcum albomyces, Penicillium dupontii* and *Sporotrichum thermophile* were found in abundance.

In paddy straw compost, *Chaetomium thermophile, Humicola* spp. and *Sporotrichum thermophile* are abundantly present (Satyanarayana, 1978). Satyanarayana and Johri (1984) observed that the colonizing ability of thermophilic fungi on paddy straw was directly proportional to the inoculum concentration. The colonization by *Humicola lanuginosa, Sporotrichum thermophile* and *Torula thermophila* increased with higher inoculum dose. During peak heating period, only a few thermophilic propagules were present exhibiting a higher rate of respiration.

Klamer *et al.* (2001) studied the succession of mycoflora during eight months of composting of miscanthus straw and pig slurry in well insulated containers. Before peak heating, *Aspergillus fumigatus* and *Rhizomucor pusillus* were dominant. Forms developing after peak heating could be divided into two groups: those appearing from day 15 to 27, and others developing from day 50 to 225. The first group was dominated by, *Paecilomyces variotii, Scytalidium thermophilum* and *Thermomyces lanuginosus*, and the second by, *Acremonium* spp. and *Thermomyces lanuginosus*. The Brillouin diversity index changed with temperature; diversity was high before peak-heating, low during elevated temperature, and increased again during the third phase of composting. Temperature was the main controlling parameter that changed fungal community during the first month of composting. Based on principal component analysis (PCA), it could be concluded that when the temperature reached the ambient level, only minor change in fungal community was detected although some changes in certain species were still discernible.

Municipal wastes generally contain substrates rich in lignohemicellulose, among other substrates. Thermophilic fungi play a significant role in the conversion of these materials into farmyard manure or single cell protein (Kane and Mullins, 1973; Eriksson and Larson, 1975). This aroused interest in studying the diversity of mycoflora in municipal compost. The unique ability of some species to degrade plastic substances envisaged special interest in their study (Eggins and Mills, 1971; Brown *et al.*, 1974).

Subrahamanyam *et al.* (1977) isolated a new genus *Thermomcor* besides other fungi from municipal waste compost in India. *Thermoascus aurantiacus* and *Myceliophthora thermophila* were the two major thermophilic fungi recovered from municipal waste compost (Sen *et al.*, 1980; Subrahmanyam, 1980). Kane and Mullins (1973) reported *Thermoascus aurantiacus* and other thermophilic fungi at the beginning of the digestion period, which persisted throughout composting. These workers were of the opinion that high temperature, acidity and anaerobic conditions could limit fungal growth in the interior of the compost, and thus restrict the role of these moulds. They recorded the presence of thermophilic fungi at all times during composting of municipal refuse and did not find any apparent succession within the species.

Thermophilic fungi grow extensively during the last phase of composting in mushroom compost from the spores that survive the pasteurization temperature (Straatsma *et al.*, 1989). Thus, they contribute significantly towards the quality of compost. However, their presence throughout the course of composting is largely responsible for the maintenance of biological equillibrium that ultimately leads to unique selectivity wherein *A. bisporus* multiplies without competition. These fungi influence growth of *A. bisporus* at three distinct levels (Weigant, 1992): First, they decrease concentration of ammonia in compost which otherwise would counteract the growth of the mycelium. Second, they immobilize nutrients in a form, which improves apparent availability to the mushroom mycelium. Third, they exert direct growth promotory influence on the mushroom mycelium viz., *S. thermophilum*. The course of fungal succession is partially dependent on the ecophysiological conditions in compost (Satyanarayana *et al.*, 1992).

In mushroom compost maximal diversity amongst thermophilic fungal morphotypes is observed with fourth turning of phase I compost (H'=2.14; E1=0.89 and D=8.88); and least by peak heat stage morphotypes (H'=0.75 and D=1.80). End of Phase I is most rich in species make up (R1=4.07 and R2=3.37). Fourth turning of phase I compost is maximally diverse for thermophilic community. The least fungal diversity is observed at peak-heat stage (Rawat, 2004). This is not unusual since only limited fungal species spectrum has been reported from this stage of composting (Straatsma *et al.*, 1994a).

The pioneer thermophilic mycoflora of mushroom compost comprises of fast growing and rapidly sporulating fungi such as *Aspergillus fumigatus* and *Rhizomucor* spp. with a pH optima below 7.0 and temperature optima of about 40°C. When self-heating and ammonification starts and pH reaches 9.0, the pioneer flora disappears and paves way for *Talaromyces thermophilus* and *Thermomyces lanuginosus*; during massive heat production these fungi possess moderate growth rate, as they exhibit high thermal death point and pH tolerance, but do not degrade cellulose. At the end of the composting process, about 50-70 per cent of the compost biomass is constituted by thermophilic fungi (Sparling *et al.*, 1982; Weigant, 1992). While most of the species are eliminated, *S. thermophilum* appears as near exclusive species after phase II composting and constitutes a climax species in the mushroom compost along with thermophilic actinomycetes (Straatsma *et al.*, 1994b). The number of CFU of *S. thermophilum* in fresh matter of phase II is about 10^6 g^{-1} compost (Bilai, 1984), however, actinomycetes and bacteria appear to play a decisive role in successful colonization by this thermophile. The presence of *S. thermophilum* throughout the composting period i.e., from zero day, dominance during phase II and at the end of phase II is supported by its relative abundance (0.68) as observed by Rawat (2004) and earlier observations of Straatsma *et al.* (1994a) on the subject.

In the beginning of phase II of mushroom compost, thermophilic fungi and actinomycetes extensively colonize the plant matter until temperature reaches 60°C, as an out come of slow peak-heating for about two days (Straatsma *et al.*, 1994a). The high temperature of the first indoor period of phase II kills most of the pathogenic and non-pathogenic microorganisms, except the spores of actinomycetes and thermophilic fungi such as *Scytalidium thermophilum* (Straatsma *et al.*, 1991); the latter was most abundant at the end of phase II compost (abundance = 0.68) (Rawat, 2004). Klamer *et al.* (1998) reported *A. fumigatus* and *Rhizomucor pusillus* as predominant species before peak heating and *P. variotii, S. thermophilum* and *Thermomyces lanuginosus* as dominant forms after peak heating. Tewari (2000) reported the presence of *H. lanuginosa*, and *S. thermophilum* during peak heat stage of phase II composting.

Thermophilic fungi of the *Torula-Humicola* complex are a necessary and dominant component of the community in mushroom compost during Phase II. *S. thermophilum* is a natural inhabitant of compost ingredients including drainage from compost, and has been documented to be present throughout composting. Dominance of *S. thermophilum* has been reported by several workers (Straatsma *et al.*, 1991; Vijay, 1996; Klamer *et al.*, 1998; Rajni *et al.*, 1998) while *H. grisea* var. *thermoidea* and *H. insolens* have been described by others (Fergus, 1964). They are inherently close partners in the degradation processes in compost and provide selectivity to compost (Straatsma *et al.*, 1989; Opden Camp *et al.*, 1990). Rajni *et al.* (1998) and Rawat (2004) observed nearly similar microbial distribution pattern in compost as reported by Straatsma *et al.* (1991) with predominance of *S. thermophilum* although inputs in the European and Indian composts are substantially different. In twenty days schedule of compost preparation, *S. thermophilum* was detected from the first turning (i.e., after 5th day of composting) till fifth turning (i.e. 17th day) whereas species of *Paecilomyces* were present only during the last turning i.e., 20th day. Two isolates of *Malbranchea cinnamomea* were recorded between the second and fifth turning stage (8th to 17th day). The presence of *Paecilomyces* sp. and *M. cinnamomea*, which are normally slow growers, provided an opportunity to evaluate their influence on *in situ* mycelial extension of *A. bisporus*. At 24th day of composting the population of *S. thermophilum* was 10^8 propagules g^{-1} of compost.

Thermophilic fungi of the *Torula-Humicola* complex are a necessary and dominant component of the community during Phase II. Dominance of *S. thermophilum* has been reported by several workers (Straatsma *et al.*, 1991; Vijay, 1996; Klamer *et al.*, 1998; Rajni *et al.*, 1998) while *H. grisea* var. *thermoidea* and *H. insolens* have been described by others (Fergus, 1964). They are inherently close partners in the degradation processes in compost and provide selectivity to compost (Straatsma *et al.*, 1989; Opden Camp *et al.*, 1990). The density of *S. thermophilum* was found to be positively correlated with mushroom yield (Straatsma *et al.*, 1989). Improved growth of *A. bisporus* mycelium in composts treated with *S. thermophilum* has been extensively reported in literature (Ross and Harris 1983; Straatsma *et al.*, 1989; 1991; Weigant, 1992; Straatsma and Samson 1993; Straatsma *et al.*, 1994 a, b). The causal relationship between the presence of *S. thermophilum* and the crop yield of mushroom remains still obscure. Straatsma *et al.* (1993) observed that this fungal species merely affects the radial extension rate rather than having a positive influence on the surface growth rate of *A. bisporus* mycelium. It reduces the growth of pathogenic microorganisms by virtue of inhibitory influence (Straatsma *et al.*, 1991). Respiratory CO_2 of this species may play a stimulatory role (Weigant *et al.*, 1992) but under different experimental conditions, neither volatiles nor CO_2 were stimulatory (Straatsma *et al.*, 1993; Straatsma *et al.*, 1995). The mere presence of *S. thermophilum* is however quite essential. Ross and Harris (1983) suggested that visible but dormant biomass of this species in composts fills an otherwise biological vacuum, which in turn allows growth of *A. bisporus* mycelium. Other thermophilic fungal species such as, *Chaetomium thermophilum, Malbranchea sulfurea, Myriococcum thermophilum, Stilbella thermophila, Thielavia terrestris* and two unidentified Basidiomycetes were also found to be promotory for mycelial growth of *A. bisporus* on sterilized compost along with *S. thermophilum* (Straatsma *et al.*, 1994a).

Among various groups actively engaged in studying the ecology of mushroom compost, Straatsma's group in Holland had laid considerable emphasis on population dynamics of *S. thermophilum* for better compost management. It is a natural inhabitant of compost ingredients, and drainage from compost, and has been documented to be present throughout composting. The disappearance of ammonia and selectivity of compost for the growth of *A. bisporus* mycelium that occurs in Phase II at temperature 45-55^{0}C are linked to the presence of *S. thermophilum* (Ross and Harris, 1983). Rajni *et al.* (1998) and Rawat (2004) observed nearly similar microbial distribution pattern in compost as reported by Straatsma *et al.* (1991) with predominance of *S. thermophilum* although inputs in the European and Indian composts are substantially different. They also observed the morphological variability of this fungus in compost with differences in their growth rate and promotion of mycelial growth. In twenty days schedule of compost preparation, *S. thermophilum* was detected from the first turning (i.e., after 5th day of composting) till fifth turning (i.e. 17th day) whereas species of *Paecilomyces* were present only during the last turning i.e., 20th day. Two isolates of *Malbranchea cinnamonea* were recorded between the second and fifth turning stage (8th to 17th day). The presence of *Paecilomyces* sp. and *M. cinnamonea*, which are normally slow growers, provided an opportunity to evaluate their influence on *in situ* mycelial extension of *A. bisporus*. At 24th day of composting the population of *S. thermophilum* was 10^8 propagules g^{-1} of compost.

Aspergillus fumigatus and *Humicola grisea* var. *thermoidea* are the dominant member of spent mushroom compost. Others include *Aspergillus flavus*,

A. nidulans, A. terreus, A. versicolor, Chrysosporium luteum, Mucor spp., *Nigorospoa* spp., *Oidiodendron* spp., *Paecilomyces* spp., and *Penicillum chromogenum*. The cultivation of mushrooms under controlled conditions in a growth room changes the quality and quantity of mycoflora in the compost. However, Klamer *et al.* (1998) reported *A. fumigatus* and *Rhizomucor pusillus* as predominant species before peak heating and *P. variotii, S. thermophilum* and *Thermomyces lanuginosus* as dominant forms after peak heating. Tewari (2000) reported the presence of *H. lanuginosa*, and *S. thermophilum* during peak heat stage of phase II.

Antagonisms, too, plays a significant role in determining the population structure. Volatile compounds and antibiotics are produced by microorganisms *in vivo* and also *in vitro*. The volatile of *Sporotrichum thermophile* and *Chaetomium thermophile* can inhibit conidial germination of *Humicola lanuginosa* by impairing essential metabolic processes. Volatiles of *Chaetomium thermophile* inhibit mycelial growth of *Humicola lanuginosa* and *Torula thermophila*. However, effect of the fungistatic volatile factors in compost ecosystem is only marginal in view of high temperature at which they grow (Johri and Satyanarayana, 1986).

(b) Genetic diversity

The genetic diversity of compost microflora has not been widely studied. It is however attracting attention in order to assign correct taxonomic status based on the traditional and molecular tools. The study of genomic DNA/RNA composition, gene structure mainly with a view to examine intron architecture/ organization and also regulatory sequences and "motifs" related to gene expression, is in progress. The GC content of DNA of all bacterial strains isolated from thermogenic compost at temperature between 65 and 820C ranges from 60.5- 63.4 mole per cent (Beffa *et al.*, 1996) and is similiar to that reported for *Thermus* spp. (Hudson *et al.*, 1987). All isolates except one showed high degree of DNA-DNA homology with *T. thermophilus* (65-71%) than with *T. acquaticus* (50-62%) and poor DNA – DNA homology with *T. filiformis* (39-48%) and *T. ruber* (30-40%).

During their early studies of *Humicola*, de Bertoldi *et al.* (1972, 1973) observed the mole per cent GC content of mesophilic and thermophilic species of *Humicola* to be newely in the same range; for the former it ranged between 30.6 and 56.9, and for the latter, 34.8 and 55.5. Although, *H. brevis* and *Torula terresteris* possess almost similar GC content (30.6 and 30.4%), these two organisms are not related suggesting base sequence dissimilarities (Meyer and Phaff 1969). Rodrigues *et al.* (1991) suggested that high mutation rates could cause variability and genomic differences in *Humicola* spp., which are further accentuated by polynucleated characteristic of this species.

The most widely applicable and rapid genetic fingerprinting techniques are based on the use of PCR. Genetic fingerprinting includes restriction fragment length polymorphism (RFLP) analysis of major components of the rDNA operon (rrn), namely, 16S, 23S, rDNA intergenic spacer region i.e., IGS, internal transcribed spacer region (ITS – PCR) and random amplified polymorphic DNA (RAPD) analysis (Blanc *et al.*, 1997). A comparison of nucleotide sequence of 5.8 S rRNA was the central focus of early studies on genetic diversity of thermophilic fungi. The nucleotide sequence of *T. lanuginosus* was closely related to other fungi, but exhibited high overall homology with other 5.8 S rRNA (Wildeman and Nazar, 1981). In hot compost (60 – 80°C) the isolates were found to have similar RFLP profiles as *Thermus thermophilus* HB 8 while strains of *T. thermophilus, T. acquaticus, T. filiformis* and *T. ruber* showed different RFLP profiles (Beffa *et al.*, 1996). A high level of intraspecific polymorphism amongst black *Aspergillus* species, representative of considerable divergence among sexual lines with no, or very little, genetic exchange, was reported based on RAPD analysis (Megnegneau *et al.*, 1993). Muthumeenakshi *et al.* (1994) studied the intraspecific molecular variation among *Trichoderma harzianum* isolates colonizing mushroom compost based on ITS sequences.

The genetic variation exhibited by *Torula-Humicola* complex has drawn wide attention. Azevedo *et al.* (1999) have distinguished homokaryotic strains of *Humicola grisea* var. *thermoidea* in two groups displaying uniform DNA profile reflecting heterogeneity in the wild genome using RAPD analysis. Straatsma and Samson (1993) studied the genetic diversity among *Scytalidium thermophilum* isolates using RAPD analysis. These strains exhibited a distinct pattern of amplified DNA bands. Rajni (1999) studied the genetic diversity between the black and white strains of *S. thermophilum* by RAPD analysis. A distinct band pattern was exhibited by these isolates. The protein profiling of *Torula-Humicola* complex exhibited *S. thermophilum* was more closely related to *H. grisea* var. *thermoidea* while the latter was similar to *H. insolens* than *H. lanuginosa; H. insolens* and *H. lanuginosa* were more distantly related.

The RAPD analysis and sequence analysis of ITS region of rDNA exhibited wide genetic variation in *Torula- Humicola* complex (Lyons *et al.*, 2000). RAPD analysis of 34 geographically diverse isolates revealed two distinct groups showing differences in the banding pattern. An examination of the genetic distance matrix indicated differences between isolates belonging to *S. thermophilum* cultural types 1 and 2. The sequence analysis of ITS 1, 5.8 S and ITS 2 region of rDNA suggested high homology between the isolates with minor sequence variation. Genetic distance values, among type 1 and 2 *S. thermophilum* isolates, varied by a value of 0.005 per cent. The RAPD groupings mirror closely the morphological and thermogravimetric data for

S. thermophilum isolates and provides further evidence of the variation, which exists between the species complex (Straatsma and Samson, 1993; Lyons and Sharma, 1998). Isolates of *S. thermophilum* bear close similarity to those of *H. grisea* var. *thermoidea* and *H. insolens*. Using RAPD analysis (Rawat, 2004) that majority of structurally or functionally dominant fungal species recovered from different stages of composting belonged to *Torula - Humicola* complex.

Beffa *et al*. (1996) reported for the first time the presence of genus *Thermus* in thermogenic (65 to 82^{0}C) composts taken from 2 to 5 week old organic waste samples. Majority of the isolates were probably *Thermus* strains, which had adapted to the conditions prevalent in hot compost ecosystem. The nutritional characteristics, total protein profiles, DNA-DNA hybridization and restriction fragment length polymorphisms (RFLP) profiles of 16S rDNA showed that *Thermus* strains isolated from host composts were closely related to *T. thermophilus* HB8 except strain JT4. All isolates except JT4 showed 65 to 71 per cent DNA-DNA homology with *T. thermophilus* and 50 to 62 per cent, with *T. aquaticus* while JT4 showed 72 per cent homology with *T. aquaticus*. A moderately high number of obiligately autotrophic *Hydrogenobacter* spp. and facultatively autotrophic *Bacillus schlegelii* growing at temperatures above 70°C were isolated from hot composts (Beffa *et al*., 1996). A number of entrobacteriaceae and members of the genus *Lactobacillus* were observed in the initial stage of composting of organic matter at 410C. Low G+C gram-positive bacteria constituted a dominant fraction of the bacterial community during hot composting (55-70°C) phase (Alfreider, 2002).

The genetic profiling techniques which are cultivation independent have great potential in identifying the population structure and community succession. These techniques utilize DNA or RNA directly extracted from environmental samples and amplification of signature genes by PCR or reverse transcription-PCR (RT-PCR) with primers, bind to conserverd regions and produce homologous gene fragments. The products can be subsequently analyzed to determine their nucleotide differences by techniques such as, denaturing gradient gel electrophoresis (DGGE), temperature gradient gel electrophoresis (TGGE), terminal restriction fragment length polymorphism (t-RFLP) and single-stranded conformation polymorphism (SSCP) (Muyzer *et al*., 1993; Lee *et al*., 1996; Liu *et al*., 1997; Schwieger and Tebbe, 1998). SSCP has the potential to be more easily applied in contrast to DGGE and TGGE, as no GC clamps or construction of gradient gel is required (Lee *et al*., 1996). However, it is quite essential to compare diversity results obtained by both cultivation-dependent and cultivation-independent methods for better understanding and for eliminating the biases associated with genetic profiling.

Rawat (2004) observed that SSCP profile (Fig. 4.1) of fungal community of different stages of composting corroborated well with the culturable fungal diversity; though the total number of fungal species culturable were only 34, a total of 95 distinct bands were obtained. The banding pattern of community underwent a rapid change with the onset of composting; this corroborated well with the reports of culturable fungal diversity by Peters *et al*. (2000). The profile patterns of two samples of zero day compost (PWI and PWII) were quite similar while different stages of phase I composting shared nearly identical pattern profile; pattern of cropping sequences was quite similar to each other. PWI and PWII compost profiles consisted of many faint bands but with the onset of composting these faint bands disappeared; during peak-heat stage only prominent bands were present. This banding pattern corroborated with the observations of Vijay (1996) that fungi encountered on the ingredients play only a minor role in composting and may disappear as soon as composting is started.

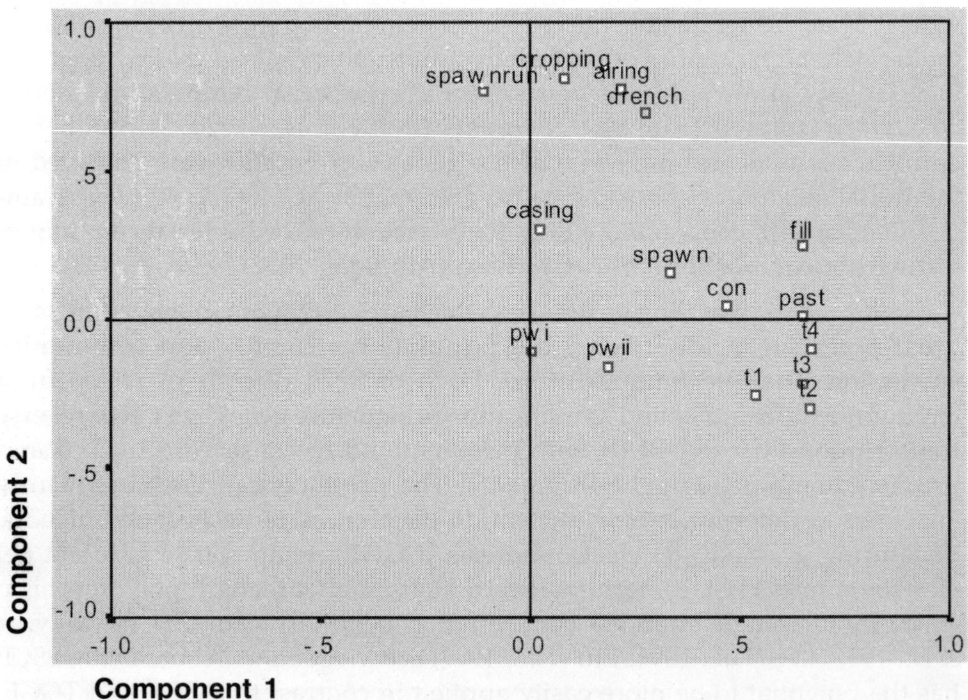

Fig. 4.1: **PCA of 18S Community of Different Stages of Mushroom Compost**

The dendrogram (Fig. 4.2) based on Jaccard's similarity coefficient exhibited a 15-66 per cent similarity amongst the community of different stages of mushroom compost. Community of all the samples could be divided into three main groups. Group I comprised of zero day (PWI & PWII) community exhibiting 26 per cent similarity. Group II could be further subdivided into two groups: Ist subgroup comprised of phase I community. Second (T2) and third (T3)turning community shared maximum similarity at 66 per cent level while first turning (T1) community shared a similarity of 32 per cent with that of second and third community. Fourth turning (T4) and end of phaseI (filling) community showed 51 per cent similarity with each other. IInd subgroup comprised of peak-heat, conditioning and end of phase II compost (spawning) community. Peak-heat and conditioning communities shared 38 per cent similarity with each other and 30 per cent similarity with end of phase II compost community. The overall similarity between the two subgroups was 30 per cent. II group had casing soil, cropping, airing and drenching communities. PWI, PWII, T2, T4, spawning, cropping, airing and drenching community shared a maximum similarity of 66 per cent with each other and 44 per cent similarity with spawn-run community. Drenching community shared 42 per cent similarity with that of spawn-run, cropping and airing community. Casing community showed 22 per cent similarity with cropping, airing and drenching community. The similarity amongst these three subgroups was quite low; 16 per cent between gp I and gp II while they both shared 15 per cent similarity with gp III.

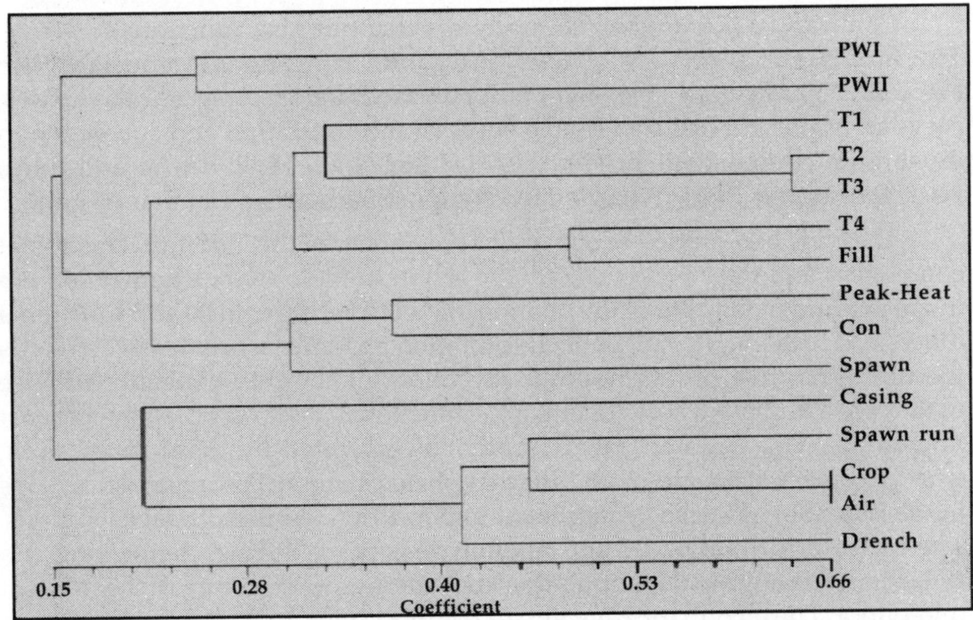

Fig. 4.2: **Cluster Analysis of 18S Community of Different Stages of Mushroom Compost Based on Jaccard's Coefficient**

The community profiles of Phase I compost were found to be identical to each other; maximum diversity was observed during end of phase I compost, casing soil and cropping stage (H′ = 0.37) and least at peak-heat stage. However, the level of diversity assigned on the basis of SSCP did not match with the culturable fungal diversity; both the approaches however described least diversity value at peak-heat stage as a common point. The diversity indices indicated maximum diversity amongst community of end of phase I compost, casing and cropping community (H′=0.37) while least at peak-heat community (H′=0.22).

The fungal phylotypes, revealed by cloning and sequencing of fungal internal transcribed spacer (ITS) region of samples of different stages of composting in a full-scale and a pilot-scale composting reactors, could be grouped into those that dominated the mesophilic low pH initial phases (sequences similar to genera *Candida, Dipodascaceae* and *Pichia*) and those found mostly or exclusively in the thermophilic phase (sequences clustering to *Candida, Rhizomucor* and *Thermomyces*), but a few were also present throughout the whole process (Hultman *et al.*, 2010).

(c) Functional diversity

Compost is not only structurally diverse but also functionally active. The *in situ* functionality of each microbial component especially the extracellular enzymatic machinery viz., polysaccharases, proteases and lipases, plays an important decisive role in successful colonization and succession in mushroom compost (Rajni *et al.*, 1998; Johri *et al.*, 1999, Rawat and Johri, 2002, Rawat and Johri, 2004). Infact, compost harbours a number of guilds.

The wide exploration of enzymatic machinery of the individual microbial component and their *in situ* enzymatic action in their own niche would help in greater understanding of the relationship between structural and functional diversity. However, the available information appears largely biased towards the functional role of thermophilic mycoflora of compost probably because of they are a dominant component of the functional niche occupied by compost microbiota. The wide enzymatic potential exhibited by these fungi along with enzyme multiplicity with different phsico-chemical characteristics helps in the functioning of each component under different biophysical conditions. The increase in cellulolytic and amylolytic activity during composting is a reflection of change in the population and community structure of the resident microflora. The enzymatic diversity of compost microbiota is known to result in specificity and successional change besides providing a niche to various species to survive in the absence of simple sugars (Rawat and Johri, 2002).

In compost the pioneer microflora in general can utilize simple sugars but such biota disappear soon and only those organisms with wide polysaccharolytic ability persist. The cellulolytic and hemicellulolytic ability of thermotolerant *Aspergillus fumigatus* allows it to persist in the wheat straw compost whereas thermophilic *Mucor pusillus* could not recur even after temperature become suitable for growth due to lack of polysaccharolytic ability. *Humicola lanuginosa* persists throughout composting due to its ability to lead commensal life with other along with its cellulolytic and hemicellulolytic ability. *Chaetomium thermophile, Humicola insolens, Humicola lanuginosa* and *Talaromyces dupontii* develop abundantly in the 'plateau' period and rapidly utilize cellulose and hemicellulose. When compost temperature drops, thermophilic *Sporotrichum thermophile* and mesophilic *Coprinus cinereus* and *Clitopilus pinsitus* appear which can utilize cellulose and hemicellulose in wheat staw at a slower rate (Chang and Hudson, 1967).

The success of microflora in competitive saprophytic colonization (CSC) such as that operative in plant residues and soil depends upon its intrinsic ability to decompose that substrate and the ability to succeed in the competition (Garret, 1963). The strongly cellulolytic and hemicellulolytic *Aspergillus fumigatus, Sporotrichum thermophile* and *Torula thermophila* exhibit greater colonization ability than the weakly cellulolytic, *Humicola lanuginosa* (Johri and Satyanarayana, 1984). The dominance of *S. thermophilum* has been attributed to the presence of complete complement of polysaccharlytic enzyme machinery (Grajek, 1987; Rawat, 1998; Khokar, 1999; Tewari, 2000). The hydrolytic potential of such thermophilic fungi is responsible for solubilization of complex ingredients of compost and making the nutrient availabile to *A. bisporus*. The stimulation of growth of mushroom mycelium by cellulose decomposing mycoflora has been well-documented (Stanek, 1969).

Considering the fact that culturable microbial populations are limited on account of our poor understanding of their nutritional requirements, detailed, *in situ* enzymatic investigations are likely to provide a better understanding of the relationship between structural and functional diversity of thermophilic fungal community. Iiyama *et al.* (1996) observed that the loss of cellulose and lignocellulose and increase in protein content during the composting period was a result of increased polysaccharolytic activity of the fungal biomass; this resulted in increased level of reducing sugars. In mushroom compost the level of enzymes was found to increase from zero day to the end of phase I compost; thereafter it decreased continuously; results were well corroborated with the population structure (Rawat, 2004).

It has been observed that *in situ* changes in lignocellulose, cellulose and loss in weight during composting is corroborated with the activity of thermophilic fungi. The analysis of plant residues after decomposition by pure thermophilic fungal cultures resulted in biochemical changes that were similar to those observed during composting of organic materials by natural mixed microflora (Satyanarayana, 1978). During the 24 day composting sequence of button mushroom, Rajni (1999) reported that the level of organic carbon decreased from 18.12 to 10.57 per cent while that of cellulose and lignocellulose from 32.3-23.0 per cent and 52.4-43.1 per cent, respectively. An increase of 77.5 per cent and 86 per cent in protein and reducing sugar level was observed. The level of amylase, endo- cellulase and exo-cellulase also changed. Based on the regression analysis between the population of *Scytalidium thermophilum* and chemical parameters, a 92.5 per cent change in lignocellulose was found as a result of rise in population of *S. thermophilum* in compost. The levels of dehydrogenase activity decreased by 72 per cent; protease by 32 per cent; xylanase and cellulase by 50 per cent during peak heat while during of phase II and post peak heat stageof mushroom compost, levels again increased by 71 per cent, 23 per cent and 33.3 per cent, respectively. These changes were found to be well corroborated with the change in population structure of compost microflora (Tewari, 2000).

In compost the pioneer microflora, in general, can utilize simple sugars but such biota disappear soon and only those organisms with wide polysaccharolytic ability persist. The cellulolytic and hemicellulolytic ability of thermotolerant *Aspergillus fumigatus* allows it to persist in the wheat straw compost whereas thermophilic *Mucor pusillus* does not recur even after temperature became suitable for growth due to lack of polysaccharolytic ability. *Humicola lanuginosa* persists throughout composting due to its ability to lead commensal life with other along with its cellulolytic and hemicellulolytic ability. *Chaetomium thermophile, Humicola insolens, Humicola lanuginosa* and *Talaromyces dupontii* develop abundantly in the 'plateau' period and rapidly utilize cellulose and hemicellulose. When compost temperature drops, thermophilic *Sporotrichum thermophile* and mesophilic *Coprinus cinereus* and *Clitopilus pinsitus* appear which can utilize cellulose and hemicellulose in wheat straw at a slower rate (Chang and Hudson, 1967).

The success of microflora in competitive saprophytic colonization (CSC) such as that operative in plant residues and soil depends upon its intrinsic ability to decompose that substrate and the ability to succeed in the competition. The strongly cellulolytic and hemicellulolytic *Aspergillus fumigatus, Sporotrichum thermophile* and *Torula thermophila* exhibit greater colonization ability than the weakly cellulolytic, *Humicola lanuginosa* (Johri and Satyanarayana, 1984). The dominance of *S. thermophilum* has been attributed to the presence of complete complement of polysaccharolytic enzyme machinery (Rawat, 1998; Tewari, 2000; Rawat *et al.*, 2005). The hydrolytic potential of such thermophilic fungi is responsible for solubilization of complex ingredients of compost and making the nutrient availabile to *A. bisporus*. The stimulation of growth of mushroom mycelium by cellulose decomposing mycoflora has been well-documented (Stanek, 1969; Straatsma *et al.*, 1994a; Johri and Rajni, 1999).

Mushroom compost that harbours high population of thermophilic flora yields more mushroom produce (Shandilya, 1982; Vijay, 1996). The selectivity of compost is brought about by the static population of thermophilic flora, which becomes inactive at the time of spawning. The thermophilic microbial biomass is a concentrated source of nutrients required for the growth of *A. bisporus*. Thermophilic fungi appear to use up all the readily available nutrients during the process of composting and thus a major portion of the available nutrients is locked up inside their cells (Betterely, 1993). *Agaricus bisporus* posseses the complement of enzymes viz., b-N-acetyl galactosaminidase, laminarinase, protease etc. by which it can degrade thermophilic bacteria, fungal and actinomycete mycelium for its own growth (Fermor and Grant, 1985; Rawat *et al.*, 2005). Sparling *et al.* (1982) reported that microbial biomass contributed less than 10 per cent to mushroom biomass and therefore *A. bisporus* probably obtained bulk of its carbon nutrition from straw. However, the microbial biomass can act as a concentrated source of nitrogen and minerals. The selectivity of compost is lost if dormant thermophilic biomass is destroyed by heat or chemicals (Ross and Harris, 1983), and growth rate of *A. bisporus* mycelium is reduced on sterilized compost (Wood and Matchman, 1980). Rawat (2004) found that dominant functional forms in mushroom compost were representatives of T3 stage.

The role of *Scytalidium thermophilum*, predominant component of compost, in compost management has been well documented by various workers (Ross and Harris, 1983; Straatsma *et al.*, 1989; Johri and Rajni, 1999; Rawat, 2004; Rawat *et al.*, 2005). The disappearance of ammonia and selectivity of compost for the growth of *A. bisporus* mycelium that occurs in Phase II at temperature 45-55°C is linked to the presence of *S. thermophilum* (Ross and Harris, 1983). The density of *S. thermophilum* was found to be positively correlated with mushroom yield (Straatsma *et al.*, 1989). The causal relationship between the presence of *S. thermophilum* and the crop yield of mushroom remains still obscure. Straatsma *et al.* (1991) observed that this fungal species merely affects the radial extension rate rather than having a positive influence on the surface growth rate of *A. bisporus* mycelium. It reduces the growth of pathogenic microorganisms by virtue of inhibitory influence. Respiratory CO_2 of this species may play a stimulatory role (Weigant, 1992) but under different experimental conditions, neither volatiles nor CO_2 were stimulatory (Straatsma *et al.*, 1994a). The mere presence of *S. thermophilum* is however quite essential. Ross and Harris (1983) suggested that visible but dormant biomass of this species in composts fills an otherwise biological vacuum, which in turn allows growth of *A. bisporus* mycelium. The disappearance of ammonia and selectivity of compost for the growth of *A. bisporus* mycelium that occurs in Phase II at temperature 45-55^{0}C are linked to the presence of *S. thermophilum* (Ross and Harris, 1983). Other thermophilic fungal species such as, *Chaetomium thermophilum*, *Malbranchea sulfurea*, *Myriococcum thermophilum*, *Stilbella thermophila*, *Thielavia terrestris* and two unidentified Basidiomycetes were also found to be promotory for mycelial growth of *A. bisporus* on sterilized compost along with *S. thermophilum* (Straatsma *et al.*, 1994a).

Considering the fact that culturable microbial populations are limited on account of our poor understanding of their nutritional requirements, detailed, *in situ* enzymatic investigations are likely to provide a better understanding of the relationship between structural and functional diversity of thermophilic fungal community. Iiyama *et al.* (1996) observed that the loss of cellulose and lignocellulose and increase in protein content during the composting period was a result of increased polysaccharolytic activity of the fungal biomass; this resulted in increased level of reducing sugars. In mushroom compost the level of enzymes was found to increase from zero day to the end of phase I compost; thereafter it decreased continuously and the results were well corroborated with the population structure (Rawat, 2004; Rawat *et al.*, 2005).

It has been observed that *in situ* changes in lignocellulose, cellulose and loss in weight during composting is corroborated with the activity of thermophilic fungi. The analysis of plant residues after decomposition by pure thermophilic fungal cultures resulted in biochemical changes that were similar to those observed during composting of organic materials by natural mixed microflora (Satyanarayana, 1978). During the 24 day composting sequence of button mushroom, Rajni (1999) reported that the level of organic carbon decreased from 18.12 to 10.57 per cent while that of cellulose and lignocellulose from 32.3-23.0 per cent and 52.4 - 43.1 per cent, respectively. An increase of 77.5 per cent and 86 per cent in protein and reducing sugar level was observed. The level of amylase, endo- cellulase and exo-cellulase also changed. Based on the regression analysis between the population of *Scytalidium thermophilum* and chemical parameters, a 92.5 per cent change in lignocellulose was found as a result of rise in population of *S. thermophilum* in compost. The levels of dehydrogenase activity decreased by 72 per cent; protease by 32 per cent; xylanase and cellulase by 50 per cent during peak heat while during of phase II and post peak heat stage of mushroom compost, levels again increased by 71 per cent, 23 per cent and 33.3 per cent, respectively. These changes were found to be well corroborated with the change in population structure of compost microflora (Tewari, 2000).

Yu *et al.* (2007) reported that hemicellulose and cellulose were partially degraded during initial stage of composting of agricultural wastes and thereafter the degrading ratio was almost unaltered due to high temperature followed by the large decomposition during the temperature falling phase (12-20d) and initial stage of the second fermentation (21-40d of composting).

Lignin was slightly decomposed during the initial stage of composting. When the temperature was lower than the maximum value during thermophilic phase, lignin was greatly degraded until the temperature began to fall.

Stanek (1969) observed stimulation of growth of mushroom mycelium by cellulase decomposing microflora mainly, actinomycetes and fungi. It is, however, difficult to draw a conclusive relationship between restricted cellulolysis and growth promotion of *A. bisporus* since species such as *Aspergillus fumigatus* and *Corynascus thermophilum* are cellulolytic but not growth promotry whereas the reverse is true for *Chaetomium thermophilum* and *Sporotrichum thermophile*. Thus, growth promotory species can be cellulolytic but not necessary pioneers colinizers of the compost biota. Such an influence is exerted by the climax species of mushroom compost, *Scytalidium thermophilum*, perhaps due to production of a complete complement of enzyme machinery (Rawat, 1998; Tewari, 2000; Rawat, 2004).

An increase in cellulase activity and decrease in laccase activity was observed after the addition of casing soil to the surface of compost colonized by *Agaricus bisporus* (Gillman *et al.*, 1994). The increase in cellulolytic and amylolytic activity during composting is a reflection of change in the population and community structure of the resident microflora. The enzymatic diversity of compost microbiota is known to result in specificity and successional change besides providing a niche to various species to survive in the absence of simple sugars.

The importance of polysaccharolytic enzymes in mushroom compost has led some to stimulate composting by supplementing the substrate with commercial enzymes. Savoie and Libmond (1994) observed that microbial enzyme activities, number of bacteria, and solubilization of carbon and nitrogen were greater in compost treated with polysaccharidases. However, this had no positive effect on mushroom yield. Libmond *et al.* (1995) observed that supplementation of wheat straw with Express (trade name of poysaccharidase complex) reduced the time of mushroom composting besides, releasing low quantities of readily available sugars, increased enzyme activities and number of microrganisms, particularly aerobic bacterial population in the substrate.

Some workers have exploited the enzymatic potential of thermophilic fungi by preinoculation of compost with thermophilic fungi. Salar and Aneja (2007) observed the growth of *Agaricus bisporus* on sterile compost pre-colonized with four thermophilic fungi *viz.*, *Chaetomium thermophile, Malbranchea sulfurea, Thermomyces lanuginosus* and *Torula thermophila*, either singly or in different combinations. A mixed inoculum of *Malbranchea sulfurea* and *Torula thermophila* was found to be the best amongst the various treatments that promoted the growth of *A. bisporus* to the plateau of 7.7 mm day^{-1} and the yield of the mushroom was almost twice compared to the pasteurized control. The effect of *T. lanuginosus* when inoculated singly or in combination with other thermophilic fungus/fungi in compost was insignificant resulting in lower growth rates. The study revealed that thermophilic fungi provide for compost selectivity and protection against negative effects of compost bacteria on mycelial growth of *A. bisporus*. Improved growth of *A. bisporus* mycelium in composts treated with *S. thermophilum* has been extensively reported in literature (Ross and Harris, 1983; Weigant, 1992; Straatsma and Samson, 1993; Straatsma *et al.*, 1994 a, b; Rawat, 2004; Salar and Aneja, 2007). Straatsma *et al.* (1994a) reported that nine thermophilic fungi viz., *Chaetomium thermophilum*, an unidentified *Chaetomium* sp., *Malbranchea sulfurea, Myriococcum thermophilum, S. thermophilum, Stilbella thermophila, Thielavia terrestris*, and two unidentified basidiomycetes, promoted mycelial growth of *Agaricus bisporus* on sterilized compost.

The study of physiological diversity of compost by techniques like phospholipid fatty acids analysis (PLFA) and metabolic fingerprinting has been instrumental in tracking changes in microbial communities and thus understanding the *in situ* community structure (Garland and Mills, 1991; Petersen *et al.*, 1991; Kennedy and Busacca, 1995; Inssam *et al.*, 1996; Boggs *et al.*, 1998; Campbell and Cooper, 1999; Cahayani *et al.*, 2002). Neither of the PLFA markers of fungi, i.e., 18:2 w6C and 18:3 w6C changed significantly over time, indicating that the proportion of fungi in the community varies little with compost maturation although the type of fungi present or active at any stage could vary significantly (Boggs *et al.*, 1998).

Community analysis of composting of dairy manure and pine shave beddings based on carbon source utilization as tool revealed that microbial utilization of g-aminobutyric acid was increased over time while histidine was utilized at similar level at all sampling times. The ability to utilize sucrose, galactose and fructose increased while trehalose utilization decreased during composting (Boggs *et al.*, 1998).

Rawat (2004) studied physiological diversity of different stages of mushroom compost by 'metabolic fingerprinting' employing Biolog. Average well colour development (AWCD) was higher for mesophilic community than for the thermophiles. Principal component analysis (PCA) analysis revealed that the thermophilic mycoflora community can be divided into two clusters (Fig. 4.3): Cluster I comprised of drenching, spawn-run, casing, cropping, airing, PW I and PWII community; Cluster II comprised of filling, conditioning, peak-heat, spawning, first turning, second turning, third turning and end of phase I composting community. The physiological distribution of community, however, did not correlate well with the structural distribution. Maximum physiological diversity was exhibited within the mesophiles representing zero day community and least amongst peak-heat community. Among thermophiles, zero day community was maximally diverse and conditioning community of phase II, the least.

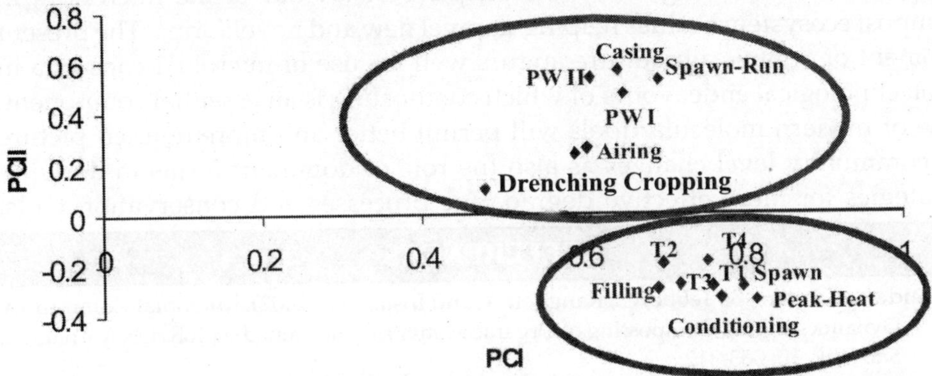

Fig. 4.3: **PCA of Physiological Diversity of Thermophilic Mycoflora in Mushroom Compost Based on Metabolic Fingerprinting**

The wide enzymatic potential exhibited by thermophilic fungi with different physico-chemical characteristics helps in the fuctioning of each component under different biophysical conditions. They also exhibit enzyme multiplicity which helps them function efficiently under different eco-physiological conditions. Multiplicity of hemicellulolytic enzymes has been widely reported in *Chaetomium thermophile* var. *coprophile*, *Humicola grisea* var. *thermoidea*, *Melanocarpus albomyces*, *Talaromyces emersonii*, *Thermoascus aurantiacus* and *Scytalidium thermophilum* (Thakur *et al.*, 1992; Tuohy *et al.*, 1993; Johri and Rajni, 1999; Rawat, 2004; Rawat *et al.*, 2005).

Conclusion

Compost represents an interesting example of thermogenic, solid-state fermentation process that results from a succession of microbial communities. While it is a complex ecosystem, study of structural diversity complemented with functional diversity provides a fair picture of the species spectrum and their associated interactions within the substrate. Application of phenotypic and genetic tools with culturable and non-culturable components of the microbial diversity, coupled to utilization of diversity indices and PCA analysis has permitted deeper insights at subtle changes that result in physico-chemical and biological conditioning of compost. The survival strategies and competitive behaviour of microflora in this interesting niche requires to be understood. The *in situ* functionality of thermophilic fungi is still poorly known whereas tapping the biopotentiality of microflora in this niche would help in hastening the composting process besides improving the quality of compost by pre-inoculation of microflora. This approach while being widely practised in mushroom compost and has currently become popular in other composting systems as Effective Microorganism Technology but is at its nascent stage. New vertical dimensions will add to our existing knowledge, which would throw light into the adaptive behaviour of the microflora in compost ecosystem besides helping unravel new and novel forms. The present moment of organic agriculture augurs well for use of microbial consortia in ecotechnological endeavours of which composting is an essential component. Use of modern molecular tools will permit better and more defined picture of community level changes as also the role of dominant forms in deriving strategies for more effective degradative processes and conservation tools.

REFERENCES

Alfreider, A., Peters, S., Tebbe, C., Rangger, A. and Insam, H. (2002). Microbial Community Dynamics during Composting of Organic Matter as Determined by 16S rDNA Analysis. *Sci. Util.*, 10: 303-312.

Antizar-Ladislao, B., Lopez-Real, J. and Beck, A.J. (2005). Laboratory Studies of the Remediation of Polycyclic Aromatic Hydrocarbon Contaminated Soil by in-vessel Composting. *Waste Mgmt.*, 25: 281-289.

Azevedo, M.O., Felipe, M.S.S. and Satyanarayana, T. (1999). Molecular and General Genetics. *In*: Thermophilic Moulds in Biotechnology (eds. B.N. Johri, T. Satyanarayana and J. Olsen), Kluwer Academic Publishers, Netherlands, 317-342.

Beffa, T., Blanc, M. and Aragno, M. (1996). Obligately and Facultatively Autotrophic, Sulfur and Hydrogen-oxidizing Thermophilic Bacteria Isolated from hot Composts. *Arch. Microbiol.*, 165: 34-40.

Betterley, D.A. (1993). Supplements, Composting, Mushroom Nutrition and Future Direction. *Mushroom News*. 41: 8-12.

Biddlestone, A.J. and Garay, K.R. (1985). Composting. *In*: Comprehensive Biotechnology (ed. M. Moo-Young). Pergamon Press, New York. Vol. 4. pp. 1059-1070.

Bilai, V.T. (1984). Thermophilic Micromycete Species from Mushroom Composts. *Mikrobiol. Zh. (Kiev).*, 46: 35-38.

Blanc, M., Marilley, L., Beffa, T. and Aragno, M. (1997). Rapid Identification of Heterotrophic Thermophilic, Spore Forming Bacteria Isolated from Hot Composts. *Int. J. Bacteriol.*, 47: 1246-1248.

Boggs, L.C., Kennedy, A.C. and Reganold, J.P. (1998). Use of Phospholipids Fatty Acids and Carbon Source Utilization Patterns to Track Microbial Community Succession in Developing Compost. *Appl. Environ. Microbiol.*, 64: 4062-4064.

Brown, B.S., Mills, J. and Hulse, J.M. (1974). Chemical and Biological Degradation of Waste Plastics. *Nature*, 250: 161-163.

Cahayani, V.R., Watanabe, A., Matsuya, K., Asakawa, S. and Kimura, M. (2002). Succession of Microbiota Estimated by Phospholipids Fatty acid Analysis and Changes in Organic Constituents during the Composting Process of Rice Straw. *Soil Sci. Plant Nut.*, 48: 735-743.

Campbell, C.D. and Cooper, J.N. (1999). Community Succession and Decomposition of Microbial Biomass during the Composting of Pot ale Liquor. *In*: Microbial Process during Composting. Proc. 8th Int. Symp. on Microbial. Ecol. (eds. C.R. Bell, M. Brylinsky and P.G. Johnson), Halifax, Canada.

Chang, Y. and Hudson, H.J. (1967). The Fungi of Wheat Straw Compost. I. Ecological Studies. *Trans. Br. Mycol. Soc.*, 50: 649-666.

Cooney, D.C. and Emerson, R. (1964). Thermophilic fungi: An Account of Their Biology, Activities and Classification (eds. D.C. Cooney and R. Emerson). Freman and Co. San Francisco Pub., p. 180.

de Bertoldi, M., Lepidi, A.A. and Nuti, M.P. (1972). Classification of the Genus *Humicola* Traeen:I. Preliminary Reports and Investigations. *Mycopathol. Mycol. Appl.*, 46: 289-304.

de Bertoldi, M., Lepidi, A.A. and Nuti, M.P. (1973). Significance of DNA base Composition in Classification of *Humicola* and Related Genera. *Trans. Br. Mycol. Soc.*, 60: 77-85.

Eggins, H.O.W. and Mills, J. (1971). *Talaromyces Emersonii,* a Possible Biodeteriogen. *Int. Biodet. Bull.*, 7: 105-108.

Ellis, D.H. (1980a). Thermophilic Fungi Isolated from a Heated Acquatic Habitat. *Mycologia,* 72: 1030-1033.

Ellis, D.H. (1980b). Thermophilic Fungi Isolated from some Antarctic and Sub-antarctic Soil. *Mycologia*, 72: 1030-1033.

Eriksson, K.E. and Larson, K. (1975). Fermentation of Waste Mechanical Fibres from Newsprint Mill by the Fungus *Sporotrichum Pulverulentum. Biotechnol. Bioeng.*, 17: 327-348.

Fergus, C.L. (1964). Thermophilic and Thermotolerant Molds and Actinomycetes of Mushroom Compost during Peak Heating. *Mycol.*, 56: 267-284.

Fermor, T.R. and Grant, W.D. (1985). Degradation of Fungal and Actinomycetes Mycelia by *Agaricus* Bisporus. *J. Gen. Microbiol.*, 131: 1729-1734.

Finstein, M.S. and Morris, M.L. (1975). Microbiology of Municipal Solid Composting. *Adv. Appl. Microbiol.*, 19: 113-151.

Forsyth, W.G. and Webley, D.M. (1948). *Proc. Soc. Appl. Bacteriol.*, p. 34.

Galler, W.S. and Davey, C.B. (1971). *In*: Livestock Waste Management and Pollution Abatement. Publ. Proc. 271, Amer. Soc. Agr. Eng. St. Joseph, Michigan. pp. 159-162.

Garland, J.L. and Mills, A.L. (1991). Classification and Characterization of Heterotrophic Microbial Communities on the Basis of Community-level Sole Carbon Source Utilization. *Appl. Environ. Microbiol.*, 57: 2351-2354.

Gillman, L., Lebeault, J.M. and Cochet, N. (1994). Influence of Casings on the Microflora of Compost Colonized by *Agaricus Bisporus. Acta Biol. Technol.*, 14: 275-282.

Grajek, W. (1987). Production of D-Xylanase by Thermophilic Fungi Using Different Methods of Culture. *Biotechnol. Lett.*, 353-356.

Herrmann, R.F. and Shann, J.F. (1997). Microbial Community Changes during Composting of Municipal Solid Waste. *Microbiol.* Ecol., 33: 78-85.

Hiraishi, A., Narihiro, T. and Yamanaka, Y. (2003). Microbial Community Dynamics During Start-up Operation of Flowerpot-using Fed-batch Reactors for Composting of Household Biowaste. *Environ. Microbiol.*, 5: 765-776.

Horng, J. M. (2003). Food Waste Utilize Effectively. Taiwan, ROC: Environmental Protection Union of Taiwan.

Hultman, J. (2009). Microbial Diversity in the Municipal Composting Process and Development of Detection methods. *Ph.D. Thesis*, University of Helsinki.

Hultman, J., Vasara, T., Partanen, P., Kurola, J., Kontro, M., Paulin, L., Auvinen, P. and Romantschuk, M. (2010). Determination of Fungal Succession during Municipal Solid Waste Composting Using a Cloning-based Analysis. *J. Appl. Microbiol.*, 108: 472-487.

Iiyama, K., Stone, B.A. and Macauley, B.J. (1996). Changes in the Concentration of Soluble Anions in Compost during Composting and Mushroom Growth. *J. Food Sci. Agric.*, 72: 243-249.

Inssam, H., Amor, K., Renner, M. and Crepaz, C. (1996). Changes in Functional Abilities of the Microbial Community during Composting of Manure. *Microbiol. Ecol.*, 37: 77-87.

Johri, B.N. and Rajni. (1999). Mushroom Compost: Microbiology and Applications. *In*: Modern Approaches and Innovations in Soil Management (eds. D.J. Bagyaraj, A. Verma, K.K. Khanna and H.K. Kheri), Rastogi Publ., Merrut, India, pp. 345-358.

Johri, B.N. and Satyanarayana, T. (1984). Ecology of Thermophilic fungi. *In*: Progress in Microbial Ecology (eds. K.G. Mukherji, V.P. Agnihotri, and R.P. Singh), Print House, Lucknow, pp. 349-361.

Johri, B.N., Satyanarayana, T. and Olsen, J. (1999). Thermophilic Moulds in Biotechnology (eds. B.N. Johri, T. Satyanarayana and J. Olsen), Kluwer Academic Publishers, Netherlands, p. 354.

Kane, B.E. and Mullins, J.T. (1973). Thermophilic Fungi in a Municipal Compost System. *Mycologia*, 65: 1087-1100.

Khiyami, M., Masmali, I. and Abu-khuraiba, M. (2008). Composting a Mixture of Date Palm Wastes, Date Palm Pits, Shrimp and Crab Shell Wastes in Vessel System. *Saudi J. Biol. Sci.*, 15(2): 199-205.

Khokar, A. (1999). Production and Characterization of Lipase from *Scytalidium Thermophilum*. *Ph.D. Thesis*, G.B. Pant University of Agril. & Technol., Pantnagar, p. 116.

Klamer, M. and Baath, E. (1998). Microbial Community Dynamics during Composting of Straw Material Studied Using Phospholipid Fatty Acid Analysis. *FEMS Microbiol. Ecol.*, 27: 9-20.

Klamer, M., Lind, A.M., Gams, W., Balis, C., Lasaridi, L., Szmidt, R.A.K., Stentiford, E. and Lopez-Real, J. (2001). Fungal Succession during Composting of Miscanthus Straw and Pig Slurry. Proc. Int. Symp. on Composting of Organic Matter, Macedonia, Greece, 30 Aug-1 Sept., *Acta Hortculturae*. 549: 37-546.

Klamer, M., Sochting, U. and Szmidt, R.A.K. (1998). Fungi in a Controlled Compost System With Special Emphasis on the Thermophilic Fungi. *Proc. Int. Symp. On Composting and Use of Composted Materials for Horticulture*, Ayr, U.K., 5-11 April 1997, No. 469, pp. 405-412.

Kleyn, J.G. and Wetzler, T.F. (1981). The Microbiology of Spent Mushroom Compost and Its Dust. *Can. J. Microbiol.*, 27: 748-753.

Korn-Wendisch, F., Rainey, F., Kroppenstedt, R.M., Kempf, A., Majazza, A., Kutzner, H.J. and Stackebrandt, E. (1995). *Thermocrispum* gen. nov., a New Genus of the Order Actinomycetales and Description of *Thermocrispoum municipale* sp. nov. and *Thermocrisporum agreste* sp. nov. *Int. J. Syst. Bacteriol.*, 45: 67-77.

Kowalchuk, G.A., Naovmenko, Z.S., Derikx, P.J.L., Felske, A., Stephen, J.R. and Arkhipchenko, I.A. (1999). Molecular Analysis of Ammonia-oxidizing Bacteria of the Subdivision of the Class Proteobacteria in Compost and Composted Materials. *Appl. Environ. Microbiol.*, 65: 396-403.

Lee, D.H., Zo, Y.G. and Kim, S.J. (1996). Non-radioactive Method to Study Genetic Profiles of Natural Bacterial Communities by PCR-single Stranded Conformation Polymorphisms. *Appl. Environ. Microbiol.*, 62: 3112-3120.

Libmond, S., Savoie, J.M. and Elliott, T.J. (1995). Stimulation of Mushroom Composting by a Polysaccharidase Complex Induction of Cellulase Production in *Bacillus subtilis*. Proc. 14th Int. Cong. Sci Cult. Edible fungi, UK, pp. 195-202.

Lindt, W. (1886). Mitteilungen Iiber Einige Neve Pathogene Schimmelpilze. *Arch. Exp. Path. Pharmakol.*, 21: 264-298.

Liu, W.T., March, T.L., Cheng, H. and Forney, L.J. (1997). Characterization of Microbial Diversity by Determining Terminal Restriction Fragment Polymorphisms of Genes Encoding 16S rRNA. *Appl. Environ. Microbiol.*, 63: 4516-4522.

Lyons, G.A., McKay, G.J. and Sharma, S.H. (2000). Molecular Comparison of *Scytalidium Thermophilum* Isolates using RAPD and ITS Nucleotide Sequence Analysis. *Mycol. Res.*, 104: 1431-1438.

Lyons, G.A. and Sharma, H.S.S. (1998). Differentiation of *Scytalidium Thermophilum* Isolates by Thermogravimetric Analysis of Their Biomass. *Mycol. Res.*, 102: 843-849.

Mantel, E.F.K., Agarwala, R.K. and Seth, P.K. (1972). A Guide to Mushroom Cultivation Ministry of Agriculture, Farm Information Unit, Directorate of Extension, New Delhi, Farm Bull, No. 2.

Margesin, R., Cimadom, J., and Schinner, F. (2006). Biological Activity during Composting of Sewage Sludge at Low Temperatures. *Int. Biodeterior. Biodegrad.*, 57: 88-92.

Megnegneau, B., Debets, F. and Hoekstra, R.F. (1993). Genetic Variability and Relatedness in the Complex Group of Black *Aspergilli* Based on Random Amplification of Polymorphic DNA. *Curr. Gen.*, 23: 323-329.

Meyer, S.A. and Phaff, H.J. (1969). Deoxyribonucleic Acid Base Composition in Yeasts. *J. Bacteriol.*, 97: 52-56.

Miehei, H. (1905). Uber Die Selbsterhitzung des Heus. Arb. Deutsch. Landwritisch-Gesellsch., 111: 76-91.

Miehei, H. (1907). Die Selbsterhitzung des Heus. Fine Biologische Studie. Gustav Fischer, Jena. pp. 1-127.

Miller, F.C. (1994). Conventional Composting System. *In*: *Agaricus* Compost (ed. N.G. Nair), Australian Mushroom Growers Association, Windsor, Australia, pp. 1-18.

Moubasher, A.H., Aboel-Hafez, S.I.I., Aboelfattah, H.M. and Moharrah, A.M. (1982). Fungi of Wheat and Broad Bean Straw Compost. *Mycopathol.*, 84: 61-72.

Mouchacca, J., Allsopp, D., Colwell, R.R. and Hawksworth, D.L. (1995). Thermophilic Fungi in Desert Soils: A Neglected Extreme Environment. *In*: Microbial Diversity and Ecosystem Function. Proc. of IUBS-IUMS Workshop, U.K., 10-13 Aug. 1993, 265-288.

Muyzer, G., deWaal, E.C. and Uitterlinden, A.G. (1993). Profiling of Complex Microbial Populations by Denaturing Gradient gel Electrophoresis Analysis of Polymerase Chain Reaction-amplified Genes Coding for 16S rRNA. *Appl. Environ. Microbiol.*, 59: 695-700.

Namkoong, W., Hwang, E.Y., Park, J. S., and Choi, J.Y. (2002). Bioremediation of Dieselcontaminated Soil with Composting. *Environ. Pollut.*, 119: 23-31.

Opden Camp, H.J.M., Stumm, C.K., Straatsma, G., Derikx, PJ.L. and van Griensven, L.J.L.D. (1990). Hyphal and Mycelial Interactions Between *Agaricus bisporus* and *Scytalidium Thermophilum* on Agar Medium. *Microb. Ecol.*, 19: 303-309.

Peters, S., Koschinsky, S., Schwieger, F. and Tebbe, C.C. (2000). Succession of Microbial Communities during Hot Composting As Detected by PCR-Single Strand-Conformation Polymorphism-based Genetic Profiles of Small Subunit rRNA gene. *Appl. Environ. Microbiol.*, 66: 930-936.

Petersen, S.O., Henriksen, K., Blackburn, T.H. and King, G.M. (1991). A Comparison of Phospholipid and Chloroform Fumigation Analyses for Biomass in Soil: Potentials and Limitations. *FEMS Microbiol. Ecol.*, 85: 257-268.

Rajni. (1999). Molecular Ecology of *Scytalidium Thermophilum. Ph.D. Thesis*, G.B. Pant Univ. of Agril. and Technol., Pantnagar, India, p. 88.

Rajni, Rastogi, S., Johri, B.N. and Singh, R.P. (1998). Microbial Dynamics and Its Influence in Cultivation Cycle of *Agaricus bisporus. Mushroom Res.*, 7: 63-70.

Rawat, S. (1998). Production and Characterization of Amylases from *Scytalidium Thermophilum. M.Sc. Thesis*, G.B. Pant Univ. of Agril. and Technol. Pantnagar, India, p. 86.

Rawat, S. (2004). Microbial Diversity of Mushroom Compost and Xylanase of *Scytalidium Thermophilum. Ph.D. Thesis*, G.B. Pant Univ. of Agril. & Technology, Pantnagar, India, p. 199.

Rawat, S., Agarwal, P.K., Chaudhary, D.K. and Johri, B.N. (2005). Microbial Diversity and Community Dynamics of Compost Ecosystem. In: *Microbial Diversity: Current Perspectives and Applications* (eds. T. Satyanarayana and B.N. Johri), I.K. International Pvt. Ltd., New Delhi, pp. 181-206.

Rawat, S. and Johri, B.N. (2002). Ecological and Functional Diversity of Thermophilic Fungi. *In*: Frontiers of Fungal Diversity in India (Prof. Kamal Festchrift) (eds. G.P.Rao, C. Manoharachari, D.J. Bhat, R.C. Rajak, T.N.Lakhanpal). Int. Book Distributing Co. Lucknow, India, pp. 205-232.

Rawat, S. and Johri, B.N. (2004). Xylanases of Thermophilic Moulds and Their Application Potential. *In*: Handbook of Fungal Biotechnology (ed. D.K. Arora), Marcel Dekker, USA, Vol. 20: pp. 299-314.

Rodrigues, E.C., Pizzirani-Kleiner, A.A., Tanaka, Y. and Jorge, J.A. (1991). Cytogenetic and Biochemical Aspects of the Cellulolytic Fungus *Humicola* sp. *Mycol. Res.*, 95: 169-177.

Ross, R.C. and Harris, P.J. (1983). An Investigation into the Selective Nature of Mushroom Compost Preparation. *Scientia Horti.*, 20: 61-70.

Ryckeboer, J., Mergaert, J., Coosemans, J., Deprins, K. and Swings, J. (2003). Microbiological Aspects of Biowaste during Composting in a Monitored Compost. *J. Appl. Microbiol.*, 94: 127-137.

Salar, R.K. and Aneja, K.R. (2007). Significance of Thermophilic Fungi in Mushroom Compost Preparation: Effect on Growth and Yield of *Agaricus bisporus* (Lange) Sing. *J. Agril. Technol.*, 3(2): 241-253.

Satyanarayana, T. (1978). Thermophilic Microorganism and Their Role in Composting Process. *Ph.D. Thesis*. Sagar University, Sagar, p. 212.

Satyanarayana, T. and Grajek, W. (1999). Composting and Solid State Fermentation. *In*: Thermophilic Moulds in Biotechnology (eds. B.N. Johri, T. Satyanarayana and J. Olsen), Kluwer Academic Publishers, Netherlands, pp. 265-288.

Satyanarayana, T. and Johri, B.N. (1981). Volatile Sporostatic Factors of Thermophilic Fungal Strains of Paddy Straw Compost. *Curr. Sci.*, 50: 763-768.

Satyanarayana, T. and Johri, B.N. (1984). Ecology of Thermophilic Fungi. *In*: Prog. Microbial Ecol. (eds. Mukherji *et al.*). Print House Publications, Lucknow, India, 349-361.

Satyanarayana, T., Johri, B.N. and Klein, H. (1992). Biotechnological Potential of Thermophilic Fungi. In: *Handbook of Applied Mycology* (eds. D.K. Arora, R.P. Flander and K.G. Mukherjee), Marcel Dekker Inc., New York, pp. 729-761.

Savoie, J.M. and Libmond, S. (1994). Stimulation of Environmentally Controlled Mushroom Composting by Polysaccharides. *World J. Microbiol. Biotechnol.*, 10: 313-311.

Schwieger, F. and Tebbe, C.C. (1998). A New Approach to Utilize PCR-single Strand Conformation Polymorphisms for 16S rRNA gene-based Microbial Community Analysis. *Appl. Enviorn. Microbiol.*, 64: 4870-4876.

Sen, T.L., Abraham, T.K. and Chakrabarthy, S.L. (1980). Utilization of Cellulolytic Wastes by Thermophilic Fungi. *In*: Advances in Biotechnology (ed. M.M. Young). Pregman Press Publ. Proc. 6th Int. Ferm. Symp. 633-638.

Shandilya, T.R. (1982). Composting and Casing Research at Mushroom Research Centre, during Past Seven Years. *Ind. J. Mushroom.* 8: 5-13.

Sinden, J.W. and Hauser, E. (1950). The Short Method of Composting during Fermentation. *Mushroom Sci.*, 1: 52-59.

Sparling, G.P., Fermor, T.R. and Wood, D.A. (1982). Measurement of the Microbial Biomass in Composted Wheat Straw and the Possible Contribution of the Biomass to the Nutrition of *Agaricus* bisporus. *Soil. Biol. Biochem.*, 14: 609-611.

Stanek, M. (1969). Diewitkung der zelulose setzenden mikroorganismen auf das waehstun des champignons. *Mushroom Sci.*, 7: 161-172.

Straatsma, G., Gerrits, J.P.G., Augustijn, M.P.A.M., OpDenCamp, H.J.M., Vogels, G.D. and Van Griensven, L.J.L.D. (1989). Population Dynamics of *Scytalidium Thermophilum* in Mushroom Compost and Stimulatory Effects on Growth and Yield of *Agaricus bisporus*. *J. Gen. Microbiol.*, 135: 751-789.

Straatsma, G., Gerrits, J.P.G., Gerrits, T.M., Op Dencamp, H.J.M. and van Griensven, L.J.L.D. (1991). Growth Kinetics of *Agaricus Bisporus* Mycelium on Solid Substrate (Mushroom Compost). *J. Gen. Microbiol.*, 137: 1471-1477.

Straatsma, G., Olijnsma, T.W., Gerrits, J.P.G., Amsing, J.G.M., OpDen Camp, H.J.M. and Van Griensven, L.J.L.D. (1994b). Inoculation of *Scytalidium Thermophilum* in Button Mushroom Compost and Its Effect on yield. *Appl. Environ. Microbiol.*, 60: 3049-3054.

Straatsma, G. and Samson, R.A. (1993). Taxonomy of *Scytalidium Thermophilum,* an Important Thermophilic Fungus in Mushroom Compost. *Mycol.* Res., 97: 321-328.

Straatsma, G., Samson, R.A., Olijnsma, T.W., Opden Camp, H.J.M., Gerrits, J.P.G., Griensven, L.J.L.D. Van and van Griensven, L.J.L.D. (1994a). Ecology of Thermophilic Fungi in Mushroom Compost with Emphasis on *Scytalidium Thermophilum* and Growth Stimulation of *Agaricus Bisporus* Mycelium. *Appl. Environ. Microbiol.*, 60: 454-458.

Straatsma, G., Samson, R.A., Olijnsma, T.W., Gerrits, J.P.G., OpDen Camp, H.J.M. and van Griensven, L.J.L.D. (1995) . Bioconversion of Cereal Straw into Mushroom Compost. *Can. J. Bot.*, 73: 1019-1024.

Strom, P.F. (1985). Identification of Thermophilic Bacteria in Solid-waste Composting. *Appl. Environ. Microbiol.*, 50: 906-913.

Stutzenberger, F.J., Kaufmar, A.J. and Lossins, R.D. (1970). Cellulolytic Activity in Municipal Solid Waste Composting. *Can. J. Microbiol.*, 16: 553-560.

Subrahmanyam, A. (1980). A New Thermophilic Variety of *Humicola grisea* var. *indica*. *Curr. Sci.*, 49: 30-31.

Subrahmanyam, A., Mehrotra, B.S. and Thirumalacher, M.J. (1977). *Thermomucor*, a New Genus of Mucorales. *Geor. J. Sci.*, 35: 1-6.

Tewari, P. (2000). Thermophilic Microorganisms from Mushroom Compost and Their Polysaccharolytic Activities. *M.Sc. Thesis*, G.B.Pant Univ. of Agril. and Technol., Pantnagar, India, p. 99.

Thakur, I. S., Rana, B. K. and Johri, B. N. (1992). Multiplicity of Xylanase in *Humicola grisea* var. *thermoidea*. *In*: Xylan and Xylanases (eds. J.Visser, M.A. Beldman, Kusters-van Someren and A.G.J. Voragen), Elsevier, Amsterdam, pp. 511-514.

Tiquia, S.M., Wan, J.H.C. and Tam, N.F.Y. (2002). Microbial Population Dynamics and Enzyme Activities during Composting. *Compost Sci. Util.*, 10: 150-161.

Troussellier, M. and Legendre, P. (1981). A Functional Evenness Index. *Microb. Ecol.*, 7: 283-296.

Tuohy, M.G., Puls, J., Claeyssens, M., Vrsanska, M. and Coughlan, M.P. (1993). The Xylan Degrading Enzyme System of *Talaromyces Emersonii* Novel Enzymes with Activity Against beta –D- xylosides and Unsubstituted Xylans. *Biochem. J.*, 290: 515-523.

Vijay, B. (1996). Investigations on Compost Mycoflora and Crop Improvement in *Agaricus bisporus* (Lange). *Ph.D. Thesis*, H.P. Univ., Shimla.

Weigant, W.M. (1992). Growth Characteristics of Thermophilic Fungus *Scytalidium Thermophilum* in Relation to Production of Mushroom Compost. *Appl. Environ. Microbiol.*, 58: 1301-1307.

White, D.C. and Findlay, R.H. (1988). Biochemical Markers for Measurement of Predation Effects on the Biomass Community Structure, Nutritional Status and Metabolic Activity of Microbial Biofilms. *Hydrobiol.*, 159: 119-132.

Wildeman, A.G. and Nazar, R.N. (1981). Studies on the Secondary Structure of 5.8S rRNA from a Thermophile *Thermomyces lanuginosus*. *J. Biol. Chem.*, 256: 5675-5682.

Wood, D.A. and Matchman, S.E. (1980). Growth of *Agaricus Bisporus* in Composted Straw. Evidence for Microbial Interaction. Second International Symposium on Microbial Ecology, Warwick, p. 233.

Yu, H., Zeng, G., Huang, H., Xi, X., Wang, R., Huang, D., Huang, G. and Li, J. (2007). Microbial Community Succession and Lignocellulose Degradation during Agricultural Waste Composting. *Biodegrad.*, 18: 793-802.

5

Seasonal Variations and Prevalence of Some External Parasites Affecting Freshwater Fishes Reared at Upper Egypt

Mahmoud A. El-Seify, ***Egypt***
Mona S. Zaki, ***Egypt***
Abdel Razek Y. Desouky, ***Egypt***
Hossam H. Abbas, ***Egypt***
Osman K. Abdel Hady, ***Egypt***
Attia A. Abou Zaid, ***Egypt***

ABSTRACT

This study was carried out to detect prevalence and seasonal variation of external parasites affecting freshwater fishes. 330 Oreochromis niloticus and 140 Clarias gariepinus were collected from three different ecosystems at Kafrelsheikh province. Obtained results revealed that, the highest infection rate was recorded among O.niloticus followed by C. gariepinus. Also, seasonal dynamics among the examined O.niloticus were recorded.The isolated ectoparasites among examined fishes were Cichlidogyrus tilapiae, Cichlidogyrus aegypticus, Cichlidogyrus cirratus, Quadricanthus aegypticus, Macrogyrodactylus clarii, Trichodina centrostrigeata, Trichodina rectinucinata, Chillodinella hexastica, Ichthyophthirius multifillis, Henneuguya branchialis, Lamproglena monody, Ergasilus sarsi and Copepodit stage (2nd stage) of Lernea cyprinacea.

Key words: External parasites, monogenetic trematodes, external protozoa, crustaceans, *O.niloticus, C. gareipinus*.

Introduction

Fish is one of our most valuable sources of protein food. Worldwide, people obtain about 25 per cent of their animal protein from fish and shell fish.

By the increasing intensification of fish production and lack of health management measures have lead to many disease problems of bacterial, viral, fungal and parasitic origin. About 80 per cent of fish diseases are parasitic especially in warm water fish (Eissa, 2002). Ecto-parasites are the most dangerous group that causes severe mortalities (Shalaby and Ibrahim, 1988). In Egypt there are a long periods of optimum warm weather that enable external parasites for more production and cause bad effects on fish. The majority of the monogenitic trematodes of fishes are ectoparasites, Monogeneans (flatworms) are among the most host-specific of parasites in general and may be the most host-specific of all fish parasites. Monogenitic trematodes usually don't cause any problems in the natural environment unless the host is continually reinvested so that massive numbers of worms build up on the fish (Woo, 1995).

The most identified protozoa are belonging to ciliates. They can easily spread among most of the fish hosts. Uncontrollable or recurrent infection with ciliated protozoans is indicative of unhygienic husbandry problems (Al-Rasheid *et al.*, 2000).

Parasitic crustaceans are increasingly serious problem in cultured fish. Most Parasitic crustacean of freshwater fish can be seen by the naked eyes as they attach to the gills, body and fins of the host and it spent a large part of their life on fish, possessing an adhesive organs and mouth parts adapted for piercing and sucking fish blood. (El Moghazy, 2008)

Materials and Methods

Fish Samples

A total number of 470 (330 *Oreochromus niloticus* and 140 *Clarias gariepinus*) freshwater fish were collected alive from three different ecosystem in Kafr El-Shiekh governorate River Nile Branch (Bahr Nashart), Drainage canal (Damroo Drainage canal) and Fish farm supplied water from damroo Drainage canal by the aid of fisher man and then transported alive to the laboratory of parasitology department-Faculty of Vetrinary Medicine-Kafrelsheikh university where they examined immediately (Table 5.1).

Parasitological Examination

Parasitological examination was carried out for the detection and identification of the external parasites on the skin, gills and the accessory respiratory organs of the samples.

Table 5.1: Number of Fish Species Examined from Different Localities

Locality / Fish spp.	Examined Number			Total Fish spp.
	River Nile Branch	Drainage Canal	Fish Farm	
Oreochromus niloticus	117	100	113	330
Clarias gariepinus	80	60	–	140
Total	**197**	**160**	**113**	**470**

Collection and Preparation of the Detected Ecto-parasites

Monogenea: Monogenea were collected under binocular dissecting microscopic by means of small pipette in small Petri-dish and cleared several times with water to remove the attached mucous and debris.

The worms were then left in refrigerator at 4C till complete relaxation. Then, they were fixed in 5 per cent formalin for permanent preparation, worms were washed carefully in water to get red of formalin traces and stained with Semichon's acetocarmine stain for about 5-10 minutes till reaching staining, the specimens were passed through ascending grades of ethyl alcohol (30, 50, 70, 90% and absolute) for dehydration. Then, cleared in clove oil, xylene and mounted in canda balsam (Pritchard and kruse, 1982), while the unstained Monogeneas were mounted in glycerin jelly (Abdel-Hady, 1998).

Protozoa

Some of the positive slides were stained according to Klein's dry silver impregnation method in which the slides were air -dried, covered with 2 per cent aqueous solution of silver nitrate ($AgNO_3$) for 8 minutes, rinse thoroughly in distilled water and exposed to UV light for 20-30 minutes or to direct sun light for 1-2 hr. The slides were allowed to dry and mount with neutral Canada balsam. This method is indispensable technique for staining *Trichodina* (Ali, 1992).

Other positive slides were also air-dried, fixed with absolute methanol and stained with 10 per cent Giemsa stain for 20-30 minutes to detect the other protozoa. (Ali, 1992).

Crustacea

The detected crustacean parasites were carefully collected by a fine brush and special needle, and transferred into Petri-dish for cleaning by using preserved and cleared in lacto phenol then mounting with polyvenylalcohol (Raef *et al.*, 2000).

Results

As shown in (Table 5.2); from 330 examined *O. niloticus* taken from different three localities, the total infected number was 226 (68.5%), While the rates of infection in the River Nile branch, the drainage canal and the fish farm were 71.8 per cent (84/117), 69 per cent (69/100) and 64.6 per cent (73/113) respectively. In addition; the total infection rate among *Clarias gariepinus* was 58.6 per cent (82/140). While the rates of infection in the River Nile branch and the drainage canal was 53.7 per cent (43/80) and 65 per cent (39/60) respectively.

As described in (Table 5.3); in *O. nilotica* the percentage of infection by monogenetic trematodes was higher in drainage canal than that of River Nile branch and fish farm, in case of infection by protozoa; it was higher in River Nile branch than that of drainage canal and fish farm, while the percentage of infection by crustacea was higher in drainage canal than that of fish farm and River Nile branch.

In case of *Cl. Gariepinus*, the percentage of infection by monogenetic trematodes was higher in drainage canal than that of River Nile branch and the infection was not detected in fish farm branch, protozoal infection among *Cl. Gariepinus* was higher in River Nile than that of drainage canal and not detected in fish farm locality. Parasitic crustacean was not detected among *Cl. Gariepinus* in all localities

Concerning the seasonal dynamics in the examined *O. niloticus* (Table 5.4) revealed that the highest seasonal prevalence of ecto-parasites in examined *O. niloticus* was recorded in spring followed by summer then autumn and finally in winter. In The River Nile branch the highest prevalence of ecto-parasites was recorded in spring then winter followed by summer and autumn. But the highest prevalence of ecto-parasites in the drainage canal was recorded in summer followed by autumn then spring and winter, while in the fish farm the highest prevalence of ecto-parasites was recorded in spring then summer followed by winter finally in autumn.

Table 5.5 showed the peak of seasonal dynamic of Monogenea in total examined *O. niloticus* was during autumn followed by summer then winter and spring. while parasitic Protozoans recorded highest infection during spring followed by summer then winter and autumn. The highest seasonal prevalence of Crustaceans among total examined *O. niloticus* was recorded during summer then spring followed by autumn and finally in winter.

Table 5.2: Prevalence of Ecto-parasites in Examined Fish spp. in Different Localities

Locality / Fish spp.	River Nile Branch			Drainage Canal			Fish Farm			Total		
	No Ex.	No Inf.	% of Inf.	No Ex.	No Inf.	% of Inf.	No Ex.	No Inf.	% of Inf.	No Ex.	No Inf.	% of Inf.
O. niloticus	117	84	71.8	100	69	69	113	73	64.6	330	226	68.5
Clarias garipienus	80	43	53.7	60	39	65	–	–	–	140	82	58.6

Table 5.3: Prevalence of Different Ecto-parasites in Examined Fish Species in Different Localities

Locality / Parasites	River Nile Branch				Drainage Canal				Fish Farm				Total			
	O. Niloticus No = 117		*C. Gariepinus* No = 80		*O. Niloticus* No = 100		*C. Gariepinus* No = 60		*O. Niloticus* No = 113		*C. Gariepinus* No = 0		*O. Niloticus* No = 330		*C. Gariepinus* No = 140	
	No Inf.	%	No Inf.	%	No Inf.	%	No Inf.	%	No Inf.	%	No Inf.	%	No Inf.	%	No Inf.	%
Monogenea	27	23	23	28.7	41	41	36	60	43	38	–	–	111	33.6	59	42
Protozoa	76	65	29	36.3	48	48	12	20	53	46.9	–	–	177	53.6	41	29.3
Crustacean parasites	16	13.7	–	–	36	36	–	–	39	34.5	–	–	91	27.6	–	–

Table 5.4: Seasonal Prevalence of Ecto-parasites in Examined *O. niloticus* in Different Localities

Locality / Season	River Nile Branch			Drainage Canal			Fish Farm			Total		
	No. Ex.	No. Inf	%	No. Ex.	No. Inf.	%	No. Ex	No. Inf	%	No. Ex.	No. Inf	%
Autumn	25	16	64	25	19	76	23	14	60.9	73	49	67
Winter	25	17	68	30	17	56.6	37	23	62	92	57	62
Spring	31	27	87	20	13	65	26	19	73	77	59	76.9
Summer	36	24	66.6	25	20	80	27	17	63	88	61	69

Table 5.5: Seasonal Dynamics of Different Ectoparasites Among Examined *O.niloticus*

Parasites / Season	Monogenea		Protozoa		Crustacea	
	No. infected	%	No. infected	%	No. infected	%
Autumn N = 73	28	38.4	32	43.8	19	26
Winter N = 92	29	31.5	46	50	21	22.8
Spring N = 77	22	28.6	51	66	22	28.6
Summer N = 88	32	36.4	48	54.7	29	33

N= Number examined.

Discussion

The present investigation revealed that Monogenetic trematodes recorded an incidence of (33.6%) which is nearly similar to those obtained byAbd El-Maged (2009) among examined O. niloticus was infected on the other hand higher value (80.76) was recorded by Abd El-Gawad (2004) which may be due to different of sample collection and changes in water quality in different localities. In total examined Clarias gariepinus, our study revealed (42%) prevalence of Monogenetic trematodes which is considered higher than obtained by Ramadan (2000) 36.28 per cent. and lower than recorded by Abd El-Maged (2009) (51.7%) Parasitic protozoa recorded an incidence of (55.5%) among total examined O. niloticus. This result is found higher than that recorded by Abd El-Maged (2009) who recorded an infection rate of (6.3%).The prevalence of parasitic protozoa among total examined Clarias gariepinus reached (29%). This result was in contrary with Abd El-hady (1998) who did not detect parasitic protozoans among Clarias gariepinus in River Nile and other water branches. This result may be related to different localities of sample collection.

The prevalence of Parasitic crustaceans in this study was (27%) in total examined *O. niloticus*. This result is higher than obtained by Abd El-Khalek (1998) who recorded that the prevalence was (24.73%), while being lower than that recorded by El-Moghazy (2008) who mentioned that the prevalence was (80%) While parasitic crustaceans not recorded is among Clarias gariepinus, being coincided with Abd El-Hady (1998). This is may be due to differences in localities and water quality in these localities.

With regard to the effect of the seasonal variation on the prevalence of *Monogenetic trematodes* in the present study, the highest rate of infection was during autumn. This result agreed with Ramadan (2000) and Abd El-Gawad (2004) Mean while, this result was in contrary with Abd El-Maged (2009) who recorded the lowest infection rate was obtained during autumn.

Regarding the seasonal dynamics of external protozoa, the highest infection rate was in spring. This result was in agreement with El-Sayed (1993) stated that the seasonal incidence of protozoal infection was high in spring.

Concerning the seasonal dynamics of crustacean's infection the maximum rate of infection was during summer. This result agreed El-Moghazy (2008) mentioned that the highest incidence was recorded during summer. But this result did not agree with Hassan (1992) who detected the crustacean during winter.

These differences in the rates and seasonal dynamics of infection between the different localities may be attributed to the differences in environmental conditions, fish species, and the differences in the degree of water pollution as well as number of examined samples.

REFERENCES

Abd EL- Hady. O. K. (1998): Comparative Studies on Some Parasitic Infection of Fishes in Fresh and Polluted Water Sources. Ph.D. Thesis (parasitalogy), Fac. Vet. Med., Cairo University.

Abd El-Gawad, R.A. (2004): Studies on Ectoparasites of Freshwater Fish. M.V.Sc. Thesis. Fac. Vet. Med., Zagazig. University.

Abd El-Khalek, H.M. (1998): Studies on the Ectoparasites of Some Freshwater Fishes in Beni-Suef Governorate. M.V.Sc. Thesis. Fac. Vet. Med., Beni-Suef. University.

Abd El-Maged, R.R. (2009): Studies on Ecto-parasites of Freshwater Fishes in Dakahlia Governorate. Ph.D. Thesis, Fac. Vet. Med., Kafrelsheikh University.

Ali, M.A. (1992): Biological and ecological studies on protozoan parasites infecting cultured *Tilapia* in Serow fish farm. M. Sc. Thesis, Fac. Science, Cairo Univ., Egypt.

Al-Rasheid, K.A.; Slim, A.; Sakran, T.; Abdel Bakr, A.A.and Abdel Ginaffer, F.A. (2000): "Trichodinid Ectoparasites (Ciliophorea: Paritrichida) of Some River Nile Fish, Egypt". Parasitol. Int. Aug., 49(2): 131-137.

Eissa, I.A.M, (2002): Parasitic Fish Diseases in Egypt, 1st Edition, pp: 52-53. Dar El-Nahdda El-Arabia Publishing.

El-Moghazy, D.F. (2008): Studies on Some Parasitic Diseases Caused by Harmful Crastaceans in Fish. Ph.D.Thesis, Fac. Vet.Med. Suez Canal University.

El-Sayed, E. (1993): Some Studies on Protozoal Infection Among Cultured Fish in Sharkia. M.V.Sc. Thesis, Zagazig University.

Hassan; M. A. (1992): Studies on Some Parasitic Affections in Fresh Water Fishes in Beni Suef governorate. Ph.D. Thesis, Fac. Vet. Med., Beni-Suef. Cairo University.

Pritchard, M.H. and Kruse, G.O.W. (1982): The Collection and Preservation of Animal Parasites. University Nebraska, Lincolin and London, p. 141.

Raef, A.M.; El-Ashram, A.M. and El-Sayed, N.M. (2000): Crustacean Parasites of Some Cultured Freshwater Fish and Their Control in Sharkia. Egypt. Vet. J., 28(2): 180-191.

Ramadan, R. A. M. (2000): Morphological and Immunological Studies on Certain Ectoparasites of Some Freshwater Fishes. Ph.D. Thesis, Fac. Vet. Med., Suez Canal University.

Shalaby, S.I. And Ibrahim, M.M. (1988): The Relationship Between the Monogenetic Trematodes *Cichlidogyrus Tubicirrus* Magnus First Record in Egypt and Morphological Lesions of Gills Among Tilapia Nilotica. Egyption J. of Comparative Pat and Clin. Path., 1(9):116-126.

Woo, P.T.K. (1995): "Fish Diseases and Disorders". Vol. 1. Protozoon and Metazoan Infections Phylum Arthropoda.

6

Pesticides in Soil Environment and Their Microbial Degradation

Tarun Kumar Sharma, ***India***
K.K. Sharma, ***India***

ABSTRACT

Pesticides have emerged as indispensible tool in modern agriculture. Currently we are using a variety of pesticides belongs to diverse chemical class including organochlorine, carbamates, anthranalic diamide, organophosphates and neonecotinoids. The injudicious application of these pesticides creates havoc. Their residue is contaminating the environment. Need of the hour is to develop an ecofriendly approach to combat this situation. Bacterial diversity of soil is a promising way to explore and exploit the degradation potential of various bacterial species. In the present review we are throwing light on the bacterial pesticide interaction, their degradation potential evolution of degradation gene and enzymes responsible for degradation of myriad of pesticides.

Key words: Pesticides, Soil environment, microbial degradation.

Introduction

Pesticide is a substance or mixture of substances which destroys pests. The word 'Pesticide' is derived from the Latin word 'Pestis' which includes organisms which are present abundantly in an area and pose an economic or medical threat to the society and its interests. They are mainly used in agriculture, public health and consumer use.

Modern synthetic pesticides have tremendously increased the yield of crops. Pesticides usually work through biological or chemical means against pests. Pesticide based on the organism it kills/destroys, is mentioned as insecticide, herbicide, fungicide and bactericide. Here we are focusing upon insecticides and herbicides.

Despite the benefits they impart, these pesticides pose potential threats mainly health hazards to non-target organisms in and around the area of their application. Pesticides hamper the balance of the eco-system by destroying predator and parasites of the target organisms, leading to the reduction of beneficial species. They contaminate the ground water by leaching. Pesticides enter the food chain and lead to bio-magnification as their residues are found on fruits and vegetables. High levels of toxicity of many of these pesticides to humans and other mammals have led to their ban in many developed countries

Classification of Pesticides

Insecticides are divided on the basis of their composition into organic and inorganic. These insecticides are also categorized, based on the difference in their mode of action. A different mode of action is necessary to prevent resistance of insects against pesticides (Brown, 2005).

Inorganic Insecticides

Silica

This is derived from the diatoms (Bacillariophyceae), thus is also known as diatomaceous earth. Its larger surface area allows it to absorb larger amounts of pesticides.

Boric Acid

It is used by making baits.

Organic Insecticides

This is the largest group of Insecticides and includes below mentioned chemical classes.

Organophosphorous

Organophosphates are phosphoric acid esters or thiophosphoric acid esters. They work by affecting the nervous system of the insects and disrupt the neurotransmitter cholinesterase. After sending the impulse cholinesterase is unable to break acetylcholine and the neurotransmitter continuously signals the neuron to send an impulse. This leads to over stimulation of the nervous system and the insect dies. Organophosphates are one of the oldest and most poisonous group of pesticides. For eg: Malathion, parathion, chlorpyrifos, etc.

Carbamates

Carbamate pesticides are esters of N-methyl carbamic acid. Carbamates work with a mode of action similar to that of organophosphates. However, carbamate poisoning is reversible since the insecticide releases the bound enzyme cholinesterase. For eg: aldicarb, carbofuran, ethineocarb, fenobucarb, etc.

Organochlorines

Organochlorines are chlorinated hydrocarbons with at least one chlorine atom. They work by inhibiting the GABA receptor with affects the chloride channel. After the binding of the insecticide onto the GABA receptor, the chloride channel does not close which sends a repeated signal down the neuron. Thus, overstimulation of the nervous system results in the death of the insect. For eg: Endosulfan, aldrin, dialdrin, endrin, pentachlorophenol, etc.

Pyrethroids

Pyrethroids are synthetic analogs of pyrethrins (naturally occurring compounds derived from the chrysanthemum family) which are designed to be more stable in the environment. They also act by keeping the sodium channel open, which leads to a continuous nerve impulse and finally death. For eg: Cypermethrin, bifenthrin, allenthrin, etc.

Neonicotinoids

They work by acting as agonists of the acetylcholine receptor Cholinesterase is not inhibited in this case but the neonicotinoid continuously stimulates the neuron causing over stimulation of the nervous system which leads to the death of the insect. For eg: Imidacloprid, thimethoxam, etc.

Anthranillic diamides

This is a relatively new class of insecticides. They are derivatives of anthranillic acid. Anthranillic diamides work with a new mode of action. They do not affect the nervous system, instead they attack the ryanodine receptors of the skeletal muscles leading them into tetany and thus causing the death of the insect. For eg: Coragen.

Herbicides

Herbicides which are usually weed-killers are pesticides used to kill unwanted herbs. Herbicides can be classified on the basis of use, mode of action and activity.

(*a*) On the basis of use herbicides can be divided into the following groups:

1. *Pre-plant incorporated:* They are applied prior to sowing of the plant.
2. *Pre-emergent:* They are applied prior to the emergence of the plant.
3. *Post-emergent:* They are applied after the crop has grown.

(b) Based on different mode of actions herbicides can be divided into:

1. ACCase inhibitors: It inhibits Acetyl Co-enzyme A Cholinesterase (ACCase) and kills grasses.
2. *ALS inhibitors:* AcetoLactate Synthase (ALS) enzyme inhibitors kill both grasses and dicots: For eg: Sulphonurea, imidazoline, etc.
3. *Photosystem inhibitors:* They affect the passage of electrons from the photosystems during the photochemical step in photosynthesis. For eg: paraquat, nitrofen, atrazine, etc.

(*c*) Lastly on the basis of activity herbicides can be divided into:

1. *Contact:* They destroy the tissue of the plant in contact with the compound.
2. *Systemic:* They destroy the herb by translocation, foliar application, etc.

Fate of the Pesticides in Enviornment

Fate of these pesticides in the environment depends on physical, chemical and biological parameters. Biologically it is dependent on the microbial activity. Chemical structure of the pesticide decides the persistence of some of these pesticides while others readily degrade. A vast number of bacteria belonging to different families have been isolated from the pesticide contaminated soils which are known to degrade pesticides. Some of these bacteria belong to *Alcaligenes, Flavobacterium, Pseudomonas, Rhodococcus and Sphingomonas species*.These microorganism's breakdown the pesticide into simpler non-toxic compounds. The breakdown of pesticide into smaller compound by a microorganism is known as 'Biodegradation'. The biodegradation of pesticides is affected by pH, organic content, temperature and other microbial population of the soil.

National and International Status of Pesticide Consumption

Application of synthetic pesticides has started in 1948-49 with the use of DDT to fight malaria and BHC for locust swarm. In India pesticide industry was setup at Rishra near Kolkata in 1952. This was a small BHC technical plant. Soon after this Hindustan insecticides Ltd. set up two units to manufacture DDT. In 1969, Union Carbide set up a small plant (Union Carbide India Ltd (UCIL)) in Bhopal (Madhya Pradesh), to formulate pesticides. The

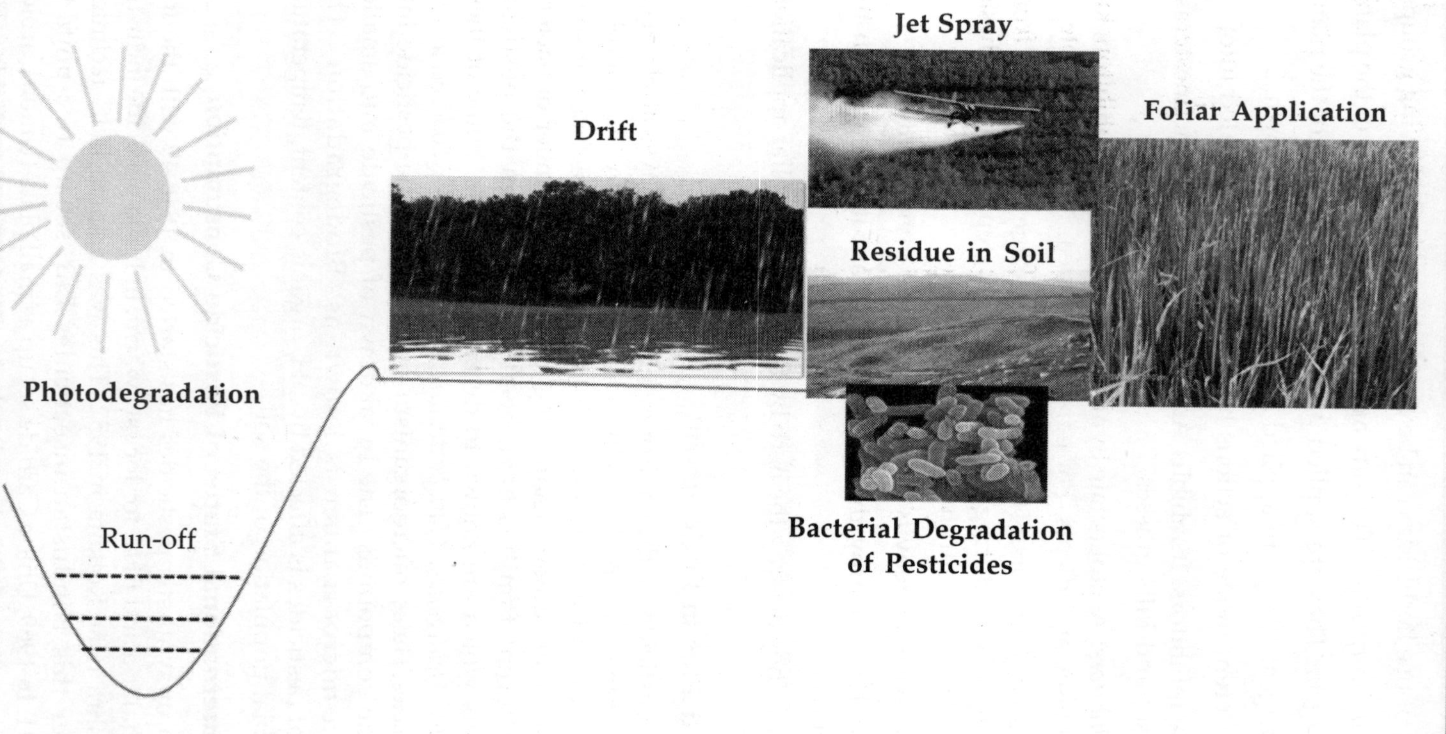

Fig. 6.1: **Fate of Pesticides in Environment**

Bhopal facility was thought an intrinsic part of India's green revolution aimed to boost the crop production. The industry produced various pesticides, mainly seven brand carbaryl insecticide and temikc brand aldicarb pesticide. The application of pesticide use differs significantly across the world. The worldwide consumption of pesticide is about two million tons per year, of which 24 per cent is consumed in the USA alone, 45 per cent in Europe and 25 per cent in the rest of the world. The usage of pesticides in India is only 0.5 kg ha″^{1}, while in Korea and Japan, it is 6.6 and 12.0 kg ha″1, respectively. Among the various pesticides used in India, organochlorine group of pesticide contribute about 40 per cent consumption of all the pesticides used (FAO Proceeding, 2005). The other major category is organophosphate pesticides. Monocrotophos, phorate, phosphamidon, methyl parathion and dimethoate are some of highly hazardous pesticides that are continually and indiscriminately used in India. A new category of pesticides namely neonecotinoids, having Imidacloprid as representative have been introduced in the market further Dupont also introduced new pesticide named coragen.

Interaction Between Microorganisms and Pesticides

Modern pesticides being used in agriculture sector are simple or complex organic compounds with poor water solubility therefore, they are available commercially in several forms which include emulsifiable concentrates, wettable powders, dusts, granules and capsules. Kruglov (1983) demonstrated and stated that the distribution of pesticides in the soil was governed by its application mode. He presents generalized schemes reflecting the formation of microflora in the pesticide treated soil distinguishing two main types of microbial distributions around the pesticide particles.

1. Broad spectrum pesticides (e.g. Endosulfan) - In this case, a sterile zone is present in periphery of pesticide particles, and bacterial flora start growing at some distance from them. The sterile zone diminishes with time, and microorganisms penetrate. This is attributed to the swift evolution of bacterial population in response to selection pressure imposed by a particular pesticide and to the decrease in pesticide concentration because of dispersion, sorption, photo degradation etc.

2. Narrow spectrum pesticides (e.g. the herbicide atrazine) - In this case no sterile zones are formed around the pesticide particles and the latter become delimited by myriad of bacterial species. As the bacterial mass accumulates, the transformation and degradation of these pesticides begins by different routes which depend on bacterial ability to produce different degradation enzymes. A variety of enzymes including monooxygenase, hydrolase, oxygenase, esterase, phosphotase, dehalogenase are involved in these degradation pathways (Kumar *et al.* 1996).

Kruglov (1987) proposed a model for the distribution of microorganisms and their action on pesticides in the soil which involved three forms of microbial distributions:

(a) Free cells in the soil solution

(b) Colonies, films and groups of microorganisms at the surface of soil particles and

(c) Microorganisms immobilized in the organo-mineral gels and structural elements of the soil.

Pesticides exist in five forms in the soil as:

(a) Particles, drops and films

(b) Dissolved forms

(c) Physically bound systems

(d) Chemically bound systems

(e) In the interlattice space of clay minerals

It is believed that microorganisms in any form of distribution are competent enough to use both forms of pesticides (soil solution and chemically bound forms) as carbon and energy source. Microorganisms restricted at the surface of soil particles utilize both pesticide preparations and their physically bound forms which are also utilized by immobilized microorganisms. The author suggests analogous mechanisms for the degradation of pesticides present in the soil solution and in a liquid microbial culture. The degradation of pesticide depends on the rate of it's desorption in the soil solution, the physio-chemical properties of the pesticide preparation, the mineral composition of the soil, and also on the humus content. The pesticides trapped in the interlattice space of clay minerals are practically unavailable to microorganisms (Galiulin et al. 2001).

There are some reports on the chemotactic movement based interaction of bacteria and xenobiotics. Renner (1997) showed role of positive chemotaxis in xenobiotic degradation (i.e. they move toward the higher concentration of the compound degraded). From the observations of Kruglov (1983), micellar forms of microorganisms (hyphae of fungi and actinomycetes) 'evade' particles of some pesticides (atrazine, basudin, and TMTD) suggesting negative chemotaxis to play a vital role in the interaction between these microorganisms and pesticides. According to the Boesten hypothesis (1993), the pesticide in the soil is not only sorbed in the solid phase or dissolved in the liquid phase but is also related to the organic matter, mainly humic substances (Vozbutskaya, 1968). It is alleged that the pesticide present in liquid phase is the biological available form of pesticide hence, the bacterial transformation of the pesticide are a function of its concentration in the liquid phase of the soil because only dissolved pesticide molecules can easily pass the biological membranes. The biological availability of the pesticide drastically decreases because of its sorption by the solid phase of the soil.

Evolution of Pesticide Degradation Genes

Unique ability of bacteria to multiply rapidly and their genetic plasticity allow them to evolve swiftly as a consequence of which they can degrade nearly all known organic materials. Xenobiotics are molecules of anthropogenic origin evidently absent from the pre existing environment. Since bacteria did not have any previous contact with these molecules they could not evolve enzymes to degrade these molecules but interestingly, a few years after the introduction of the xenobiotics into the soil environment, soil bacteria succeeded in development of novel degradative pathways resulting in destruction of the environmentally detrimental molecules (Seffernick and Wackett, 2001; Johnson and Spain, 2003). The evolution of these degaradative pathways occurs in Darwinian fashion allowing only those bacteria to survive which have the capability to surpass the selection pressure posed by xenobiotics. Agricultural soil contains approximately 10 per cent organic matter which is available in limited amount due to its slow degradation rate in lieu of the absence of potential degrading agents hampering bacterial growth and fitness. Thus availability of newer organic compounds of anthropogenic origin gives ample opportunity to soil bacterium to utilize these molecules as carbon source to increase their fitness by switching on the expression of previously silent genes induced by selection pressure via the evolutionary processes. The concept of the selfish gene is especially pertinent to degradation genes in bacteria since many of them are mobile; carried by plasmids or other transposable insertion elements (Top and Springael, 2003). In this regard, a gene with higher fitness is expected to proliferate in the environment in different bacterial hosts. These genes can "select" the most apposite host for a given environment and "as a reward" would increase the fitness of their host. Evolution of degradation genes induced by dichloropropionic acid (DCPA) can be studied in-vitro under selective pressure (Senior *et al.*, 1976). In other cases, biochemical, genetics and bioinformatics based approach are used in combination to elucidate the evolutionary pathways (Werlen *et al.*, 1996; Copley, 2000, Seffernick and Wackett, 2001; Johnson *et al.*, 2002). Such evidences include- bits and bobs of genetic material from lateral gene transfer, scattered organization of the genes encoding the enzymes, primitive or inefficient regulation of enzyme synthesis, and poorly adapted degradative enzymes attributed to high Km, low Kcat, and low substrate specificity. Studies of primitive pathways reveal that bacteria keep on evolving employing new mechanisms and also provide insights about the origin of catabolic steps (Johnson and Spain, 2003). Atrazine metabolism is the best example of evolution of pesticide degradation genes (Seffernick and Wackett, 2001). During the first 35 years of atrazine utilization, atrazine and its triazine degradation products were known to accumulate both in natural agricultural soil and laboratory media. Studies with pure and mixed microbial cultures demonstrated that the catabolism of atrazine occurs mainly through N-dealkylation reactions and there were no reports of microbial dechlorination of atrazine (Seffernick and Wackett, 2001). However, Mandelbaum *et al.* (1995) reported rapid microbial dechlorination of atrazine. Shortly thereafter bacteria that can dechlorinate atrazine were isolated (Mandelbaum *et al.*, 1995; Struthers *et al.*, 1998; Topp *et al.*, 2000a, b; Rousseaux *et al.*, 2001). The transformation of atrazine to cyanuric acid by these bacteria transpired via a novel route involving atrazine chlorohydrolase (AtzA), the dechlorinating enzyme which shared 98 per cent homology (a difference in only nine nucleotide) to the enzyme melamine deaminase (TriA) which catalyzes the removal of two of the three amino groups from melamine (Seffernick *et al.*, 2001). Melamine (2, 4, 6-triamino-1, 3, 5-triazine) was introduced in market 40 years before atrazine (Partington, 1961). Sequence comparison of triA and atzA suggested a lack of silent mutations and the authors suggested that atzA evolved from triA under the influence of strong selective pressure (Seffernick *et al.*, 2001).

Attempts were made to further improve the efficiency of the dechlorination associated with this gene by artificial evolution (1600 different mutation) which resulted in only slightly enhancement of activity (1.4 times faster), implying that atzA had optimal structure for catalyzing the dechlorination of atrazine and had already evolved to a great extent (Raillard *et al.*, 2001). Although mutations seemed to play an important role in the evolution of atzA, but gene transfer of all the six enzymes responsible for dechlorination of atrazine in a single plasmid was the crucial requirement (Martinez *et al.*, 2001).

Based on the GC content, different genes evolved in variety of bacterium (Martinez *et al.*, 2001). These genes (98–100% identity) were found in different bacteria belonging to different families and sharing different geographic regions (de Souza *et al.*, 1998; Rousseaux *et al.*, 2001), demonstrating the rapid dispersion of the newly evolved genes throughout the world.

Enzymes Involved in Degradation of Pesticides

Microbial possess a unique and highly controlled machinery that can metabolize a number of pesticides belongs to diverse chemical classes. Metabolism has proved to be very adaptable and diverse. This ability allowed many different bacterial species to develop survival strategies in presence of various pesticides which offer an additional advantage to be used in bioremediation of pesticide residue. On site bacterial remediation of pesticides provides an inexpensive and efficient solution for their final disposal or for treatment of agricultural soils, contaminated water bodies or polluted ecosystems. Moreover microbial degradation has advantages as large variety of compounds can be degraded completely under placid conditions in comparison to degradation using physico-chemical means. Most of the research on pesticide degradation are focused on microorganisms specifically on bacteria because they are easy to culture in simple media and grow faster than other microbes; besides, they are easy to manipulate at genetic level to improve their degradation potential. Emerging tool of genetics and molecular biology provide an ample opportunity to identify and characterize bacterial gene cluster which participate in the degradation process (Zhang *et al.* 2005). As a matter of fact in mother nature pesticide mineralization is accomplished by metabolic prowess of microbial communities rather than a single isolated bacterial species, suggesting in nature several co-metabolic pathways are involved in degradation of pesticides. Since pesticides used in agriculture sector posses a variety of structure, individual reactions of degradation–detoxification pathways are versatile and include oxidation, reduction, hydrolysis, esterification, dehalogenation and conjugation. These pesticides are degraded by different routes by exploiting the catalytic ability of enzymes including dehydrogenases (Bourquin, 1977; Singh & Singh, 2005), dioxygenases (Nadeau *et al.*, 1994; Van Eerd *et al.*, 2003), cytochrome p450 (Castro *et al.*, 1985; Jauregui *et al.*, 2003), ligninases (Pizzul *et al.*, 2009) and, in the case of organohalogenate compounds, dehalogenases (Franken *et al.*, 1991; Sharma *et al.*, 2006). Conjugation with glutathione is most common detoxification route, in plants and insects; further this mechanism has also been reported in bacteria (Vuilleumier, 2001; Wei *et al.*, 2001; Chaudhry *et al.*, 2002). Metabolism of these pesticides may involve three-steps. In very first step of metabolism, the parent compound is usually transformed through oxidation, reduction, or hydrolysis to generally produce a water-soluble and a less toxic product than the parent. The second step engrosses subsequent conjugation of a pesticide or pesticide metabolite to a sugar or amino acid, which further increases the water solubility and reduces toxicity. The third and final step involves conversion of step two metabolites into secondary conjugates, which are also non-toxic. All these degradation steps are enzyme (Table 6.1) dependent and involve several extra or intracellular enzymes (Scott *et al.* 2008).

Conclusion

Increasing population and decreasing agriculture land creating a grave situation. Further whatever crop we are growing is constantly being damaged by various pests. In order to protect our crop from various pests we have to

Table 6.1: Enzyme Dependent Degradation Steps

Sl. No.	Enzymes	Source Organisms	Co-factor Required	Targeted Pesticide(s)	Bioremediation Strategies Required
1.	Oxidoreductase	*Pseudomonas* sp LBr; *Agrobacterium* strain T10	Flavin (FAD)	Glyphosate	In planta
2.	Monooxygenase	*Mycobacterium* sp. *Arthrobacter* sp F	FAD and NADH	Endosulfan and Endosulphate	Not yet in use
3.	Cytochrome oxidoreductase (P450)	*Pseudomonas putida*	Fe^{2+} and NADH	Hexachloro-benzene and Pentachloro-benzene	Transgenic Sphingobium chlorophenolicum
4.	Dioxygenase	*Pseudomonas putida*	Fe^{2+} and NADH	Trifluralin	Not yet in use
5.	Phosphotriesterases	*Agrobacterium radiobacter; Pseudomonas diminuta; Flavobacterium*	Fe^{2+} and $Zn2^{+}$	Malathion, Parathion, Methyl parathion and Monocrotophos	Free-enzyme bioremediation
6.	Haloalkane dehalogenases	Sphingobium sp.; *Sphingomonassp* *Pseudomonas sp.* ADPNocardioides sp.	Fe^{2+} and $Zn2^{+}$	Hexachlorocyclohexan (β– and δ–isomers, Atrazine	Bioaugmentation of Sphingobium indicum

rely on various pesticides. Injudicious application of these hazardous chemical are affecting the human and animal population significantly. Ironically in developing world no attention is giving on the detoxification technologies of these hazardous chemical even though India is blessed by huge biodiversity. There is an urgent need to develop a simple, cheap and efficient method to overcome this problem of non-target toxicity. Microbes present in soil gave offered an opportunity to tackle this situation. Further the advancement in genetic engineering and molecular biology can improve the degradation potential of a particular bacterial strain. We need to focus upon it followed by technology transfer from lab to field to benefit the mankind.

REFERENCES

Brown, A.E. (2005). Mode of Action of Insecticides and Related Pest Control Chemicals for Production Agriculture, Ornamentals, and Turf. Pesticide Information Leaflet No. 43, (Revised May, 2006).

Zhang, R., Zhongli C., Jiandong J., Jian He, Xiangyang Gu and Shunpeng Li (2005). Diversity of Organophosphorus Pesticide-degrading Bacteria in a Polluted Soil and Conservation of Their Organophosphorus Hydrolase Genes. *Canadian Journal of Microbiology*, 51:(4) 337-343.

Galiulin, R.V., Bashkin V.N., Galiulina R.A. and Birch P. (2001). The Theoretical Basis of Microbiological Transformation and Degradation of Pesticides in Soil. *Land Contamination & Reclamation*, 9 (4): 367-376.

Kruglov, Yu.V. (1987) Microbial Transformation of Pesticides in the Soil. *In Bull. Sci. Res. Inst. Agric. Microbiology*, 46: 3-5. Leningrad (in Russian).

Kruglov, Yu.V. (1983) The Distribution of Microorganisms in the Soil After the Pesticide Treatment. *In Proc. Sci. Res. Inst. Agric. Microbiology*, 52: 32-36. Leningrad (in Russian).

Kumar, S., Muketji K.G. and La1 R. (1996). Molecular Aspects of Pesticide Degradation by Microorganisms. *Critical Reviews in Microbiology*. 22(1): 1-26.

Boesten, J.J.T.I. (1993) Bioavailability of Organic Chemicals in Soil Related to Their Concentration in the Liquid Phase: A Review. *Sci. Total Environ. Suppl.*, Part 1, 397-407.

Renner, R. (1997). On the Trial of Bioremediating Microbes. *Environ. Sci. Technol.*, 31(4): 188A-189A.

Vozbutskaya, A.E. (1968) Soil Chemistry. Vysshaya Shkola Publishing House, Moscow (in Russian).

Singh, J. & Singh D. K. (2005). Dehydrogenase and Phosphomonoesterase Activities in Groundnut (Arachis Hypogaea L.) Field After Diazinon, Imidacloprid and Lindane Treatments. *Chemosphere*. 60 (1): 32-42.

Sharma, P., Raina V., Kumari R., Malhotra S., Dogra C., Kumari H., Kohler H.P.E., Buser H.R., Holliger C. & La R. (2006). Haloalkane Dehalogenase LinB is Responsible for b- and d-Hexachlorocyclohexane Transformation in Sphingobium Indicum B90A. *Appl. Environ. Microbiol*. 72 (9), 5720-5727.

Vuilleumier, S. 2001. Bacterial Glutathione S-transferases and the Detoxification of Xenobiotics: Dehalogenation Through Glutathione Conjugation and Beyond. Pages

240-252 in J. C. Hall, R. E. Hoagland, and R. M. Zablotowicz, eds. Pesticide Biotransformation in Plants and Microorganisms: Similarities and Divergences. ACS Symposium Series 777. Washington, DC: American Chemical Society. ISBN 0-8412-3704-2.

Pizzul, L., Castillo M. P. & Stenström J. (2009). Degradation of Glyphosate and Other Pesticides by Ligninolytic Enzymes. *Biodegradation*. 20: 751-759.

de Souza, M, Newcombe D, Alvey S, Crowley D, Hay H, Sadowsky M, Wackett L (1998). Molecular Basis of a Bacterial Consortium: Interspecies Catabolism of Atrazine. *Appl. Environ. Microbiol*. 64: 178-184.

Franken, S.M., Rozeboom H.J., Kalk K.H. & Dijkstra D.W. (1991). Crystal Structure of Haloalkane Dehalogenase: An Enzyme to Detoxify Halogenated Alkanes, *EMBO J*. 10: 1297-1302.

Chaudhry, Q., Schröder P., Werck-Reichhart D., Grajek W. & Marecik R. (2002). Prospects and Limitations of Phytoremediation for the Removal of Persistent Pesticides in the Environment. *Environmental Science and Pollution Research*. 9(1): 4-17.

Castro, C.E., Wade R.S. & Balser N.O. (1985). Biodehalogenation: Reactions of Cytochrome P-450 with Polyhalomethanes. *Biochemistry*. 24: 204-210.

Bourquin, A. W. (1977). Degradation of Malathion by Salt-marsh Microorganisms. *Appl. Environ. Microbiol*. 33: 356-362.

Copley, SD (2000). Evolution of a Metabolic Pathway for Degradation of a Toxic Xenobiotic: The Atchwork Approach. *Trends Biochem*. Sci. 25: 261-265.

Top, EM, Springael D (2003). The Role of Mobile Genetic Elements in Bacterial Adaptation to Xenobiotic Organic Compounds. *Curr. Opin. Biotechnol*. 14: 262-269.

Nadeau, L.J., Fu-Min M., Breen A. & Sayler, G. S. (1994) Aerobic Degradation of (l,l, 1 richloro-2,2-bis (4-chlorophenyl) ethane) DDT by Alcaligenes eutrophus A5. Appl. *Environ. Microbiol*. 60: 51-55.

Van-Eerd, L.L., Hoagland R.E., Zablotowicz R. M., & Hall J. C. (2003). Pesticide Metabolism in Plants and Microorganisms. *Weed Science*. 51(4): 472-495.

Wei, S.H., Clark A.G. & Syvanen M. (2001). Identification and Cloning of a Key Insecticide-metabolizing Glutathione S-transferase (MdGST-6A) from a Hyper Insecticide-resistant Strain of the Housefly Musca Domestica. *Insect Biochemistry and Molecular Biology*. 31(12): 1145-153.

Jauregui, J. Valderrama B. Albores A. & Vazquez-Duhalt R. (2003). Microsomal Transformation of Organophosphorus Pesticides by White Rot Fungi. *Biodegradation*. 14: 397-406.

Scott, C., Pandey G., Hartley C.J., Jackson C.J., Cheesman M.J., Taylor M.C. Pandey R., Khurana J.L., Teese M., Coppin C.W., Weir K.M., Jain R.K., Lal R., Russell R.J., and Oakeshott J.G. (2008). The Enzymatic Basis for Pesticide Bioremediation. *Indian J. Microbiol*. 48: 65-79.

Mandelbaum, RT, DL. Allan and LP Wackett (1995) Isolation and Characterization of a Pseudomonas sp. that Mineralizes the S-triazine herbicide Atrazine. *Appl Environ Microbiol* 61: 1451-1457.

Seffernick, JL, de Souza ML, Sadowsky MJ and Wackett LP (2001) Melamine Deaminase and Atrazine Chlorohydrolase: 98 per cent Identical but Functionally Different. *J Bacteriol* 183: 2405-2410.

Raillard, S, Krebber A, Chen Y, Ness JE, Bermudez E, Trin-idad R, Fullem R, Davis C, Welch M, Seffernick J, Wackett LP, Stemmer WPC and Minshull J (2001) Novel Enzyme Activities and Functional Plasticity Revealed by Recombining Highly Homologous Enzymes. *Chem Biol* 8: 891-898.

Werlen, C, Kohler HPE, van der Meer JR (1996). The Broad Substrate Chlorobenzene Dioxygenase and Cis-chlorobenzene Dihydrodiol Dehydrogenase of Pseudomonas sp. P51 are Linked Evolutionarily to the Enzymes for Benzene and Toluene Degradation. *J. Biol. Chem.* 271: 4009-4016.

Senior, E., Bull, A.T. & Slater, J.H. (1976). Enzyme Evolution in a Microbial Community Growing on the Herbicide Dalapon. *Nature, London* 263: 476-479.

Martinez, B., Tomkins, J., Wackett, L.P., Wing, R. and Sadowsky, M.J. (2001) Complete Nucleotide Sequence and Organization of the Atrazine Catabolic Plasmid pADP-1 from Pseudomonas sp. Strain ADP. *Journal of Bacteriology*, 183: 5684-5697.

Mandelbaum, R.T., Allan, D.L. and Wackett, L.P. (1995) Isolation and Characterization of a Pseudomonas sp. that Mineralizes the s-triazine Herbicide Atrazine. *Applied and Environmental Microbiology*, 61: 1451-1457.

Struthers, J.K., Jayachandran, K. and Moorman, T.B. (1998) Biodegradation of Atrazine by Agrobacterium Radiobacter J14a and Use of this Strain in Bioremediation of Contaminated Soil. *Applied and Environmental Microbiology*, 64: 3368-3375.

Rousseaux, S., Hartmann, A. and Soulas G. (2001) Isolation and Characterisation of New Gram-negative and Gram-positive Atrazine Degrading Bacteria from Different French Soils. *FEMS Microbiology Ecology*, 36: 211-222.

Topp, E, Mulbry WM, Zhu H, Nour SM & Cuppels D (2000a) Characterization of s-triazine Herbicide Metabolism by a Nocardioides sp. Isolated from Agriculture soils. *Appl Environ Microb* 66: 3134-3141.

Topp, E, Zhu H, Nour SM, Houot S, Lewis M & Cuppels D (2000b) Characterization of an Atrazine-degrading Pseudaminobacter sp. Isolated from Canadian and French Agricultural Soils. *Appl Environ Microb* 66: 2773-2782.

Seffernick, JL &Wackett LP (2001) Rapid Evolution of Bacterial Catabolic Enzymes: A Case Study with Atrazine Chlorohydrolase. *Biochemistry*, 40: 12747-12753.

Johnson, G.R. and Spain, J.C. (2003). Evolution of Catabolic Pathways for Synthetic Compounds: Bacterial Pathways for Degradation of 2, 4-dinitrotoluene and Nitrobenzene. *Appl. Microbiol. Biotechnol.* 62: 110-123.

Johnson, G.R., Jain, R.K. and Spain, J.C. (2002). Origins of the 2, 4-dinitrotoluene Pathway. *J. Bacteriol.* 184: 4219-4232.

Partington, J.R. (1961). A History of Chemistry. Macmillan, London,England.

FAO, (2005). Increasing the Contribution of Small-scale Fisheries to Poverty Alleviation and Food Security. FAO Technical Guidelines for Responsible Fisheries No. 10. Rome. p. 79.

Web resources

http://www.epa.gov/pesticides/about/types.htm

http://www.epa.gov/pesticides/reregistration/REDs/aldicarb_red.pdf

http://npic.orst.edu/factsheets/diazinontech.pdf - Accessed 12/14/09

7

Dose Phenol Toxicity Affected Endocrine Status in African Catfish (*Clarias gariepinus*)

Mona S. Zaki, ***Egypt***
Nabila El-Batrawy, ***Egypt***
Nadia M. Taha, ***Egypt***

ABSTRACT

The influence of dietary phenol on immunity, and hormonal profile was studied in catfish. The results revealed that, treatment of Catfish (Clarias gariepinus) with 12mg/l phenol for 3 months decreased IgM, Insulin, Thyroxin, however there was elevation in cortisol hormone level. Phenol may induce an immunosuppressive effect on humoral immune response of African Catfish which was suggested by reduction of immunoglobulin.

Key words: Phenol; Endocrine; African Catfish (*Clarias gariepinus*)

Introduction

Phenol and phenolic compounds are examples of toxic chemicals acts as endocrine disruptors; which mimic or antagonize hormones and disrupt the endocrine system. It is also has great potential for compromising the immune system and increases susceptibility of fish to secondary infections (Writer *et al.*, 2010).

Phenols are discharged into water from the effluents of a variety of industries such as coal refineries, phenol manufacturing, pharmaceuticals, industries of resin, paint, dyeing, textile, leather, petrochemical, and pulp mill. Natural processes such as the decomposition of plant matter also contribute to phenol accumulations in the aquatic environment (BuBuikema *et al.*, 1979 and Ali *et al.*, 2011). Phenols are of growing concern due to their high persistent and toxicity in the aquatic environment in addition to the difficulty in detecting them given their lack of taste and odor (Tilak *et al.*, 2007).Unfortunately, there is a lack of information regarding phenol pollution and its effect in the Egyptian aquatic environment.

The record level of phenol in Egyptian waste water was 0.05 ppm (Nazih *et al.*, 2008). *C. gariepinus* was extensively used as fish model by many scientists to monitor microbial, pathological or environmental studies (Ibrahem *et al.*, 2011). Unfortunately, there is a lack of information about the toxicity and pathological consequences in *C. gariepinus* exposed to phenol (Ibrahem, 2011)

Material and Methods

One hundred and twenty African Catfish (*Clarias gariepinus*) were used in the present study. Their live body weight was averaged 37.5 grams. The fish were healthy and clinically free from external and internal parasites. They were maintained in tanks containing well aerated water at atmospheric temperature for two weeks before the experiments began. Fish were randomly distributed into two groups; each of 60 fish. Group one not given any treatment and considered a control group, the second group treated with sublethal dose of phenol at a dose level of 12mg/L (Verma, *et al.*, 1980).

Analytical grade phenol, C6H5OH (purity 99%; E. Merck, made in Germany) was used as test chemical. Test fish were not fed from 2 d prior to the end of the experiments. The test medium was replaced in both control and experimental tanks.

The experimental fish were fed on ration composed of 16.3 per cent crude protein, 2.5 per cent crude fat and 14 per cent crude fiber, the digestible energy was 26 per cent cal/kg. The diet contained feed additives which included minerals, vitamins and amino acids. Body weight measured every month for four month.

Samples

Serum samples were collected 4 times at one month interval and Sera were frozen at -20°C for later analysis. Serum cortisol, IgM, T4, and insulin were determined using kits.

IgM Determination

The serum IgM was measured according to Fuda *et al.* (1991).

Preparation of Antisera

Antisera for catfish were prepared by immunizing rabbits with catfish antigen as described by Hara (1976).

Catfish IgM antibody

The procedure for labeling antibody fragment with enzyme was performed according to the method of Bagee *et al*. (1993).

EIISA Assay Procedure

Assays were carried out in 96-well polystyrene ELISA microtiter plates (Titertex, Horsham, PA). The micortiter plates were coated with rabbit antitilapia IgM which was fractionated by DE-52 according to the method described by Bagee *et al*. (1993).

Incubation of Samples and Standards

After washing as described above 100 µL of sample and standard were placed into the appropriate wells in the microtiter plates and incubated at room temperature.

Incubation with peroxidase labeled antibody. After washings as described above, each well received 150µ1 of peroxidase labeled antibody 1: 1600 in PBS-BSA, followed by incubation for 12 hrs at room temperature.

Enzymatic Colour Reaction

The plates were washed as described above and O-phenylenediamine (3mg/ml O.1M citric acid-phosphate buffer (pH 5.0) containing 0.02% H_20_2) were added to each well for enzymatic color reaction. The reaction was stopped after 30min at room temperature by adding 100ul of 4N HCL. The results were recorded at absorbance of 492nm.

Double antibody sandwich Elisa according to the method of Matsubara *et al*. (1985) was used for determination of IgM.

Cortisol was estimated using radio immunoassay technique according to the method of Wedemyer (1970) and Pickering and Potinger (1983).

Serum thyroxin was estimated using radioimmunoassay (RIA) using coat (A) count provide by diagnostic product corporation Los Angelos U.S.A. (Defetoff, 1979).

Insulin was determined by RIA according to the method described by Sundly (1991).

Statistical Analysis

The difference between the groups were calculated according to Snedecor and Cochran (1967) by t-test.

Results

Table 7.1showed the influence of phenol on IgM. Highly significant decrease of IgM levels was detected in treated group with phenol.

Table 7.1: Effect of Phenol Toxicity (12mg/l) on IgM Level of Catfish (*Clarias gariepinus*)

Groups/Duration (Months)	1 Months	2 Months	3 Month
Control	1.84± 0.72	1.80± 0.45	1.23± 0.40**
Phenol (12mg/l)	1.20± 0.14	1.14± 0.19**	0.98**± 0.84

**P<0.01 M Month Number of catfish each group 60

Table 7.2 (*See on next page*) showed the serum hormonal changes in infected fish treated with phenol. The results revealed decrease level of insulin, and thyroxin while a highly significant elevation of cortisol level was observed.

Discussion

IgM level was determined to find out information about catfish immune system, which was previously investigated in different species by many authors as Matsubara *et al.* (1985) and Fuda *et al.* (1991).

In this work the purified IgM revealed a single preciption in this work reacted against specific polyvalent antiserum to catfish IgM a similar result was obtained by Bagee *et al.* (1993). They found that chum salmon (IgM) was detected by specific anti (IgM) antibodies.

While the lower limit was 5 mg/ml reported, by Fuda (1991). There is a significant decrease in IgM level in fish treated with phenol in comparison with control group. Anderson *et al.* (1982) found a relation between cortisol and IgM as when cortisol increased IgM decreased.

The significant increase of cortisol level in intoxicated group with phenol could be attributed to stress factors and the intoxication has examined response of fish to stress factors e.g. crowding, continuous handling infection. Wedemyer (1970); Strange (1978); Barton *et al.* (1980) and John *et al.* (1994), reported that the elevation of cortisol in phenol treated fish may be attributed to intoxication, and continuous handling of fish. These observations emphasize the extreme care needed during design and analysis of experiments, involving the (HPI) axis of test fish due to extremely sensitive HPI axis. Similar results were reported by Pickering and Pottinger (1983).

Serum thyroxin (T4) concentrations in the serum of Cat fish species decreased in the intoxicated group. It has been shown that intoxication, and chronic stress in a marked long lasting depression of serum T_4 levels in catfish

Table 7.2: Effect of Phenol Toxicity (12mg/l) on Some Hormonal Profile in Catfish (*Clarias gariepinus*)

	Insulin µg/dl			Thyroxin			Cortisol µg/dl		
	1M	2M	3M	1M	2M	3M	1M	2M	3M
Control	10.1± 0.40	10.2± 1.2	10.00± 1.50	0.0780± 0.065	0. 750± 0.059	0.740± 0.054	0.764± 0.1286	0.752± 0.113	0.740±0.103
Phenol (12mg/l)	10.00*± 0.16	15.00± 0.24	18.40± 4.8	0.0654± 0.072	0.0554*± 0.081	0.0500*±0.044	0.870± 0.65	0.945* ± 0.70	0.982**± 0.84

* P<0.05

** P<0.01 M Month

(Osborn *et al.*, 1978 and Milne and Leatherland, 1980). The response of thyroid gland of tested catfish needs further investigation with particular attention to possible relationship between the HPI axis and pituitary thyroid axis. Mooreoud *et al.* (1977); Osborn *et al.* (1978) and Milne and Leatherland (1980) using histological approach concluded that cortisol reduced thyroidal activity in sock eye salmon. The significant decrease of insulin values may be attributed to phenol which may somehow reduce the metabolic activities in the phenol treated catfishes. The decrease in body weight was observed, while detectable agrees with Ostrowski (1984), Hilton *et al.* (1987) and Sundly *et al.* (1991) as they observed a detectable decrease in body weight of duck infected with phenol.

The perfuse skin mucous secretion was prominent in phenol intoxicated catfish. This can be explained by the fact that skin in among the first to be in close contact with the dissolved pollutants. Hence, reactions in the skin cells are spontaneous as a protection mechanism through increasing level of mucous secretion over the body surface, forming a barrier between the body and the toxic medium, minimizing its irritation effect, thus, scavenge or even eliminates toxicants through the epidermal mucous (Chebbi and David, 2010).

Nervous manifestation; skin expressed perfuse mucous, black patches with skin erosion and ulceration in the later stages. All observation were correlated to the time and dose exposure ((Ibrahem, 2011).

In conclusions phenol reduces of the hormonal immune response as detected by decrease of IgM level and cortisol elevation. Suppress IgM, Thyroxin *(T4)* hormone and insulin levels.

REFERENCES

Ali, S. M., Sabac, S. Z., Fayez, M, Monib, M. and Hegazi, N. A. (2011): The Influence of Agro-industrial Effluents on River Nile pollution. J. Adv Res.; 2: 850-895.

Anderson, D.P.; Roberson, B.S. and Dixon, O. W (1982): Immunosuppression Induced by Corticosteroid or an Alkylating Agent in Rainbow Trout. Dev, Comp. Immunol. Suppl., 2: 197-204.

Bagee, M.; Fuda, HI; .Mara, H.; Kawamura, H. and Yamauchi (1993): Changes in Serum Immunoglobulin M (IgM) Concentrations during Early Development of Chum Salmon as Determined by Sensitive Elisa Technique, Comp. Biochem. Physiology, 106A: 69-74

Barton, B.A.; Peter, R.E. and Paulence C.R. (1980): Plasma Cortisol Level of Fingerling Rainbow Trout at Rest and Subjected to Handling Continent Transport and Stocking Fish . Aqua Sci., 37: 805-811.

BuBuikema Jr. Al, McGinniss M. J. and Carirns Jr J. (1979): Phenolics in Aquatic Ecosystems: A Selected Review of Recent Literature. Mar. Environ. Res.; 2: 8181.

Chebbi, SG, and David M. (2010): Respiratory Responses and Behavioural Anomalies of the Carp *Cyprinus Carpio* Under Quinalphos Intoxication in Sublethal Doses. Sci Asia, 36: 12-7.

Defetoff, S. (1979): Thyroid Function Tests Endocrinology. Degvoated Philadelphia Crume and Spratton. , 1: 387-428.

Fuda, H.; Sayano, K; Yamaji, F. and Haraj (1991): Serum Immunoglobulin M (IgM) during Early Development of Masu Salmon on Corhyrchus Masu. Comp. Biochem. Physiol., 99A: 637-643.

Hara, A. (1976): Iron Binding Activity of Female Specific Serum Proteins Rainbow Trout Salm'o and Chum Salman Oncorchynchus. Journal of Biochem. Physiology, 427: 549-557.

Hilton, J. W.; Plisetskeya, E.M. and Leatheland, J.F. (1987): Dose oral 3, 5, 3 Triiododthyroxine Affect Dietary Glucose Utilization and Plasma Insulin Levels in Rainbow Trout. Fish Physiol. Biochem., 4: 113-120.

Ibrahem MD.(2011): Experimental Exposure of African Catfish *Clarias Gariepinus* (Burchell, 1822) to Phenol: Clinical Evalution, Tissue Alterations and Residue Assessment. Journal of Advanced Research (in press).

Ibrahem, M.D., Shaheed, I.B. , Abo El Yazeed H, Korani H. (2011): Assessment of the Susceptibility of Polyculture Reared African Catfish and Nile tilapia to Edwardsiella. J. Am Sci., 7: 779-786.

John, F.; Carragler, and Christine, M.R (1994): Primary and Secondary Stress Responses in Golden Pereh Macquoria Ambigua (J. comp. Biochem. Physiol., 107A (1): 40-56.

Matsubara, A.; Mihara, S. and Kusuda, R. (1985): Quantitation of Yellow Tail Immunoglobulin by Enzyme-linked Immunosorbent Assay (Flisa) Bull. Japan Sac, Sci. Fish, 51: 921-925.

Milne R.S. and Leatherland J. F. (1980): Changes in Plasma Thyroid Hormones Following Administration of Exogenous Pituitary Hormones and Steroids Hormones to Rainbow Trout, Comp. Biochem. Physiol., 66A: 679-686.

Mooreoud, M.M, Mazeaud F & Donaldson E.M (1977): Primary and Secondary Effects of Stress Fish some New Data with a General Review Trans Am Fish Soc., 106: 201-212.

Nazih, M. Adel Haliam W, Halim H. A. S, and Abo Elaa S. (2008): Pollution Control and Waste Minimization of Chemical Products Industry: A Case Study of Polymers Production Industry. In: Twelfth International Water Technology Conference (IWTC12), Alexandria, Egypt, pp. 415-436.

Osborn, R.H.; Sinpson, T.H. and Yaungson, A.F. (1978): Seasonol and Diurnal Rhythms of Thyroidal Status in the Rainbow Traut J. Fish Biol., 12: 531-540.

Ostrowski, M. (1984): Biochemical and Physiological Responses of Growing Chickens and Ducklings of Dietary Aflatoxins. Comp. Biochem. Physio., 79:1, 193-204.

Pickering, A.D. and Pottinger, P. (1983): Seasonal and Diet Changes in Plasma Cortisol Levels of the Brown Trout, Salmo Trutta L. Gen. Corn. Endocrinol., 49; 232-239.

Snedecor, G.W. and Cochran, W.G. (1967): Statistical Methods Iawa State University Press, Ames USA. pp 327-329.

Strange, R.J. (1978): Changes in Plasma Cortisol Concentrations of Juvemile Salmonids during Stress. Ph.D Thesis Oregan State University U.S.A.

Sundly, A.; Fliassen, K A. Blom, A.K. and Asyard, T. (1991): Plasma Insulin, Glucogen like Peptide and Glucose Levels in Response to Feeding, Starvation, Life Long Restricted Fed Starvation in Salmonids, Fish Journal of Physiol. & Biochem., 9 (3): 253-259.

Tilak, K.S., Veeaiah K, and Butchiram M. S. (2007): Effect of Phenol on Haematological Components of Indian Major Carps *Catla catla, Labeo rohita* and *Cirrhinus mrigala*. J. Environ Biol,. 28: 177-179.

Verma, SR. Rani, S., Tyagi AK., Dalela, RC. (1980): Evaluation of Acute Toxicity of Phenol and its Chloro-and Nitro-derivatives to Certain Teleosts. Water Air Soil Poll., 14: 95-202

Wedemyer, G.A (1970):The Role of Stress in the Disease Resistance of Fishes spec. Publs Am. Fish Soc., 5: 30-35.

Writer, J. H. Barber, L. B.; Brown G. K., Taylor H. E. Kiesling, R. L., Ferrey, M. L. *et al.* (2010): Anthropogenic Tracers, Endocrine Disruption in Minnesota Lakes. Sci. Total Environ., 409: 100-111.

8

RNA Interference
An Advanced Technique in Agriculture Biotechnology

Anubhuti Sharma, *India*
Gajra Garg, *India*
Ruchi tyagi, *India*
Jaswant Roy, *India*
Renu Bisht, *India*

ABSTRACT

Ribonucleic acid interference (RNAi) technology has now been identified as a breakthrough technology for applications in target validation and therapeutics. It's an important tool for development of therapies based on short interfering RNA (siRNA). Nowadays, RNAi technology is using for those diseases where aberrant protein production is a problem. Long molecules (about 21-25 nucleotide long) of double stranded RNA (dsRNA) triggers the process. An enzyme complex called DICER then recognizes dsRNA, and cuts it into roughly 22- nucleotide long fragments. These fragments termed as siRNAs or "small interfering RNAs". Antisense strand binds to the RNA-induced silencing complex (RISC) and target the complementary mRNA resulting gene silencing. Thus these siRNAs are suitable for gene target validation and this emerging technique gaining popularity in several organisms including humans.

Keywords: RNA interference, RISC, Agriculture biotechnology.

Introduction

The gene expression process is of fundamental importance for all living organisms. Basically, most of the genes reside in the chromosomes located on the nucleus and express themselves by protein synthesis in the cytoplasm. The process of central dogma described that the genetic information is transcribed from DNA to RNA and translated from RNA into protein. In this process, RNA is believed to play a role of messenger between DNA and protein. RNA can act as a catalyst, i.e. it able to catalyze its own replication and the synthesis of other RNA molecules (the ribozyme concept) and play an active role in gene expression mechanisms. Most of the small RNA molecules work in conjunction with proteins in ribonucleoprotein (RNP) complexes. There are non-coding RNA molecules that affect transcription (e.g. human7SK snRNA bound to elongation factors), translation (e.g. SRP RNA in the signal recognition particle), replication (e.g. telomerase RNA) and chromosome structure (e.g. XIST RNA causing X chromosome inactivation). Others regulate RNA processing (e.g. M1 RNA in RNase P, snRNAs and snoRNAs) and RNA editing (guide RNAs). These various RNP particles are now being extensively investigated to understand their specific roles in the cell.

Prior to study about the mechanism of RNA interference, it is necessary to discuss the phenomenon of gene silencing in living organisms. A cloned gene incorporated into the genome (a transgene) could not only induce or stimulate gene activity but could also inhibit the expression of homologous sequences, a phenomenon called homology-dependent gene silencing. The inhibition of gene activity could take place at the transcriptional level (transcriptional gene silencing, TGS), or at the posttranscriptional level (posttranscriptional gene silencing, PTGS). Although it was evident that RNA played a key role in gene silencing, the phenomenon was remained mysterious until the discovery of RNA interference provided a most unexpected explanation with many profound consequences.

Brief History of RNAi

Research in RNAi is a fast-developing field and a lot of knowledge has accumulated since its discovery in 1998. Andrew Fire and Craig Mello published their break-through study on the mechanism of RNA interference in *Nature* in 1998. They shared a Nobel Prize in Physiology and Medicine for their work on RNA interference in nematode worm *Caenorhabditis elegans*. Earlier, it was discovered that antisense RNA (Izant and Weintraub, 1984) and Sense RNA (Guo and Kemphues, 1995) could silence genes, but the results were not consistent. The information gave by Izant and Guo that sense and antisense RNA could silence genes, Mello disagreed this fact and established that annealed sense/antisense RNA, but neither antisense nor sense RNA alone, caused interference. He reported that the mechanism could not just be a pairing of antisense RNA to mRNA, and coined the term RNA interference for the unknown mechanism (Rocheleau *et al*, 1997). Fire and Mello published their work in *Nature* in which they tested the phenotypic effect of RNA injected into the worm *Caenorhabditis elegans*. Injected double-stranded RNA, but not single-stranded RNA, induced the twitching phenotype in the progeny.

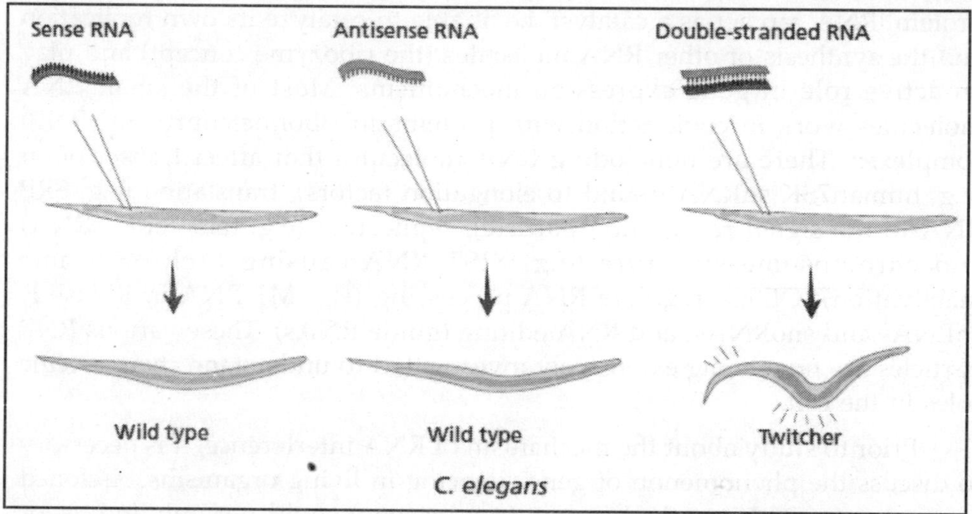

Fig. 8.1: **Phenotypic Effect in Gonad of *C. elegans* (http://nobelprize.org)**

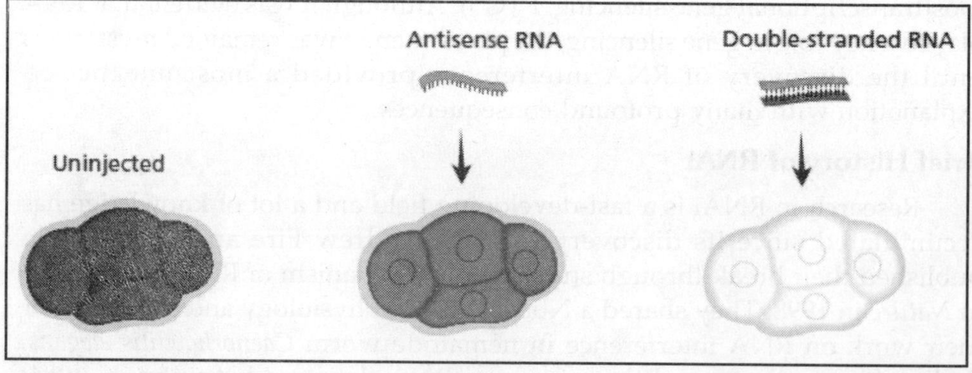

Fig. 8.2: **Effect on m-RNA Content in Embryos of *C. elegans* After Injected with Single Strand and Double Strand RNA. The Extent of Brown Colour Reflects the Amount of mRNA Present. (http://nobelprize.org**

Fire and Mello described following six conclusions from their study:

1. Silencing was triggered efficiently by injected dsRNA, but weakly or not at all by sense or antisense single stranded RNAs.
2. Silencing was specific for an mRNA homologous to the dsRNA, other mRNAs were unaffected.
3. The dsRNA had to correspond to the mature mRNA sequence; neither intron nor promoter sequences triggered a response.
4. The targeted mRNA disappeared suggesting that it was degraded. Fifth, only a few dsRNA molecules per cell were sufficient to accomplish full silencing.
5. Only a few dsRNA molecules per cell were sufficient to accomplish full silencing.
6. The dsRNA effect could spread between tissues and even to the progeny, suggesting a transmission of the effect between cells.

Avery good evidence was came out from the studies of. Fire i.e. mRNA is the target for dsRNA (recognition via complementary strands), and that the targeted mRNA is degraded prior to translation, i.e. dsRNA exerts its effect at the posttranscriptional level (Montgomery *et al*, 1998). The presence of RNAi had been documented in many other organisms, including fruit flies, trypanosomes, plants, planaria, hydra and zebrafish (Tuschl *et al*, 1999). Some experiments has done by researchers on mammalian cultured cells, initially they found no specific RNAi response due to predominant nonspecific physiological reaction of these cells to long dsRNA. Later on, when cells were exposed to short, 21 nucleotides long, dsRNA, an efficient targeted silencing was obtained in these cells (Elbashir *et al*, 2001). Similarly, when the same experiment was performed with budding Yeast (*S. cerevisiae*), it was proven to be a remarkable exception. After the research done by K. Suk *et al*, 2011, the team thus came to the conclusion that the human RNAi system may be reconstituted in *Saccharomyces cerevisiae* by simply introducing the human RNAi genes Ago2, Dicer and TRBP into the cells – making yeast an even better model organism than it is already.

Mechanism of RNAi

RNA interference (RNAi) is a specific and efficient natural mechanism for controlling gene expression. RNAi is a process in which a dsRNA precursor can trigger transcriptional or post transcriptional repression of a homologous gene. PTGS (Post Transcriptional Gene Silencing) in plants is correlated to the presence of a population of small RNAs (about 25 nucleotides long), and that this RNA contains both sense and antisense RNA sequences (Hamilton and Baulcombe, 1999). Subsequently, Fire and Mello established that long dsRNA is cleaved to small RNA (about 25 nucleotides long). There are two types of naturally-occurring small RNAs that can act as gene silencers: short, interfering RNA (siRNA) and microRNA (miRNA). Each of these arises from different triggers of the RNAi pathway. SiRNAs derive from long dsRNA duplexes. These duplexes are often produced during the course of viral reproduction within cells (foreign dsRNA), or by hybridization of overlapping transcripts from repetitive sequences in the genome, such as transposons or latent viruses (foreign DNA). These SiRNAs guide target recognition or cleave mRNA. In brief we can summarize few steps of RNAi mechanism as follows:

- The long dsRNAs are cleaved into 21–22-nt siRNAs by the enzyme Dicer (Bernstein *et al*, 2001).
- The antisense strand is loaded into the RISC complex.
- It links the complex to the mRNA strand by base-pairing.
- The RISC complex cuts the mRNA strand.
- The mRNA is subsequently degraded.

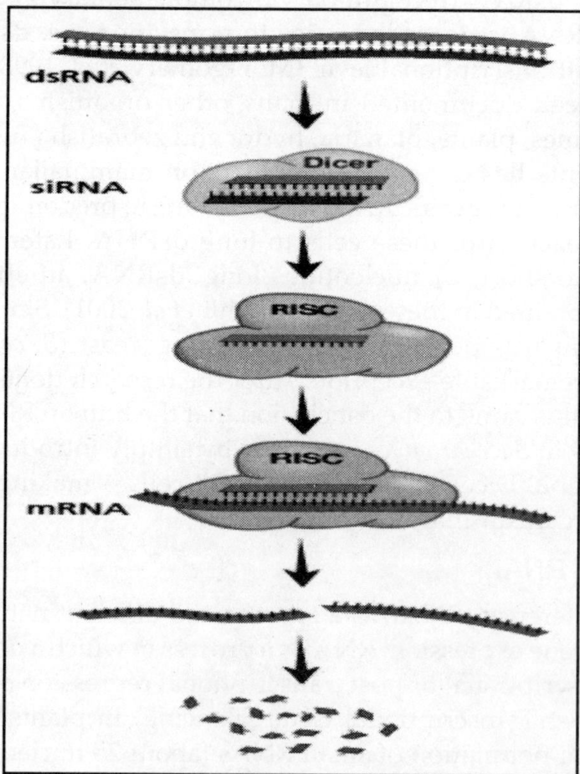

Fig. 8.3: **Overview of Double-stranded RNA (dsRNA) Mediated Gene Silencing in the cell. (http://nobelprize.org)**

Now, it is required to describe the role of specific proteins and protein complexes involved in RNAi and have to be focus on molecular details of the particular step in the process.

Dicer is a large protein (220 KD) containing a dsRNA binding domain (dsRBD), two catalytic RNAse III domains (Green colour domains in fig. 8.4), and a helicase domain (Blue colour domain in fig.4), as well as a piwi-argonaute- zwille (PAZ) interaction domain (yellow colour domain in fig.4) (Bernstein et al., 2003). This protein can unwind and cleave long dsRNA duplexes into small 21-bp duplexes with 5′ phosphates and dinucleotide 3′ overhangs.

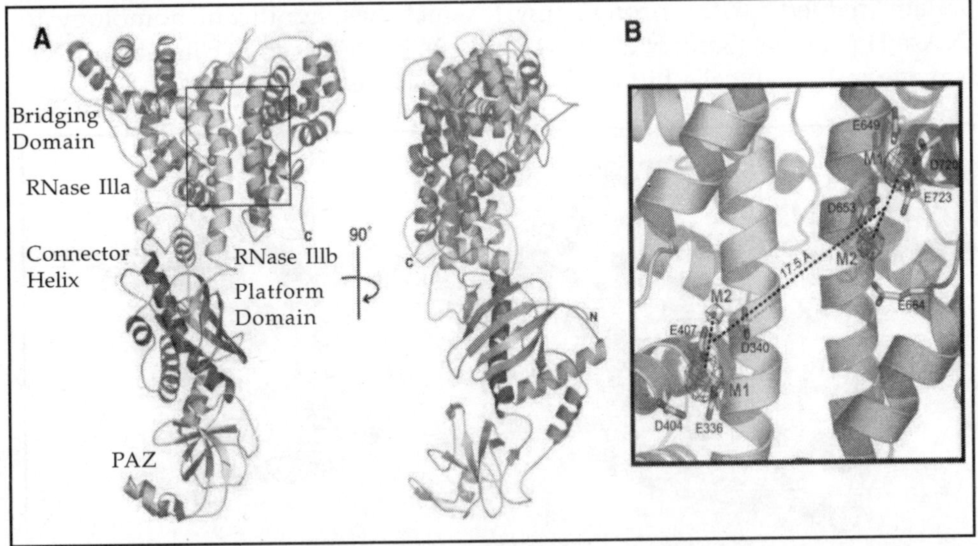

Fig. 8.4: **The Crystal Structure of Dicer Protein Isolated from *Giardia intestinalis* (MacRae *et al*, 2006)**

Some organisms, such as mammals and *C. elegans*, have only one copy of this gene. Others have several paralogs that are each responsible for processing RNA from different sources. For example, *Drosophila melanogaster* has two Dicer paralogs DCR-1 and DCR-2. Long dsRNA processing is managed by DCR-2 in association with the dsRBD-containing protein R2D2, while miRNA processing is assigned to DCR-1 (Lee et al., 2004). Another species difference with regard to Dicer activity is ATP-dependence. While human Dicer does not use ATP, Drosophila DCR-2 activity requires ATP hydrolysis (Nyka¨ nen et al., 2001; Zhang et al., 2002). Hairpin precursors are first processed into shorter premiRNAs (70 nt long) within the nucleus by the enzyme Drosha, a ribonuclease III similar to Dicer (Lee et al., 2003b). These pre-miRNAs are then exported to the cytosol, where they are converted into mature 21–23-nt-long miRNAs by Dicer before they go on to inhibit translation of complementary mRNAs (Bernstein *et al*, 2001). miRNA mediated silencing plays a particularly important role in developmental processes.

As it is clear in fig. 8.4 (1 & 3) that both of the posttranscriptional effects of RNAi, translational repression and mRNA degradation begin with the assembly of siRNAs or miRNAs into ribonucleoprotein (RNP) complexes called RISC (RNA induced silencing complex) or miRNPs, respectively (Hammond et al., 2000; Mourelatos et al., 2002). These RNP complexes consist of the unwound RNA duplex tightly bound to a member of the Argonaute (Ago) family of proteins. Ago proteins contain two conserved domains, a PAZ domain which binds small RNAs (Ma et al., 2004) as well as a PIWI domain (named for the protein piwi), which has significant homology to RNAse H proteins (Song et al., 2004) and has been shown to catalyze mRNA cleavage in human cells Liu et al., 2004; Meister et al., 2004).

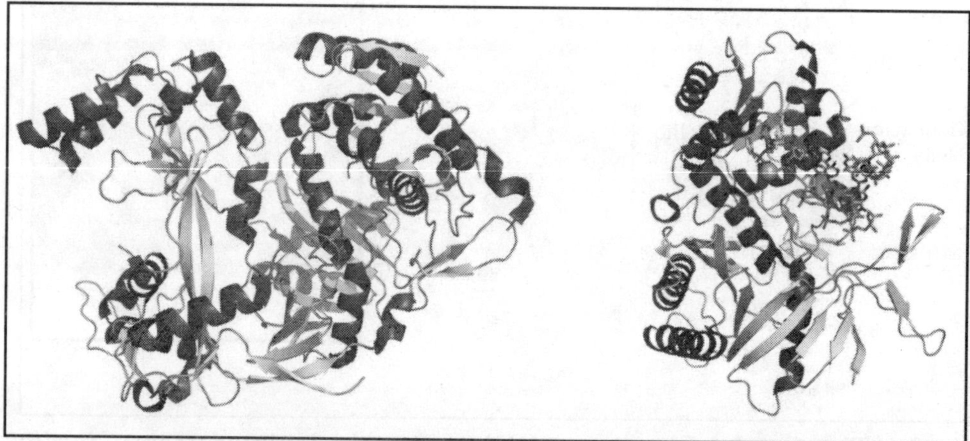

Fig. 8.5: **Argonaute Protein Isolated from the Archaea Species *Pyrococcus furiosus* (http://en.wikipedia.org/wiki/Argonaute)**

Once bound to this complex, the single-stranded siRNA serves as a template for sequence-specific degradation of homologous mRNAs (Martinez et al., 2002). While miRNAs in plants function exactly as siRNAs, in animals they are thought to have insufficient homology to target mRNAs to catalyze cleavage (Bartel, 2004).

According to Ketting *et al*, 1999 and Tabara *et al*, 1999 when components of the RNAi machinery are mutated in *C. elegans*, transposons are activated and the mobile elements cause disturbances in the function of the genome. Close to 50 per cent of our genome consists of viral and transposon elements that have invaded the genome at the time of evolution. As it is also clear in fig. 8.4 (1 & 2) that in transposon-containing regions of the genome both DNA strands are transcribed, dsRNA is formed, and the RNAi process eliminates these undesirable products. As short dsRNAs can also operate directly on chromatin and suppress transcription. This could keep transposon in inactive mode.

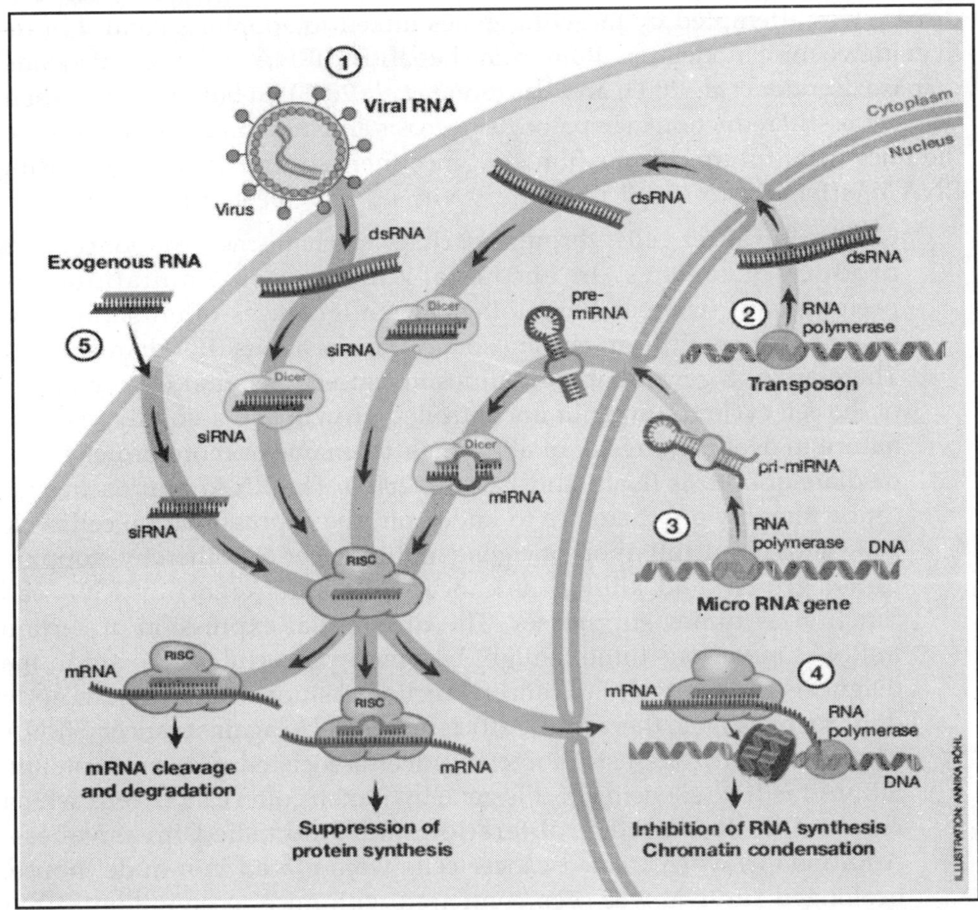

Fig. 8.6: **Cellular Process in RNAi Machinery (http://nobelprize.org)**

Applications of RNAi

RNA as Therapeutic Agent

RNAi is a biological mechanism controlling normal gene expression. The silencing functions occur at the levels of transcription, post-transcription and translation. Gene expression also increased due to RNAi as it directly effects translation (Crom *et al.*, 2008). RNAi is also regarded as a natural defense mechanism against mobile endogenous transposons and invasion by exogenous viruses. With this defense mechanism, organisms maintain genetic integrity and prevent infection (Tuschl, 2001). The most important role of RNAi against diseases is a selective depletion of one or a few specific proteins. RNAi may proved good as it provide new therapeutics for treating viral infections, neurodegenerative diseases, macular degeneration, cancer and other diseases (Dallas and Vlassov, 2006). For the first time, the liver disease was attempted by targeting genes linked to apoptosis control in the liver in two mice models of autoimmune hepatitis. SiRNA was directed against caspase (Zender *et al.*, 2003) and Fas (Song *et al.*, 2003). In both the cases there was successful reduction in hepatocyte necrosis and inflammation, and protect the mice from future chronic fibrosis. Since then, several experiments using RNA interference to target respiratory viruses have been attempted.

1. *Cancer:* In cancer cells, through various mechanisms proto-oncogenes produce oncogenes. In epithelial tumors, point mutations are predominant whereas hematological malignancies often show gene fusions that result from chromosomal translocations (Borkhardt, 2002). There are two general abnormalities in cancer cells, first dysregulation of the cell cycle resulting in uncontrolled growth and secondly resistant nature to death as a result of abnormalities in one or more proteins that mediate apoptosis (Nam and Parang, 2003). The RNAi approaches for cancer therapy are therefore to knock out the expression of a cell cycle gene and/or an anti-apoptotic gene in the cancer cells thereby stopping tumor growth and killing the cancer cells. Interference of RNA can function as tumor suppressor. The differential expression of certain miRNAs in various tumors might become a powerful tool to aid in the diagnosis and treatment of cancer. Preclinical studies have been recently done to investigate therapeutic efficiency of RNAi against cancer. SiRNA was used *in vivo* against colorectal cancer-associated gene beta-catenin. SiRNA mediate silencing of this gene in human colon cancer cells which resulted in decreased proliferation and diminished invasiveness. Additionally, when treated cancer cells were placed in a nude mouse, prolonged survival was seen compared with mice receiving untreated cancer cells (Verma, 2003). Similarly, silencing the oncogene H-ras led to inhibition of *in vivo* tumour growth of human ovarian cancer in a SCID mouse model (Liu *et al.*, 2007). The oncogenic cells expressing siRNAs against oncogenic K-ras V12 lost their ability to grow independent of anchorage when plated in semisolid media, and they lost their ability to form tumors in nude mice when transplanted.

Clinical trials with RNAi therapies are in progress (Table 8.1). First application is siRNA for age-related macular degeneration (AMD). AMD is caused by the abnormal growth of blood vessels behind the retina. The treatment strategy is inhibition of the vascular endothelial growth factor pathway by siRNA. These RNAi therapies are designed to be administered directly to the sites of disease in the eye (Takeshita and Ochiya, 2006). Studies in mouse models suggest that the anti-angiogenesis effect is not caused by RNAi, but instead induced in a non-specific manner by RNAs that vary in sequence.

Table 8.1: RNAi Based Therapies (Liu *et al.*, 2007)

Indication	Company	RNA Platform (Target)	Clinical Stage
Wet AMD	Acuity	Modified siRNA (VEGFR)	Phase I
	Sirna	Modified siRNA (VEGF)	Phase I/II
	Alnylam	siRNA	Phase I
Infectious Disease	Alnylam	siRNA for RSV (viral gene)	Phase I

2. *Infectious diseases:* Diseases caused by viruses and bacteria continue to be major causes of death worldwide. There is an increasing concern because of the emergence of resistant strains and the potential use of infectious pathogens. The HIV and other prominent infectious diseases include Influenza, Hepatitis and West Nile virus. The ability of RNAi to inhibit the replication or cellular uptake of viruses and other infectious agents has been demonstrated in cell culture studies and holds promise for the treatment of human patients. Transfection of human cells with siRNAs directed against different genes in the poliovirus genome resulted in resistance of the cells to infection with poliovirus.

   (a) *HIV:* HIV (Human immunodeficiency virus) was the first infectious agent targeted by RNAi, because its lifecycle and pattern of gene expression is well understood. Synthetic siRNAs and expressed shRNAs have been used to target several early and late HIV-encoded RNAs in cell lines and in primary haematopoietic cells including the TAR element (Jacque *et al.*, 2002), tat (Coburn and Cullen, 2002; Surabhi and Gaynor, 2002), rev (Lee *et al.*, 2002; Coburn and Cullen, 2002), gag (Novina et al., 2002; Park, 2002), env (Park, 2002), vif (Jacque *et al.*, 2002), nef (Jacque *et al.*, 2002) and reverse transcriptase (Surabhi and Gaynor, 2002). An approach to relying solely upon RNAi as an anti- HIV approach is mixing a single shRNA with other antiviral genes to provide a potent combinatorial approach. This has been successfully accomplished by co-expressing an anti-tat/rev shRNA, a nucleolar localizing TAR decoy and an anti-CCR5 ribozyme in a single vector backbone (Li *et al.*, 2005). An example of how HIV-1 can be targeted by this approach is shown in Fig. 8.7.

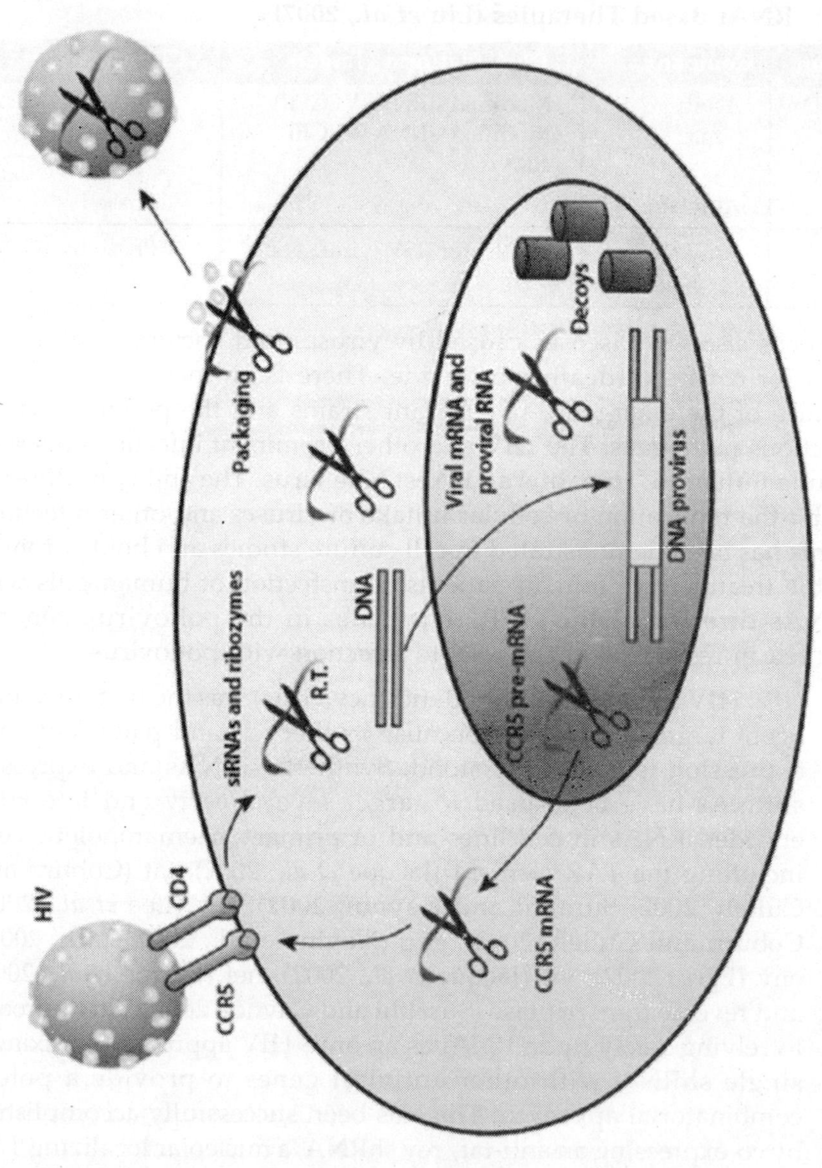

Fig. 8.7: **Proposed Multiplexing RNA Interference (RNAi) with Ribozymes and Decoys for the Treatment of Human Immunodeficiency virus (HIV) infection (Reddy *et al*, 2007)**

HIV-1 binds to the CD4 receptor and CCR5 co-receptor, which triggers entry and uncoating. The proviral RNA is reverse transcribed into DNA, which integrates randomly in the host chromosomes. Different stages of the HIV-1 replicative cycle can be attacked using RNAi and combinations of other RNA-based inhibitors. The scissors represent either small interfering RNAs (siRNAs) or ribozymes, and the decoy for binding viral Tat or Rev is depicted as a barrel in the nucleus. The virus may be exposed to RNAi or ribozymes at the preintegration step blocking proviral DNA formation and integration. Postintegration, siRNAs targeting all classes of HIV transcripts can be used. The CCR5 co-receptor RNA is targeted by either a siRNA or a ribozyme (Reddy *et al.*, 2007).

(b) *HBV (Hepatitis-B virus) as an RNAi target:* Although a vaccine is available for hepatitis A and B virus, treatment options for chronically infected patients are limited and particularly ineffective in case of hepatitis C virus (HCV) infection. A promising new opportunity currently being explored is to harness the power of RNA interference for development of an antiviral therapy. HBV is an excellent candidate for therapeutic RNAi, as its compact genome with lack of redundancy results in very limited sequence flexibility and prevents the virus from evading RNAi by mutation. Thus, ideally, a single siRNA can potentially target multiple-viral transcripts simultaneously and efficiently inhibit not only viral gene expression, but also DNA replication, because HBV amplifies through RNA intermediate (Wieland and Chisari, 2005).

3. *Cardiovascular and cerebral vascular diseases:* Cardiovascular disease is the leading cause of death in most of industrialized countries. It results from the progressive blockage of arteries in a process called atherosclerosis, which can ultimately end in a myocardial infarction or stroke. The severe problem that occurs in heart or brain cells during a myocardial infarction results in the death of cardiac muscle cells or neurons. It may be possible to use RNAi technology to intervene in the process of atherosclerosis or to reduce the damage to heart tissue and brain cells that patients suffer following a myocardial infarction or stroke.

4. *Neurodegenerative disorders:* Advances in targeted multiple delivery of RNAi-inducing molecules has raised the possibility of using RNAi directly as a therapy for a variety of human genetic and other neural and neuromuscular disorders. RNA interference (RNAi) is a powerful new gene knockdown technique that permits tissue-specific, temporally controlled suppression of gene expression. Alzheimer's disease, Parkinson's, Huntington's disease and Amyotrophic lateral sclerosis

(ALS) are examples of relatively common age related neurodegenerative disorders that are increasing as average life expectancy increases. Each disorder is characterized by the dysfunction and death of populations of neurons. Pro-apoptotic members of the Bcl-2 family (Colussi *et al.*, 2000) and caspases (Quinn *et al.*, 2000) have been effectively targeted and neuronal death prevented, using RNAi methods.

5. *Malaria:* Despite intense efforts, malaria remains a leading cause of mortality worldwide. Recent evidence suggests that RNAi can play a key role in identifying the genetic factors crucial in controlling mosquito-borne diseases (Vlachou and Kafatos, 2005; Brown *et al.*, 2003). RNAi can been made inheritable in *Anopheles* mosquitoes by stably transforming the mosquito with a transgene that contains two copies of the target gene arranged in an inverted repeat configuration (Brown *et al.*, 2003). More studies will be needed to elucidate the mechanisms of gene silencing observed in *Plasmodium* and to assess the therapeutic potential of RNAi in malaria control.

Table 8.2: Exogenous and Endogenous Disease-associated Genes Successfully Targeted by RNAi (Dillon *et al.*, 2005)

Type of Disease	Targe
(1)	(2)
Viral diseases	HIV (viral genes-genome)
	HIV (cellular receptors/enzymes)
	HBV
	HCV
	HDV
	Cytomegalovirus (CMV)
	Influenza virus
	Rhinovirus
	SARS coronavirus
	Prions
	Gamma herpes virus
Autoimmune/inflammatory disorders	TNF-α
	Fas/CD95/Apo1
	Caspase-8
Neurological diseases	Mutated SOD (amyotrophic lateral sclerosis)
	BACE1 (Alzheimer's disease)
	SCCMS (myastenic disorders)
	Polyglutamine proteins

(Contd...)

(1)	(2)
Cancer/malignant hyperproliferative disorders	Bax
	CXCR4
	Focal adhesion kinase (FAK)
	EphA2
	Matrix metalloproteinase
	AML1/MTG8
	BCR-Abl
	BRAF(V599E)
	Brk
	Epstein-Barr virus (EBV)
	EGFR
	Fatty acid synthase (FASE)
	HPV E6
	Livin/ML-IAP/KIAP
	MDR
	BCL-2
	CDK-2
	MDM-2
	PKC-α
	TGF-β
	H-Ras
	K-Ras
	VEGF
	PLK1
	Telomerase
	S100A10
	STAT3
	NPM-ALK

RNAi in Agriculture

RNAi technology has established a most powerful expression in plant biology. This application covers a wide range, from developing medical therapeutics in plants to developing designer flower colors. RNAi is both systemic and heritable. RNAi technology evolved crops with novel traits for plant health management. The major advantage in RNAi technology is due to SiRNA, which can move between cells through transport channels, present in cell wall. Further, it enables communications and transport throughout the plant. In plants, endogenously encoded miRNA are perfect complementary to their target genes and induce mRNA cleavage by interaction with RISC complex (Perrimon *et al*, 2010). The exciting application of RNAi is the improvement of essential crops such as rice and corn. As well as RNAi is being used to engineer plants to be rich in dietary proteins. For example: cotton seeds could be made useful for human consumption just to lower the levels of natural plant toxin. RNAi modified plant products are regularly producing in agriculture. A number of applications have emerged in RNAi technology such as resistance in plants to common plant viruses (Zadeh and Foster, 2004) and strengthening of plants such as tomatoes with dietary antioxidants (Niggeweg et al. 2004). RNAi applications have been taken as remedy for CCD (Colony Collapse Disorder) in European honeybees. In recent years, millions of beehives have disappeared, most likely because of the spread through bee colonies of a lethal virus, the Israeli acute paralysis virus (IAPV) (Perrimon *et al*, 2010). RNAi is becoming a potential technique to combat insect pests. RNAi applications have provided fundamental insight in insect defense mechanisms (Blandin *et al*, 2004).

Scientists have developed "tear less onion" by shutting down its lachrymatory factor synthase gene and redirected the valuable sulphur toward making more nutritive and flavouring compound. RNAi have also revolutionized the floriculture industry, by developing a BLUE ROSE, which has been the holy grail of rose breeders since 1840 (Developed by two companies namely Florigen and Suntory). It involves a package of three genes:

- A synthetic RNAi gene that switches off the RED ROSE dihydroflavanol reductase (DFR).
- Adelphinidin gene from blue pansy.
- A DFR gene from iris that had an affinity for producing delphinidin.

Limitations of RNAi

Despite the proliferation of promising cell culture studies for RNAi-based drugs, some concern has been raised regarding the safety of RNA Interference, especially the potential for "off-target" effects in which a gene with coincidentally similar sequence in the targeted gene is also repressed. A better understanding of the mechanisms that lead to nonspecific effects of short dsRNAs is essential before the use of siRNAs or shRNAs can be tested in patient trials.

REFERENCES

Bartel DP (2004). MicroRNAs: Genomics, Biogenesis, Mechanism, and Function. Cell, 116: 281-297.

Bernstein E, Caudy AA, Hammond SM, Hannon GJ (2001). Role for a Bidentate Ribonuclease in the Initiation Step of RNA Interference. Nature, 409: 363-366.

Bernstein E, Kim SY, Carmell MA, et al. (2003). Dicer is Essential for Mouse Development. Nat Genet., 35: 215-217.

Blandin S, Shiao SH,Moita LF, Janse CJ,Waters AP, Kafatos FC, Levashina EA. 2004. Complement-like Protein TEP1 is a Determinant of Vectorial Capacity in the Malaria Vector *Anopheles gambiae*. Cell, 116: 661-670.

Borkhardt A (2002). Blocking Oncogenes in Malignant Cells by RNA Interference-New hope for a Highly Specific Cancer Treatment? Cancer Cell, 23: 167-168.

Brown AE, L Crisanti BA and Catteruccia F, (2003). Stable and Heritable Gene Silencing in the Malaria Vector *Anopheles stephensi*. Nucleic Acids Res., 31: e85.

Coburn GA and Cullen BR, (2002). Potent and Specific Inhibition of Human Immunodeficiency Virus Type-1 Replication by RNA Interference. J. Virol., 76: 9225-9231.

Colussi PA, Quinn LM, Huang DC, Coombe M, Richardson H and Kumar S, (2000). Debcl, a Proapoptotic Bcl-2 homologue, is a Component of the Drosophila Melanogaster Cell Death Machinery. J. Cell Biol., 148: 703-714.

Dallas A and Vlassov AV, (2006). RNAi: A Novel Antisense Technology and Its Therapeutic Potential. Med Sci Monit., 12(4): RA67-74.

Dillon CP, Sandy P, Nencioni P, Kissler S, Rubinson DA, and Parijs LV, (2005). RNAi As An Experimental and Therapeutic Tool to Study and Regulate Physiological and Disease Processes. Annu. Rev. Physiol., 67: 147-73.

Elbashir SM, Harbort J, Lendeckel W, Yalcin A, Weber K, and Tuschl T (2001). Duplexes of 21- nucleotide RNAs mediate RNA Interference in Cultured Mammalian Cells. Nature, 411: 494-498.

Guo S and Kemphues KJ (1995). Par-1, a Gene Required for Establishing Polarity in C. *elegans* embryos, encodes a putative Sex/Thr kinase that is Asymmetrically Distributed. Cell, 81: 611-620.

Hamilton AJ and Baulcombe DC (1999). A Species of Small Antisense RNA in Posttranscriptional Gene Silencing in Plants. Science, 286: 950-952.

Hammond SM, Bernstein E, Beach D, Hannon GJ (2000). An RNA-directed Nuclease Mediates Post-transcriptional Gene Silencing in Drosophila Cells. Nature, 404: 293-296.

Izant JG and Weintraub H (1984). Inhibition of Thymidine Kinase Gene Expression by Anti-sense RNA: A Molecular Approach to Genetic Analysis. Cell, 36: 1007-1015.

Jacque JM, Triques K and Stevenson M, (2002). Modulation of HIV-1 Replication by RNA Interference. Nature, 418: 435-438.

K. Suk *et al*. (2011) Nucleic Acids Research, Vol.39, e43.

Ketting RF, Haverkamp TH, van Luenen HG, and Plasterk RH (1999). Mut-7 of *C. elegans*, Required for Transposon Silencing and RNA Interference, is a Homolog of Werner Syndrome Helicase and RNase D. Cell, 99: 133-141.

Lee Y, Jeon K, Lee JT, Kim S and Kim VN, (2002). MicroRNA Maturation: Step Wise Processing and Subcellular Localization. EMBO J., 21: 4663-4670.

Lee YS, et al. (2004). Distinct Roles for Drosophila Dicer-1 and Dicer-2 in the siRNA/miRNA Silencing Pathways. Cell, 117: 69-81.

Li MJ, Kim S, Li J, Zaia JK, Yee J, Anderson R, Akkina and Rossi JJ, (2005). Long-term Inhibition of HIV-1 Infection in Primary Hematopoietic Cells by Lentiviral Vector Delivery of a Triple Combination of Anti-HIV shRNA, Anti-CCR5 Ribozyme and a Nucleolar-localizing TAR decoy. Mol. Ther., 12: 900-909.

Liu G, Wong-Staal F and Li QX, (2007). Development of New RNAi Therapeutics. *Histol* Histopathol., 22: 211-217.

Liu J, Carmell MA, Rivas FV, et al. (2004). Argonaute2 is the Catalytic Engine of Mammalian RNAi. Science, 305: 1437-1441.

Ma JB, Ye K, Patel DJ. (2004). Structural Basis for Overhang-specific Small Interfering RNA Recognition by the PAZ domain. Nature, 429: 318-322.

Macrae I, Zhou K, Li F, Repic A, Brooks A, Cande W, Adams P and Doudna J (2006). Structural Basis for Double-stranded RNA Processing by Dicer. Science, 311: 195-8.

Martinez J, Patkaniowska A, Urlaub H, et al. (2002). Single-stranded Antisense siRNAs Guide Target RNA Cleavage in RNAi. Cell, 110: 563-574.

Matzke M, Primig M, Trnovsky J and Matzke A (1989). Reversible Methylation and Inactivation of Marker Genes in Sequentially Transformed Plants. EMBO J., 8: 643-649.

Meister G, Landthaler M, Patkaniowska A, et al. (2004). Human Argonaute2 Mediates RNA Cleavage Targeted by miRNAs and siRNAs. Mol Cell, 15: 185-197.

Montgomery MK, Xu S, and Fire A (1998). RNA As Target of Double-stranded RNA-mediated Genetic Interference in *Caenorhabditis Elegans*. Proc. Natl Acad. Sci., 95: 15502-15507.

Mourelatos Z, Postle J, Paushkin S, et al. (2002). miRNPs: A Novel Class of Ribonucleoproteins Containing Numerous MicroRNAs. Genes Dev., 16: 720-728.

Nam NH and Parang K, (2003). Current Targets for Anticancer Drug Discovery. Curr. Drug Targets, 4: 159-179.

Napoli C, Lemieux C. and Jorgensen R (1990). Introduction of a Chimeric Chalcone Synthase Gene into Petunia Results in Reversible Co-suppression of Homologous Genes *in trans*. Plant Cell, 2: 279-289.

Niggeweg R, Michael AJ, Martin C. (2004). Engineering Plants with Increased Levels of the Antioxidant Chlorogenic Acid. Nat Biotechnol 22: 746-754.

Novina CD, Murray MF, Dykxhoorn DM, Beresford PJ, Riess J, Lee SK, Collman RG, Lieberman J, Shankar P and Sharp PA, (2002). siRNA-directed inhibition of HIV-1 infection. Nat. 6: R71. Med., 8:681-686.

Nyka nen A, Haley B, Zamore PD (2001). ATP Requirements and Small Interfering RNA Structure in the RNA Interference Pathway. Cell, 107: 309-321.

Orom UA, Nielsen FC and Lund AH, (2008). MicroRNA-10a Binds the 5'UTR of Ribosomal Protein mRNAs and Enhances Their Translation. Mol Cell, 30(4): 460-471.

Park WS *et al*., (2002). Prevention of HIV-1 Infection in Human Peripheral Blood Mononuclear Cells by Specific RNA Interference. Nucleic Acids Res., 30: 4830-4835.

Park Y-D, Moscone EA, Iglesis VA, Vaucheret H , Matzke AJM and Matzke MA (1996). Gene Silencing Mediated by Promoter Homology Occurs at the Level of Transcription and Results in Meiotically Heritable Alterations in Methylation and Gene Activity. Plant J., 9: 183-194.

Quinn LM, Dorstyn L, Mills K, Colussi PA, Chen P, Coombe M, Abrams J, Kumar S and Richardson H, (2000). An Essential Role for the Caspase in Developmentally Programmed Cell Death in Drosophila. J. Biol. Chem., 275: 40416-40424.

Reddy LS, Sarojamma V and Ramakrishna V, (2007). Future of RNAi in Medicine: A Review. World Journal of Medical Sciences. 2(1):01-14.

Reddy LS, Sarojamma Vand Ramakrishna V (2007). Future of RNAi in Medicine: A Review. World Journal of Medical Sciences, 2(1): 1-14.

Rocheleau CE, Downs WD, Lin R, Wittman C, Bei Y, Cha YH, Ali M, Priess JR and Mello CC (1997). Wnt Signaling and an APC-relatred Gene Specify Endoderm in Early *C. elegans* embryos. Cell, 90: 707-716.

Song E, Lee S, Wangj, Ince N, Ouyang N, Min J, Chen J, Shankar P and Lieberman J, (2003). RNA Interference Targeting Fas Protects Mice From Fulminant Hepatitis. Nat Med., 9:347-351.

Song JJ, Smith SK, Hannon GJ, Joshua- Tor L. (2004). Crystal Structure of Argonaute and its Implications for RISC Slicer Activity. Science, 305: 1434-1437.

Surabhi RM and Gaynor RB, (2002). RNA Interference Directed Against Viral and Cellular Targets Inhibits Human Immunodeficiency Virus Type-1 Replication. J. Virol., 76: 12963-12973.

Tabara H, Sarkissian M, Kelly WG, Fleenor J, Grishok A, Timmons L, Fire A and Mello CC (1999). The rde-1 gene, RNA Interference, and Transposon Silencing in *C. elegans*. Cell, 99: 123-132.

Takeshita F and Ochiya T, (2006). Therapeutic Potential of RNA Interference Against *Cancer.* Cancer Sci., 97(8): 689-696.

Tuschl T, (2001). RNA Interference and Small Interfering RNAs. Chembiochem., 2(4): 239-45.

Tuschl T, Zamore PD, Lehmann R, Bartel DP, and Sharp PA (1999). Targeted mRNA Degradation by Double-stranded RNA *in vitro*. Genes Devel., 13: 3191-3197.

Van Blokland, K van der Geest, N Mol, J, and Kooter J (1994). Transgene-mediated Suppression of Chalcone Synthase Expression in *Petunia hybrida* Results from an Increase in RNA Turnover. Plant J., 6: 861-877.

Verma UN, (2003). Small Interfering RNAs Directed Against Beta-catenin Inhibit the *in vitro* and in vivo Growth of Colon Cancer Cells. Clin Cancer Res., 9: 1291-1300.

Vlachou D and Kafatos FC, (2005). The Complex Interplay Between Mosquito Positive and Negative Regulators of Plasmodium Development. Curr. Opin. Microbiol., 8: 415-421.

Wieland SF and Chisari FV, (2005). Stealth and Polyglutamine Cunning: Hepatitis B and Hepatitis C viruses. J. Virol., 79: 9369-9380.

Zadeh AH, Foster GD. 2004. Transgenic Resistance to Tobacco Ringspot virus. Acta Virol 48: 145-152.

Zender L, Hutker S, Liedtke C, Tilmann HL, Zender S, Mundt B, Waltemathe M, Gosling T, Flemming P, Malek NP, Trautwein C, Manns MP, Kuhnel F and Kubicka S, (2003). Caspase 8 Small Interfering RNA Prevents Acute Liver Failure Trans" in Mice. Proc Nat Acad Sci., 100:7797-7802.

Zhang H, Kolb FA, Brondani V, et al. (2002). Human Dicer Preferentially Cleaves dsRNAs at Their Termini without a Requirement for ATP. EMBO J., 21: 5875-5885.

9

Using Potato Processing Waste in Sheep Rations

Hamed A.A. Omer, ***Egypt***
Soha S. Abdel-Magid, ***Egypt***
Fatma M. Salman, ***Egypt***
Sawsan M. Ahmed, ***Egypt***
Mamdouh I. Mohamed, ***Egypt***
Ibrahim M. Awadalla, ***Egypt***
Mona S. Zaki, ***Egypt***

ABSTRACT

Twenty-seven male growing Rahmani lambs aged 6 months with an average weight 27.17 ± 0.31 kg were used to determine the effects of inclusion potato processing waste (PPW) on performance of Rahmani lambs. Animals divided into three equal groups and assigned for control and two experimental diets containing PPW which was at 0 per cent PPW (TMR_1), 7 per cent PPW (TMR_2), and 14 per cent PPW (TMR_3), respectively. The results showed that dietary treatments had no significant effect on feed intake, while water intake insignificantly ($P>0.05$) increased. Digestibility coefficients of organic matter, crude protein and nitrogen-free extract significantly ($P<0.05$) improved. However, dietary treatment had no significant effect on dry matter and ether extract digestibilities. Values of total digestible nutrient significantly ($P<0.05$) increased while, digestible crude protein insignificantly ($P<0.05$) increased. Nitrogen retention was positive for all groups. Inclusion PPW in sheep rations had no significant effect on ruminal pH, ammonia nitrogen and total volatile fatty acid concentrations. Both ruminal NH3-N and TVFAS concentrations were significantly ($P<0.05$) increased, while ruminal pH was significantly ($P<0.05$)

decreased after 3 hours post feeding compared with before feeding. Molar proportion of volatile fatty acids and all blood plasma constituents insignificant affected. Final weight, body weight gain, and average daily gain were significantly ($P<0.05$) decreased, while feed conversion ratio insignificantly decreased. Total daily feeding costs of experimental rations were decreased. It could be concluded that potato processing waste can be successfully fed to lambs without any adverse effect on digestibility coefficients, ruminal fermentation, blood plasma constituents and performance. Also, PPW can be used economically in formulation of sheep rations.

Keywords: Potato processing waste, Sheep, Digestibility, Ruminal fermentation, Performance, Blood plasma constituents, Economical evaluation.

Introduction

The total world potato waste production is estimated to 12 million tons per year (El-Boushy and Van der Poel 1994).

In Egypt, the yield of potatoes crop was two million tons (A.E.S.I. 2008). Smith and Huxsoll (1987) estimated the peeling losses of the potato chips industry which used abrasion peeling extensively to be 10 per cent. Also, in Egypt, potato processing industry produced several by-products all the time of the year. In addition to the obtaining on potato by-products and transportation is easy and economical, but it needs to be dried to use it all the time of the year.

Potato waste is an excellent energy source for feedlot cattle. It has energy values similar to corn and barley while being low in protein and calcium. The biggest problem that has to be managed with potato waste is the water, where moisture content in potatoes are reach to 80 per cent. In most feedlot rations silage is being used which could contain from 45-65 per cent water as well. The water content of potato waste is not constant and it ranged from 72 to 83 per cent (Murphy, 1997).

The starch in potato waste is fermented rapidly, limiting inclusion levels due to problems such as acidosis and bloat. Due to the wet nature of the product, spoilage can be a concern, especially during the summer (Radunz et al. 2003).

Potato waste is the product remaining after potatoes have been processed to produce frozen potato products for human consumption. The product can include peelings, cull potatoes, and other potato products. Potatoes have a feeding value similar to cereal grain but lower in CP. Potatoes are high in energy and low in protein and vitamin A. (Lardy and Anderson 2009).

Potatoes are primarily a source of energy, on a 100 per cent dry matter (DM) basis, it has 81-82 per cent total digestible nutrient (TDN) and only about 10 per cent protein. The crude protein is in the form of non-protein nitrogen, and only 60 per cent of the total may be digestible (Boyles, 2006). Because of potatoes' very low fiber content, it should not be considered a forage substitute but rather should be thought of as a high moisture source of starch. Potatoes are quite low in protein content and, when given in high amounts without protein supplementation, will not give good animal performance or feed efficiency.

Toxic components of potato called glycoalkaloids (usually solanine and chaconine). Glycoalkaloids are normally found at low levels in the tuber, and occur in the greatest concentrations just beneath the skin (FAO, 2008).

Gado et al. (1998) reported that replacement of concentrate feed mixture by potato waste at level 25 per cent of DM significantly increased digestibility of DM and nitrogen balance. Using potato by-product in growing goat ration saved 50 per cent of yellow corn, which is used in the ration and used at 60 per cent of the control ration without any adverse effect on goat performance (Omer and Tawila 2008). Potato products can be an economical substitute for grains (Murphy 1997 and Omer et al. 2010).

The main objectives of this study was to make a good cheap ration for growing Rahmani lambs and to investigate the effect of inclusion sun-dried potato processing waste on performance, digestion coefficients, rumen fermentation, blood plasma constituents and economical evaluation.

Materials and Methods

The present experiment was carried out at the Sheep and Goats' Units in El-Bostan area in Nubaria, which belongs to the Animal Production Department, National Research Center, Dokki, Giza, Egypt.

Experimental Animals and Feeds

Twenty-seven growing male Rahmani lambs, aged at approximately 6 months with average live weight of 27.17 ± 0.31 kg, were divided randomly into three equal groups (nine animals in each) and used to evaluate the effect of inclusion potato processing waste (PPW) at 0 per cent, 7 per cent and 14 per cent of total mixed ration (TMR). The composition of different total mixed rations are presented in Table 1 The animals were individually fed with the experimental rations that cover the requirements for total digestible nutrients and protein for growing sheep according to the NRC (1985), and feed allowance was adjusted every 2 weeks according to their body weight changes. Animals were housed in individual semi-open pens. Experimental animals received one of the three experimental rations of PPW. The feeding trial lasted for 105 days, diets were offered twice daily (0700 and 1300 hours) while feed residues (if any) were removed and weighed once daily before morning feeding. Fresh water was available all the time in plastic containers. Water intake was recorded weekly. Live body weights were recorded weekly before morning feeding and after fasting overnight (feed and water). Potato processing waste was obtained from potato chips factory, Borg El-Arab city, Alexandria governorate, this potato processing waste composed of peel potatoes only.

Digestibility Trials

At the end of the feeding experiment, five animals from each group were selected randomly and used to determine digestion coefficients and nutritive values of the experimental rations. The nutritive values expressed as the total digestible nutrients (TDN) and digestible crude proteins (DCP) of the experimental rations were calculated according to Abou-Raya (1967).

Rumen Fluid

Rumen fluid samples were collected from 15 animals (five animals for each treatment) at the end of the digestibility trial before feeding and 3 h post feeding via stomach tube and strained through four layers of cheesecloth to study the effect of dietary treatments on ruminal fermentations, ruminal pH, ammonia nitrogen (NH3-N), total volatile fatty acid (TVFA) concentrations, and molar proportion of volatile fatty acids.

Blood Plasma Constituents

Blood samples were collected from the same lambs at the end of digestibility trials from the left jugular vein in heparinized test tubes at about 3 hours post feeding and centrifuged at 5.000 rpm for 15 minuets. Plasma were kept frozen at -20° C for subsequent analysis of glucose, total proteins, albumin, urea, triglycerides and cholesterol.

Analytical Procedures

Representative samples of ingredients, experimental rations, feces, and ruminal NH3-N concentrations were analyzed according to A.O.A.C (1995) methods. Neutral detergent fiber (NDF), acid detergent fiber (ADF), and acid detergent lignin (ADL) were also determined in the ingredients and experimental rations according to Goering and Van Soest (1970) and Van Soest et al. (1991). NDF and ADF were expressed, inclusive of residual ash. Ruminal pH was immediately determined using digital pH meter. Ruminal TVFA concentrations were determined by steam distillation according to Kromann *et al*. (1967). Molar proportions of volatile fatty acids were determined according to Erwin *et al*. (1961). Plasma total proteins were determined as described (Armstrong and Carr, 1964); albumin (Doumas et al., 1971); urea (Patton and Crouch, 1977); triglycerides (Fossati and Principe,

1982); cholesterol (Allain et al., 1974) and Plasma glucose was measured using the enzymatic glucose oxidase method (Bauer et al., 1974). Globulin and albumin: globulin ratio (A: G ratio) were calculated. Gross energy (mega calories per kilogram DM) was calculated according to Blaxter (1968), where, each gram of crude protein (CP) = 5.65 kcal, each gram of ether extract (EE) = 9.40 kcal, and each gram crude fiber (CF) and nitrogen-free extract (NFE) = 4.15 kcal.

Economic Evaluation

The relation between feed costs and gain was calculated for the different experimental groups. The general equation by which the costs of 1 kg of live body weight gain was calculated as follows:

The cost for 1-kg gain = total cost (Egyptian pound (LE)) of feed intake/ total gain (kilogram).

Statistical Analysis

The analysis of variance for completely randomized design experiments using SAS (1998) examined the effects of dietary treatments. Differences among means were evaluated using Tukey's test.

Results and Discussion

Composition, chemical analysis, and cell wall constituents of feed ingredients and experimental rations

Results of chemical analysis and cell wall constituents of feed ingredients are presented in Table 9.1. The results showed that yellow corn recorded the highest values of organic matter (OM) and nitrogen-free extract (NFE) while wheat bran showed the lowest value of OM. On the other hand, undecorticated cotton seed meal showed the highest values of CP and the lowest value of NFE. While, pea straw (PS) showed the highest value of Neutral detergent fiber (NDF) and Acid detergent fiber (ADF), however PPW showed the highest values of hemi cellulose and lowest value of cellulose. Gross energy of potato processing waste (PPW) was nearly from yellow corn (4.274 vs. 4.423 Mcal/kg dry matter. These results were within the ranges obtained by Omer and Tawila (2008), Tawila *et al.* (2008) and Omer et al. (2010) who recorded that chemical composition of potato waste ranged from 40 to 146 g/kg DM for CP, 16 to 175 g/kg DM for CF, 780 to 820 g/kg DM for TDN, 400 to 415 g/kg DM for NDF, 58 to 64 g/kg DM for ADF, 36 to 42 g/kg DM for ADL, 323 to 347 g/kg DM for hemicellulose, and 25 to 43 g/kg DM for cellulose, respectively.

Table 9.1: Chemical analysis and cell wall constituents of feed ingredients (g/ kg DM)

Item	Feed ingredients				
	PPW	UDCSM	YC	WB	PS
Dry matter (DM; g/kg)	941.1	878.8	913.0	902.0	942.9
Chemical analysis on DM basis					
Organic matter	965.4	942.0	988.0	883.0	885.6
Crude protein	129.2	248.2	93.0	140.0	115.1
Crude fiber	30.6	277.5	23.0	112.2	297.6
Ether extract	14.0	27.1	35.0	30.0	25.3
Ash	34.6	58.0	12.0	117.0	114.4
Nitrogen-free extract	791.6	389.2	837.0	600.8	447.6
Gross energy (Mcal/kg dry matter)	4.274	4.424	4.423	4.032	3.981
Cell wall constituents					
Neutral detergent fiber (NDF)	410.0	506.3	326.3	442.1	546.0
Acid detergent fiber (ADF)	63.0	361.8	224.5	321.6	425.0
Acid detergent lignin (ADL)	38.0	204.6	21.3	40.5	134.0
Hemi cellulose	347.0	144.5	101.8	120.5	121.0
Cellulose	25.0	157.2	203.2	281.1	291.0

Hemicellulose = NDF - ADF, Cellulose = ADF - ADL

PPW potato processing waste, UDCSM undecorticated cotton seed meal, YC Yellow corn, WB wheat bran, PS pea straw.

Composition, chemical analysis, and cell wall constituents of the experimental rations are presented in Table 9.2. Experimental rations were in the same trend of gross energy (GE). Hemicellulose content was increased while cellulose content was decreased by adding PPW in the diet. These results in agreement with those obtained by Omer et al. (2010).

Table 9.2: Composition (fresh kilogram per ton), chemical analysis and cell wall constituents (g/ kg DM) of the experimental rations

Item	Experimental Rations		
	TMR_1	TMR_2	TMR_3
1	2	3	4
Composition (fresh kg/ton)	000	70	140
Potato processing waste			
Undecorticated cotton seed meal	240	205	168
Yellow corn	280	280	280
Wheat bran	150	135	122

(Contd...)

1	2	3	4
Pea straw	300	280	260
Lime stone	20	20	20
Sodium chloride	7	7	7
Vit. and mineral mixture[a]	3	3	3
Price of ton (LE)	1,220	1,090	0,995
Chemical analysis (g/kg DM)			
Dry matter	913.8	916.6	920.5
Organic matter	933.8	934.6	938.1
Crude protein	141.1	137.0	132.8
Crude fiber	179.1	163.8	148.5
Ether extract	28.4	27.6	26.7
Nitrogen-free extract	585.2	606.2	630.1
Ash	66.2	55.4	61.9
GE (Mcal/ kg DM)	4.236	4.229	4.232
Cell wall constituents			
Neutral detergent fiber (NDF)	443.0	436.5	430.2
Acid detergent fiber (ADF)	325.4	303.9	282.2
Acid detergent lignin (ADL)	101.4	93.6	85.4
Hemi cellulose	117.6	132.6	148.0
Cellulose	224.0	210.3	196.8

LE= Egyptian pound equals 0.18 USS approximately, TMR_1 = control ration contained 0 per cent potato processing waste, TMR_2 = second experimental ration contained 7 per cent potato processing waste of total mixed ration, TMR_3 = third experimental ration contained 14 per cent potato processing waste of total mixed ration.

[a] Each 3 kg vitamins and mineral mixture contains: vitamin A 12,000,000 IU, vitamin D3 2,200,000 IU, vitamin E 10,000 mg, vitamin K3 2,000 mg, vitamin B1 1,000 mg, vitamin B2 5,000 mg, vitamin B6 1,500 mg, vitamin B12 10 mg, pantothenic acid 10 mg, niacin 30,000 mg, folic acid 1,000 mg, biotin 50 mg, choline 300,000 mg, manganese 6,0000 mg, zinc 50,000 mg, copper 10,000 mg, iron 30,000 mg, iodine 100 mg, selenium 100 mg, cobalt 100 mg, CaCo3 to 3,000 g.

Feed and water intakes, nutrient digestibility coefficients and nitrogen utilization by the experimental group lambs

Feed and water intakes, nutrient digestibility coefficients, and nitrogen utilization by the experimental group lambs are presented in Table 9.3. The results showed that inclusion PPW in the diet insignificant decreased ($P>0.05$) feed intake. Dry matter, total digestible nutrient and crude protein intakes were decreased gradually with increasing quantity of PPW in the TMR. The present results might indicate that the PPW had adverse effect on palatability. These results were in agreement with those obtained by Omer and Tawila (2008) and Omer et al. (2010) found no significant effect on feed intake when

Baladi goats or Ossimi sheep fed diets replaced yellow corn by 25 per cent and 50 per cent PPW. Sugimoto et al. (2006) noted that dry matter intake increased (linear; P<0.01) as the feeding level increased and was not affected by the diet. Onwubuemeli et al. (1985) fed lactating Holstein cows for 12 wk rations contained, on a dry matter basis, 0, 10, 15, and 20 per cent potato waste and were substituted for high moisture corn in diets. They noticed that substituting potato waste for corn did not significantly affect dry matter intake.

Table 9.3: Feed Intake (gram), Water Intake (milliliter), Nutrient Digestibilities Coefficient (g/kg DM) and Nitrogen Utilization (gram) by the Experimental Group Lambs

Item	Experimental rations			SEM
	TMR_1	TMR_2	TMR_3	
1	2	3	4	5
Feed intake; gram as Dry matter (DM)	1,448	1,373	1,336	59.0
Total digestible nutrient (TDN)	1,093	1,048	1,044	44.7
Crude protein (CP)	204	188	177	8.3
Digestible crude protein (DCP)	132	132	124	5.5
Average body weight[a]	39.65a	37.95ab	36.65b	0.42
Water intake ml/h/day	4259	4330	4285	51.0
L/100 kg body weight (BW)	10.74b	11.41a	11.69a	0.13
L/ kg dry mater intake	2.94	3.15	3.21	0.14
Nutrient digestibilities coefficient				
Dry matter	792.2	801.7	796.4	0.23
Organic matter	779.7 c	789.8 b	805.0 a	0.32
Crude protein	646.5 b	701.2 a	700.3 a	0.92
Crude fiber	679.4 a	649.9 b	662.1 ab	0.44
Ether extract	748.6	735.6	754.0	0.70
Nitrogen-free extract	844.1 b	850.1 ab	864.2 a	0.38
Nutritive values (%)				
Total digestible nutrient (TDN)	754.7 b	763.6 b	781.1 a	0.34
Digestible crude protein (DCP)	91.2	96.1	93.0	0.10
Nitrogen utilization (g)				
Nitrogen intake	33.34	33.13	32.56	0.51
Fecal nitrogen	8.80	8.31	8.02	0.17

(Contd…)

1	2	3	4	5
Digested nitrogen	24.54	24.82	24.54	0.45
Urinary nitrogen	8.02	8.36	8.61	0.16
Total nitrogen losses	16.82	16.67	16.63	0.23
Nitrogen retention	16.52	16.46	15.93	0.43

a, b and c = means in the same row having different letters differ significantly (P<0.05)

SEM = standard error of the mean

[a]Average body weight = (Initial weight + Final weight/2)

Increasing level of PPW in the diets leads to insignificantly increasing (P>0.05) water intake as ml/h/d or L/kg dry mater intake, whoever, it significantly increased (P<0.05) water intake as L/100 kg body weight. These results were in agreement with those obtained by Omer and Tawila (2008) who noted that replacement of yellow corn (60% of control diet) by PPW at 25 per cent and 50 per cent in Baladi goats insignificantly increased water intake. On contrast Omer et al. (2010) noted that increasing level of PPW in sheep diets leads to insignificantly decreasing (P>0.05) water intake.

Inclusion of PPW in the diet insignificantly (P<0.05) improved digestibility coefficients of DM and EE, however, it significantly improved (P<0.05) OM, CP and NFE digestibility coefficients. On the other hand, except for OM digestibility increasing quantity of PPW in the diet from 7 per cent to 14 per cent had no significant effect on the other nutrients digestibility coefficients. Omer et al. (2010) reported that instead of 25 per cent or 50 per cent of yellow corn with PPW in sheep diets significantly (P<0.05) improved digestibility coefficients of (DM, OM and CP), while, dietary treatment had no significant effect on CF and NFE digestibilities. Tawila et al. (2008) found no significant differences among rations which were detected for DM, OM, CF, EE, and NFE digestibilities when yellow corn was replaced with PPW in Baladi goat diets at 0 per cent, 25 per cent, and 50 per cent. However, the digestibility of CP was significantly lower (P< 0.05) in R3 (50%) than in R1 (0%) and R2 (25%). Also, Radunz et al. (2003) noted that decrease in total apparent nitrogen disappearance was occurred with increasing potato waste levels in beef finishing diets to a less digestible protein with potatoes or more bacterial fermentation in the large intestine which would lead to greater fecal nitrogen extraction. Sugimoto et al. (2006) noticed that digestibility was not affected by any treatments when steers fed diets contained 0.2, 0.4 and 0.6 per cent of Body weight (BW) on a dry matter basis potato pulp silage-based diet (PPS). Szasz et al. (2005) examined the main effects and interactions of pasteurization (54.4° C for 2 h) of potato slurry (PS) and grain type on total tract digestion of beef finishing diets. They recorded that steers fed barley-based diets had greater (P=0.02) DMI and lesser (P<0.05) total tract digestibility of DM and ADF compared with steers fed corn diets. Pasteurization increased (P=0.10) total tract starch digestibility. Onwubuemeli et al. (1985) tested digestibility and nitrogen utilization of potato waste substituted for corn at 0, 10, and 20 per cent of the ration dry matter in steers diets. Potato waste did not significantly affect digestibility of crude protein or dry matter, but at 20 per cent substitution digestibility of acid detergent fiber decreased.

Inclusion PPW in the rations significantly (P<0.05) improved TDN and insignificantly (P>0.05) DCP, which is mainly due to the increase in CP and NFE digestibilities. The TMR3 had the highest TDN while, TMR2 had the highest DCP value. Tawila *et al*. (2008) noted that replacement concentrate feed mixture with PPW at 50 per cent decreased TDN by 7.52 per cent and by 29.09 per cent for DCP, respectively, compared to the control ration. Diets containing PPW significantly increased (P < 0.05) nitrogen retention. Omer et al. (2010) noted that Instead yellow corn with PPW at 0 per cent, 25 per cent and 50 per cent in sheep rations significantly (P<0.05) increased TDN and DCP values. The diet replaced 25 per cent of corn with PPW (R_2) improved TDN by 1.85 per cent and by 21.90 per cent for DCP, respectively, compared to the control diet (R_1). While, diet replaced 50 per cent of corn with PPW R_3 improved TDN by 2.06 per cent and by 29.65 per cent for DCP, respectively, with respect to the control diet (R1).

Nitrogen retention was insignificant decreased (P>0.05) when PPW introduced in the diet at 7 per cent or 14 for TMR_2 and TMR_3 compared to the control diet (TMR_1). In contrast, Omer *et al*. (2010) and Tawila *et al*. (2008) observed that nitrogen retention was improved when sheep fed diets replaced 25 per cent or 50 per cent of corn with PPW.

Rumen Fluid Parameters of the Experimental Group Lambs

Results of mean effects of rumen fluid parameter of the experimental rations (Table 9.4) indicated that dietary treatment had no significant effect on ruminal pH, NH_3–N and TVFAS concentrations. Ammonia nitrogen was insignificant (P>0.05) decreased with inclusion PPW in the diet. However, pH value and total volatile fatty acids were in significant increased. These results are in agreement with those obtained by Omer and Tawila (2008) with Baladi goats and Tawila et al.(2008) and Omer *et al*. (2010) with Ossimi sheep. The reduction of ammonia-N in the rumen liquor appears to be the result of increased incorporation of ammonia-N into microbial protein, and it was considered as a direct result to stimulated microbial activity while increasing TVFAS might be related to the more utilization of dietary energy and positive fermentation in the rumen. Feeding Baladi goats on diets replaced by 0 per cent, 25 per cent, 50 per cent, or 100 per cent of concentrate feed mixture by potato waste had no significant effect on ruminal pH, TVFAS, and ammonia-N concentrations (Gado *et al*. 1998). The rate of VFAS production may in this situation exceed the rate of VFAS absorption through the rumen epithelium, and VFAS concentration in the rumen juice is increased (Van't Klooster 1986). Also, Radunz *et al*. (2003) found that increasing levels of PW lead to increased ruminal TVFAS concentration (linear, $P < 0.01$; quadratic, $P = 0.03$). It should be noted that TVFAS concentration in the rumen is governed by several factors such as dry matter digestibility, rate of absorption, rumen pH, transportation of the digesta from the rumen to the other parts of the digestive tract, and the microbial population in the rumen and their activities (Allam *et al*. 1984). Onwubuemeli et al. (1985) substituted corn with 0, 10, 20, and 30 per cent potato waste in steers diet. They reported that rumen ammonia, acetate, acetate to propionate ratios, and total volatile fatty acids were lower at high intakes of potato waste and pH was increased. The shift in rumen fermentation when large amounts of potatoes were fed explains the depressed butter fat on these rations. Sugimoto et al. (2006) fed steers at 0.2, 0.4 and 0.6 per cent of BW, potato pulp silage-based diet (PPS) and a grain-based diet (GRAIN).They reported that steers fed the grain diet had a lower ($P<0.1$) ruminal pH compared with steers fed the PPS diet. Ruminal pH was not significantly affected by feeding level; however, it was numerically higher for steers supplemented at 0.2 per cent per BW than that for the steers supplemented above 0.4 per cent per BW due probably to the higher starch intake.

Table 9.4: Effect of Dietary Treatments and Sampling Time on the Basic Patterns of Rumen Fermentation by the Experimental Group Lambs

Item	TMR_1	TMR_2	TMR_3	SEM
pH value	6.22	6.25	6.30	0.02
NH_3–N (mg/dl)	24.69	23.88	23.98	0.41
TVFAs (mEq/dl)	7.47	7.64	7.52	0.21
Sampling time	Before feeding	3 hrs post feeding		
pH value	6.32a	6.16b	0.02	
NH_3–N (mg/dl)	23.3b	25.05a	0.41	
TVFAs (mEq/dl)	6.42b	8.66a	0.21	
Molar proportion of VFAs and acetate/propionate ratio				
Acetic acid (A; %)	42.59	42.93	42.50	0.21
Propionic acid (P; %)	24.53	24.65	24.70	0.18
Butyric acid (%)	18.21	18.34	18.50	0.15
A:P ratio	1.74	1.74	1.72	0.02

a, b and c = means in the same row having different letters differ significantly ($P<0.05$)

[a] *NH_3–N* ruminal ammonia nitrogen [b] *TVFAs* total volatile fatty acids

Sampling time has a significant effect on rumen fluid parameters. Inclusion Potato processing waste in the sheep diets significantly decreased (P<0.05) ruminal pH at 3 hours post feeding compared with before feeding. However, it significantly increased (P<0.05) NH_3–N and TVFS concentrations at 3 hours post feeding compared with before feeding. These results are in agreement with those found by Omer and Tawila (2008) and Omer et al. (2010). In contrast, these results were not in agreement with those found by Onwubuemeli et al. (1985) who studied the effect of sampling time at 0, 2, 4, and 8 hours on rumen fermentation of diets containing 0 per cent, 10 per cent, 20 per cent, and 30 per cent PPW fed to dairy cattle. They suggested that the higher percentages of dietary PPW decreased (P<0.05) rumen ammonia concentrations, which peaked 2 hours post feeding. Also, the same authors observed that TVFAS concentration was decreased while pH value was increased at 4 hours post feeding.

Inclusion PPW in sheep diets had no significant effect on molar proportion of volatile fatty acids. Omer et al (2010) with sheep and Gado et al. (1998) with goat fed diets containing potato processing waste found significant increased (P<0.05) of acetic acid and butyric acid and insignificantly increased (P>0.05) both propionic acid and acetic/propionic ratio compared to the control diet. Neither diet nor the feeding level had any effects on the proportion of ruminal propionate (Sugimoto *et al*. 2006).

Blood Plasma Constituents by the Experimental Group Lambs

Data of Table 9.5 showed that inclusion PPW in sheep diets had no significant effect on blood plasma glucose, total protein, albumin, glubulin, albumin: glubulin ratio, urea, triglycerides and cholesterol. These results are inagreement was those obtained by Gado et al (1998) who indicated that partial replacing concentrate by potato processing waste at 0, 25, 50 or 100 per cent in growing Baladi goats had no significant (P>0.05) effect on the serum urea nitrogen.

Table 9.5: Effect of Dietary Treatments on Blood Plasma Constituents by the Experimental Group Lambs

Item	Experimental Rations			SEM
	TMR_1	TMR_2	TMR_3	
Glucose (mg per100 ml)	63.43	64.25	65.00	0.43
Total protein (g per100 ml)	7.91	7.86	7.84	0.03
Albumin (g per100 ml)	1.81	1.80	1.80	0.004
Globulin (g per100 ml)	6.10	6.06	6.04	0.03
Albumin: Globulin ratio	4.37	4.37	4.36	0.02
Urea (mg per100 ml)	22.51	22.93	23.11	0.19
Triglycerides (mg per100 ml)	30.09	30:11	30.16	0.04
Cholesterol (mg per100 ml	219.00	221.00	220.00	0.76

Growth Performance of the Experimental Group Lambs

Growth performance of the experimental group animals is presented in Table 9.6. The results showed that increasing level of PPW in the experimental rations significantly (P<0.05) decreased final weight, body weight gain, average daily gain (ADG), and relative gain, while feed conversion expressed as kilogram intake of DM per kilogram gain insignificantly decreased. These results were in agreement with those obtained by Omer et al (2010) when sheep fed diets contained PPW replaced 25 per cent or 50 per cent of yellow corn in basal diet. Sauter et al. (1980) recorded a 17 per cent decrease in ADG and 5 per cent decrease in efficiency with inclusion of 50 per cent potato by-product as compared with 25 per cent potato by-product in barley-based diets. Also, Radunz et al. (2003) recorded that increasing PPW decreased ADG and feed efficiency from 0 per cent to 30 per cent and then increased at 40 per cent (quadratic, P < 0.01) when they used PPW from frozen potato products industry in high grain beef cattle finishing diets. In contrast, these results were not in agreement with those found by Omer and Tawila (2008) with Baladi goats and Makkar et al. (1984) with buffalo calves. They found that ADG and feed efficiency were better when potato waste substituted cereal grains in the rations. On the other hand, Duynisveld et al. (2004) attributed that the replacement of corn with potato processing by-product in beef cattle rations did not affect (P>0.05) average daily gain and improved (P<0.05) feed conversion efficiency.

Table 9.6: Growth Performance of the Experimental Groups

Item	Experimental Rations			SEM
	TMR_1	TMR_2	TMR_3	
No. of animals	9	9	9	–
Initial weight (kg)	27.30	27.20	27.00	0.31
Final weight (kg)	52.00 a	48.70 b	46.30 c	0.64
Gain (kg)	24.70 a	21.50 b	19.30 c	0.55
Experimental duration, days	105	105	105	–
ADG (g/day)	235 a	205 b	184 c	5.20
Relative gain (% of initial weight)[a]	90.48 a	79.04 b	71.48 c	2.12
Feed conversion (kg intake /kg gain) of Dry matter (DM)	6.16	6.70	7.26	0.29
Total digestible nutrient (TDN)	4.65	5.11	5.67	0.23
Crude protein (CP)	0.87	0.92	0.96	0.04
Digestible crude protein (DCP)	0.56	0.64	0.67	0.03

a, b and c = means in the same row having different letters differ significantly (P<0.05)

[a] Relative gain (percent of initial weight)= gain/initial weight x 100

Economic Evaluation of the Experimental Group Lambs

Economic efficiency was represented by daily profit over feed cost. The costs were based on average values of year 2010 for feeds and live body weight. Feeding costs and profit above feeding costs are shown in Table 9.7. Inclusion PPW in sheep diets lead to the decrease of total daily feeding costs of experimental rations by 15.56 per cent for TMR_2 while 25.34 per cent for TMR_3 in comparison with the control diet TMR_1. Meanwhile, average daily gain, daily profit above feeding cost, and relative economical efficiency for TMR_2 and TMR_3 were less compared to the control diet TMR_1. Feed cost LE per kilogram gain was improved by 3.16 per cent and 4.62 per cent for TMR_2 and TMR_3, respectively, compared to control diet TMR_1. These results are in agreement with those found by Omer et al. (2010). Potato by-products or potato waste can be economical substitute for feedlot cattle (Murphy 1997) and for sheep (Omer and Tawila 2008 and Omer et al., 2010).

Table 9.7: Economic Evaluation for the Experimental Rations

Item	Experimental Rations		
	TMR_1	TMR_2	TMR_3
Daily feed intake (fresh; kg)	1.585	1.498	1.451
Value of 1-kg feed (LE)	1.220	1.090	0.995
Daily feeding cost (LE)[a]	1.934	1.633	1.444
Average daily gain (kg)	0.235	0.205	0.184
Value of daily gain (LE)[b]	6.345	5.535	4.968
Daily profit above feeding cost (LE)	4.411	3.902	3.524
Relative economical efficiency[c]	100.000	88.460	79.890
Feed cost (LE/kg gain)	8.23	7.97	7.85

LE = Egyptian pound equals 0.18 USS approximately

a Based on prices of year 2010

b Value of 1- kg live body weight equals 27 LE (2010)

c Assuming that the relative economic efficiency of control diet equals 100

Conclusions

From the results of this study it could be concluded that potato processing waste can be successfully fed to sheep. Quality of the product and dry matter intake must be monitored for maximum performance. Potato processing waste can be an economical substitute for sheep rations. Optimal inclusion of PPW in sheep rations may depend on the cost of transportation and other dietary ingredients used in formulation of rations.

Abbreviations used in chapter

ADF	Acid detergent fiber
ADL	Acid detergent lignin
ADG	Average daily gain
BW	Body weight
CF	Crude fiber
CP	Crude protein
DCP	Digestible crude protein
DM	Dry matter
DMI	Dry matter intake
EE	Ether extract
LE	Egyptian pound
Mcal/kg	Megacalories per kilogram
NDF	Neutral detergent fiber
NFE	Nitrogen-free extract
NH_3–N	Ammonia nitrogen
NRC	National Research Center
OM	Organic matter
PS	Pea straw
PPB	Potato processing by-product
PPW	Potato processing waste
TMR	Total mixed ration
TMR_1	Control ration contained 0 per cent potato processing waste
TMR_2	Second experimental ration contained 7 per cent potato processing waste of total mixed ration
TMR_3	Third experimental rations contained 14 per cent potato processing waste of total mixed ration
UDCSM	Undecorticated cotton seed meal
WB	Wheat bran
YC	Yellow corn

REFERENCES

Abou-Raya, A.K., 1967. Animal and Poultry Nutrition. 1st Edit. Pub. Dar El-Maarif, Cairo (Arabic Text book).

A.E.S.I., 2008. Agriculture Economic and Statistics Institute, Agric., Economics, Pub. By Agric. Res. Center, Egypt.

Allain, C.C., Poon, L.S., Chan, C.S., Richmond, W. and Fu, P.C., 1974. Enzymatic Determination of Total Serum Cholesterol. Clin. Chem., 20: 470-475.

Allam, S.M., Abou-Raya, A.K., Gihad E.A. and El-Bedawy T.M., 1984. Nutritional Studies by Sheep and Goats Fed NoaH Treated Straw. 1st Egyptian British Conference on Animal and Poultry Production, Zagazig, 11-13 Sep. p. 53.

A.O.A.C., 1995. Association of Official Analytical Chemists: Official Methods of Analysis. 16th ed. Washington D.C. USA.

Armstrog, W.D.and Carr C.W., 1964. Physiological Chemistry: Laboratory directions 3: 75 Buger Puplishing Co. Minneapolis, Minnesota, U.S.A.

Bauer, T.D., Ackermann, P.G. and Toro, G., 1974. Methods in Clinical Chemistry. Clinical Laboratory Methods. The C.V. Mosley Company, Saint Louis, p. 946.

Blaxter, K.L., 1968. The Energy Metabolism of Ruminants. 2nd ed. Charles Thomas Publisher. Spring field. Illinois, U.S.A.

Boyles, S., 2006. Feeding Potato Processing Wastes and Culls to Cattle. OSU Extension Beef Specialist. http://beef,osu.edu/library/potato. html.

Doumas, B., Wabson, W.W. and Biggs, H., 1971. Albumin Standards and Measurement of Serum with Bromocrfsol Green. Clin. Chem. Acta, 31: 87.

Duynisveld, J.L., Charmely E., Mandell I. and Aalhus J., 2004. Replacing Corn or Barley with Potato Processing by-product in Beef Finishing Diets Improves Feed Conversion Efficiency and Alters Carcass Fat Distribution. Journal of Animal Science 82, Suppl. 1.

El-Boushy, A.R.Y. and Van der Poel, A.F.B., 1994. Poultry Feed from Waste Processing and Use. Chapman and hall (Ed).

Erwin, E.S., Marco, C.J. and Emery, E.M., 1961. Volatile Fatty Acid Analysis of Blood and Rumen Fluid by Gas Chromatography. Journal of Dairy Science 44: 1768.

F.A.O., 2008. Potatoes, Nutrition and Diet. International Year of the Potato, 2008 www.potato 2008.org

Fossati, P and Principe, L., 1982. Clin. Chem. 28, 2077.

Gado, H., Mansour, A.M., Metwally, H.M. and El-Ashry, M.A., 1998. The Effect of Partial Replacing Concentrate by Potato Processing Waste on Performance of Growing Baladi Goats. Egyptian Journal of Nutrition and feeds 1 (2): 123-129.

Goering, H.K. and Van Soest, P.J., 1970. Forage Fiber Analyses (Apparatus, Reagents, Procedures and Some Applications). USDA, Agr. Hand. Book 379.

Kromann, R.P., Meyer, J.H. and Stielau, W.J., 1967. Steam Distillation of Volatile Fatty Acids in Rumen Digesta. Journal of Dairy Science 50: 73.

Lardy, G and Anderson, V., 2009. Alternative feeds for ruminants. NDSU.permission@ndsu.edu. North Dakota State University Agriculture and University Extension Dept. 7070, Morrill 7, P.O. Box 6050, Fargo, ND 58108-6050.

Makkar, G.S., Kakkar, V.K., Bhullar M.S. and Malik, N.S., 1984. Potato Waste As a Substitute for Cereal Grains in the Rations of Buffalo Calves. Indian Journal of Animal Science 54: 1060-1061.

Murphy, S., 1997. Feeding Potato by-products. Prince Edward Island, Agriculture and Foresty, Fact Sheet, AGDEX 420-68. http://www.gov.pe.ca/af/agweb/library/factsheet/wastpot. Php3.

N.R.C., 1985. Nutrient Requirements of Domestic Animals. Nutrient Requirements of Sheep. National Academy of Sciences, Washington. D.C.

Omer, H.A.A., Abdel-Magid, S. S., Ahmed S. M., Mohamed, M. I. and Awadalla, I.M., 2010. Response to Partial Replacement of Yellow Corn with Potato Processing Waste As Non-traditional Source of Energy on the Productive Performance of Ossimi Lambs. Trop Anim Health Prod 42: 1195-1202.

Omer, H.A.A and Tawila, M.A., 2008. Growth Performance of Growing Baladi Goats Fed Diets Containing Different Levels of Sun Dried Peel Potato Waste. Egyptian Journal of Nutrition and feeds 11 (3): 453-468.

Onwubuemeli, C., Huber, J.J., King, K.J. and Johnson, C.O., 1985. Nutritive Value of Potato Processing Wastes in Total Mixed Rations for Dairy Cattle. Journal of Dairy Science 68: 1207-1214.

Patton, C.J. and Crouch, S.R., 1977. Spectrophotomattic and Kinetics Investigation of the Berthelot Reaction for the Determination of Ammonia. Anal. Chem. 49: 464.

Radunz, A.E., Lardy, G.P., Bauer, M.L., Marchello, M.J., Loe, F.R. and Berg, P.T., 2003. Influence of Steam-peeled Potato Processing Waste Inclusion Level in Beef Finishing Diets: Effects on Digestion, Feedlot Performance and Meat Quality. Journal of Animal Science 81: 2675-2685.

SAS., 1998. Statistical Analysis System. SAS Users Guide. Version 6. 12 Ed. Basics SAS Institute Inc., Cary, NC, USA.

Sauter, E.A., Hinman, D.D., Bull, R.C., Howes, A.D., Parkinsson, J.F., and Stanhope, D.L., 1980. Studies on the Utilization of Potato Processing Waste for Cattle Feed. University of Idaho Agric. Exp. Sta. Res. Bull 112, Moscow, ID.

Smith, T.J. and Huxsoll, C.C., 1987. Peeling Potatoes for Processing (Eds W.F. Talburt and O. Smith) AVI - Van Nostrand Rein Hold Company, New York, pp. 333-369.

Sugimoto, M. Saito W., Ool M., Sato Y., Saito T. and Mori K. 2006. The Effects of Potato Pulp and Feeding Level of Supplements on Digestibility, *in situ* Forage Degradation and Ruminal Fermentation in Beef Steers. Animal Science Journal 77, 587-594.

Szasz, J.I., Hunt, C.W., Turgeon, O. A., Szasz, Jr. P. A. and Johnson, K.A., 2005. Effects of Pasteurization of Potato Slurry by-product Fed in Corn-or Barley Based Beef Finishing Diets J. Anim. Science 83: 2806-2814.

Tawila, M.A., Omer, H.A.A and Gad, Sawsan M., 2008. Partial Replacing of Concentrate Feed Mixture by Potato Processing Waste in Sheep Rations. American-Eurasian Journal of Agricultural & Environmental Science 4 (2): 156-164.

Van Soest, P.J., Robertson, J.B. and Lewis, B.A., 1991. Methods for Dietary Fiber, Neutral Detergent Fiber and Non-starch Polysaccharides in relation to Animal Performance. Journal of Dairy Science 74: 3583-3597.

Van't Klooster, A.T., 1986. Pathological Aspects of Rumen Fermentation. In: New Developments and Future Perspectives in Research on Rumen Function (Neimann-Sorensen, A., Ed). Commission of the European Communities, Luxembourg, 259-276 (C.F Gado et al., 1998).

10

Effect of FYM, Vermicompost, Vermiwash and NPK Treatments on Growth, Microbial Biomass C and Yield of Soybean

Mahendra Singh, *India*
Narendra Kumar, *India*
K.K. Sharma, *India*

ABSTRACT

A field experiments was conducted at the Crop Research Centre of G.B. Pant University of Agriculture and Technology, Pantnagar during kharif season 2006 and 2007 to study the effect of nutrient management in soybean (Glycine max. L. Merrill)" on its nodulation, growth and yield on cultivar PS- 1347. The experiment was laid out in randomized block design (RBD) with three replications. The application of FYM @ 5 t /ha, vermicompost @ 2.5t /ha and vermiwash @ 10 per cent in combitions with 50 per cent NPK showed superiority for nodule number and dry weight per plant, shoots dry weight, number of trifoliate, plant height, microbial biomass C, 100-seed weight and grain yield over the sole application of recommended NPK level in both years (2006 and 2007). The combined application of FYM @ 5 t /ha + VC @ 2.5 t /ha + V W @ 10 per cent + 50 per cent NPK recorded the highest nodule number (18.33, 49.00, 37.66: 33.66, 53.0, 35.66 per plant), nodule dry weight (142.41, 384.08, 235.42: 257.27, 304.0 mg per plant, respectively) But at 60 DAS in 2007-08 it was under FYM @ 5 t /ha + VC @ 2.5 t /ha + 50 per cent NPK. This treatment also gave maximum number of trifoliate (16.2, 32.0 and 34.0: 19.66, 41.0 and 38.0 per plant), plant height (44.3, 76 and 75.63: 51.53, 79.66 and 78.66 cm per plant) during 2006 and 2007, respectively.

All the applied treatment numerically increased microbial biomass C in comparison to recommended dose of NPK. The highest microbial biomass carbon (323.06 and 292.01 µg-1) at 50 per cent flowering stage than at harvesting stage (302.5 and 277.63 µg-1) due to the increase in microbial population of soil during the both years 2006 and 2007, respectively. The maximum grain yield (3209.87 and 3230.88 kg /ha, respectively) recorded under the combined application of FYM @ 5 t /ha + VC @ 2.5 t /ha + V W @ 10 per cent + 50 per cent NPK. However, 100-seed weight remained unaffected.

Key words: FYM, vermiwash, vermicompost, nodulation, soybean, microbial biomass C, yield)

Introduction

Soybean (*Glycine max* L. Merrill) is one of the most important oil seed crop of the world. It contain exceptionally high and well balanced protein (42-45%) and edible oil (20- 22%) with higher biological value, unsaturated fatty acids viz, linoleic fatty acid (19.4%) and amino acids argentine, aspartic acids glutamic acid, glycine, isolucine, lucine and valine etc.(Smith and Circle, 1972). Soybean requires high amount of nutrients due to its high yield potential. The crop removes a large quantity of nitrogen, phosphorus and potash. A good crop producing 6720 kg /ha biomass removes about 514 kg nitrogen, 480 kg phosphorus and 485 kg potash /ha (Nelson, 1989). In case of nitrogen, full nitrogen requirement is not met by symbiosis. However, ability of soybean plant for symbiotic nitrogen fixation (about 240-250 kg / ha) (Chandel *et al*., 1989). But it also gets reduced at seed development stage when requirement of nitrogen is maximum. Gracia and Hanway (1976) also reported that N, P and K fertilization of soybean during pod filling increased the yield up to 27 to 31 per cent. At higher rate of nitrogen, more protein has been synthesized and lipid metabolism favored.

Organic manures are known to improve physical, chemical and biological properties of soil. Because of their low nutrient content and slow acting nature, organic manures alone could not the nutritional requirement of crops and therefore, chemical fertilizers also have their own importance. Farm yard manure is the most widely used organic source. It serves as a source of plant nutrients and has important role in improving soil fertility and productivity. Earthworms significantly increase soil fertility and productivity by decomposing and converting organic waste into useful compost. Vermicompost is rich in NPK and is widely used now a days. There is a great scope to increase soybean production utilizing judicious combinations of organic and inorganic fertilizer in appropriate dose. This can counter balance the correct storage of costly fertilizers and provide sustainable fertile soil for plant growth. With these ideas, the above investigation was undertaken to study the effect of various sources of nutrients on the growth and yield of soybean.

Materials and Methods

An experiment was conducted in E-5 block of the Crop Research Centre of Govind Ballabh Pant University of Agriculture and Technology, Pantnagar, District Udham Singh Nagar, for two years during rainy season (*kharif*) 2006 and 2007 to study the effect of organic and inorganic sources of nutrients on soybean (PS 1347). The experimental soil was silty clay loam, well drained (pH 7.4), high in organic carbon (0.86%), medium in available phosphorus (19.19 kg /ha) and low in available potassium (130.71 kg /ha) and nitrogen (240.17 kg /ha) content. There were 16 treatments (Table 10.1) replicated thrice in randomized block design (RBD). NPK (20:60:40) through urea, single super phosphate and murate of potash, FYM and vermicompost were applied at the time of sowing and two sprays of vermiwash were given at 30 and 45 DAS. The microbial biomass C by Vance *et al.* (1987).

Thinning and gap filling was done wherever necessary to maintain optimum plant population. For recording observation on various growth parameters, five plants were randomly selected and labeled from each plot. Nodules were carefully separated from the washed roots and counted at 30, 60 and 90 DAS, nodule of each replication after counting were dried in open glass Petri dishes at 65 + 2°C for 48 hours in an oven till constant dry weight and shoot dry weight was recorded by taken five plants from sampling area of each plot after dry in shade than put in hot oven at 65 + 2°C for 48 hours and take the weight gram per plant at 30, 60 and 90 DAS, plant height and number of branches per plant were recorded at 30, 60 and 90 DAS. Standard procedure was adopted for these biometric observations. After threshing and proper cleaning the plot grain, yield of individual plot was recorded with single pan balance and converted into kg /ha and one sample of 100 grain was drawn from each replication and weighed, recorded as 100-grain weight.

Result and Discussion

Combined application of vermicompost, vermiwash and FYM along with recommended NPK was numerically better in terms of nodule number and their dry weight over the single application of different composts and NPK. The findings corroborate with the findings of Mahto and Yadav (2005) who reported that application of vermicompost (25 q /ha equivalence) and DAP (100 kg /ha equivalence) + foliar spray of vermiwash (10%) at 30 DAS

Table 10.1: Effect of FYM, Vermicompost, Vermiwash and Recommended NPK on Nodule Number and Dry Weight (mg plant^{-1}) of Soybean at 30, 60 and 90 DAS

Treatment	Nodule Number plant^{-1}						Nodule dry weight (mg plant^{-1})					
	Year (2006-07)			Year (2007-08)			Year (2006-07)			Year (2007-08)		
	30	60	90	30	60	90	30	60	90	30	60	90
NPK 100%	15.6	25.0	15.6	26.0	36.6	17.3	131.7	182.0	140.6	210.1	282.0	167.0
NPK 50%	15.0	30.0	21.3	28.0	33.0	23.3	135.0	206.5	181.7	244.03	273.1	153.6
FYM @ 10 t ha^{-1}	16.6	33.3	22.6	28.0	41.0	21.0	136.4	200.1	181.4	215.5	330.1	161.3
VC @ 5 t ha^{-1}	15.3	35.0	25.0	27.0	37.0	28.3	137.5	253.8	192.6	227.0	320.5	181.6
VW @ 10% (Two sprays at 30 and 45 DAS)	13.3	36.0	24.6	28.0	38.6	29.0	131.4	240.5	197.7	250.2	307.2	195.6
FYM @ 5 t ha^{-1} + VC @ 2.5 t ha^{-1}	17.0	45.3	34.3	28.3	39.0	24.6	138.9	370.5	211.8	256.3	370.5	138.6
FYM @ %t ha^{-1} +VW @10%	16.3	37.3	27.0	23.0	40.6	29.3	135.5	303.5	200.1	220.1	303.5	166.0
VC @2.5t ha^{-1} +VW @10%	15.6	32.0	20.0	28.3	40.6	27.3	130.0	363.8	145.0	200.4	363.8	164.0
FYM @ 5 t ha^{-1} + VC @ 2.5 t ha^{-1} + VW @ 10%	16.0	38.6	23.6	28.0	40.6	32.0	138.8	383.3	143.7	230.4	316.6	188.3
FYM @ 5 t ha^{-1} + VC @ 2.5 t ha^{-1} + NPK 50%	17.3	48.3	37.0	29.6	41.3	26.3	137.7	377.0	158.5	213.8	377.0	163.0
FYM @ 5 t ha^{-1} +VW@ 10% +50% NPK	14.3	41.6	31.6	26.0	41.0	28.3	130.7	292.0	219.0	215.2	292.0	238.0
VC @ 2.5 t ha^{-1} + VW@10% + 50% NPK	16.0	40.0	31.3	28.6	40.3	27.0	135.1	322.0	214.9	208.4	322.0	184.6
FYM@5tha^{-1} +VC @2.5tha^{-1} +VW@ 10% + 50% NPK	18.3	49.0	37.6	33.6	53.0	35.6	142.4	384.0	235.4	257.2	324.8	304.0
FYM @ 10 t ha^{-1} 50% NPK	17.3	48.6	36.6	29.3	40.3	32.3	137.2	372.2	234.5	205.1	372.2	251.6
VC @2.5tha^{-1} +50% NPK	16.6	41.0	33.3	30.0	49.0	28.3	136.0	342.0	228.7	213.5	342.0	233.3
VW@10% + 50% NPK	16.3	39.3	28.0	24.3	49.3	27.6	129.7	269.6	205.9	202.9	319.6	185.6
SEm (±)	6	2.68	1.92	2.17	2.24	1.95	9.5	2.48	9.06	7.42	4.13	20.72
CD (P=0.05)	NS	7.7	5.6	1.2	6.4	5.8	7.1	26.5	22.7	NS	59.8	55.6

increased nodule number per plant in vegetable pea by 23.6 per cent over the control. The maximum nodule number (Table 10.1) were found with the treatments of FYM @5 t /ha + VC @ 2.5 t /ha + VW @ 10 per cent + 50 per cent NPK at all growth stages (30, 60 and 90 DAS) it may be due to the improvement in the soil porosity and more availability of nutrients to the plant.

Application of FYM @5 t /ha +VC @ 2.5 t /ha + 50 per cent NPK numerically increased shoot dry weight at all the growth intervals of the soybean plant over the recommended dose of NPK. It may be due to the improvement in the soil porosity and more availability of nutrients to the crops for its growth and development. Khutate et al. (2005) observed that the application of 75 per cent NPK + 25 per cent vermicompost (5.76 q /ha) or FYM (50%) recorded the highest shoot dry weight per plant over the control. Shoot dry weight was increased with the advancement of plant age. This is the result of synthesis of more plant tissues due to more availability of N and P with the given treatments. In both the year (2006-07 and 2007-08) maximum shoot dry weight g per plant (Table 1) at all the growth stages except at 60 DAS in 2007 it was found in the treatment FYM @ 5 t /ha+ VC @ 2.5 t /ha+ VW @ 10 per cent +50 per cent NPK, it might be due to the improvement in the soil porosity and more availability of nutrients to the plant. These findings corroborate with Khutate et al. (2005) observed that the application of 75 per cent NPK + 25 per cent vermicompost (5.76 q /ha) or FYM (50%) recorded the highest shoot dry weight per plant over the control.

Addition of FYM @ 10 t /ha +50 per cent NPK numerically increased number of trifoliate leaves per plant and plant height (cm) over the recommended dose of 100 per cent and 50 per cent NPK, it might be due to the improvement in soil porosity, structure and nutrients concentration in soil for uptake by the plant. Similarly, a field experiment conducted at Pantnagar on integrated nutrient management in soybean cv. PK-416 and maximum numbers of branches per plant were in recorded with the application of FYM @ 10 t /ha with recommended dose of NPK /ha which showed the essentiality of nitrogen for better growth of the crop (AICRP on Soybean, 1999). The maximum number of trifoliate leaves and plant height cm (Table 10.2) at all the growth intervals during the both year (2006 and 2007) recorded by the application of FYM @ 5 t /ha+ VC @ 2.5 t /ha+ VW @ 10 per cent +50 per cent NPK, it might be due to the improvement in the soil porosity and more availability of nutrients to the plant.

The microbial biomass is positively related with microbial biomass carbon. The microbial biomass carbon in soil at 50 per cent flowering stage was more in comparison to the harvesting stage, which might be due to the fact and

Table 10.2: Effect of FYM, Vermicompost, Vermiwash and Recommended NPK on Number of Trifoliate Leaves Plant^{-1} of Soybean at 30, 60 and 90 DAS

Treatment	Number of Trifoliate Leaves Plant^{-1}						Plant Height (cm)					
	Year (2006-07)			Year (2007-08)			Year (2006-07)			Year (2007-08)		
	30	60	90	30	60	90	30	60	90	30	60	90
NPK 100%	11.2	24	25.33	9.33	29.66	28.66	31.46	66.33	69.42	31.16	67.66	69
NPK 50%	12	26.66	28	11	31	31.66	33.26	68.16	68.25	31.93	68.5	71
FYM @ 10 t ha^{-1}	12.66	24.66	25.66	9.66	29.33	30.66	31.46	70.03	70.98	33.9	72.2	71.33
VC @ 5 t ha^{-1}	14	27	29	10.33	39.66	33.66	37.86	68.16	69.78	41.13	72.23	71.33
VW @ 10% (Two sprays at 30 and 45 DAS)	11.33	22	20	12	32.33	33	36.03	72.33	69.25	37.46	67.4	69.66
FYM @ 5 t ha^{-1} + VC @ 2.5 t ha^{-1}	14.1	30	31.66	9	33.66	31	41.38	75.03	75.03	39.6	71.7	75
FYM @ %t ha^{-1} +VW @10%	14.66	26.33	28	11.66	33	33	36.03	70.4	73.03	40.44	73.2	68.66
VC @2.5t ha^{-1} +VW @10%	14	24.03	26.66	12.33	40.33	33.66	37.83	72.06	70.69	32.53	70.03	66.66
FYM @ 5 t ha^{-1} + VC @ 2.5 t ha^{-1} + VW @ 10%	13.66	24.33	26	10	39.66	33.33	31.66	67.03	68.33	39.98	69.63	73
FYM @ 5 t ha^{-1} + VC @ 2.5 t ha^{-1} + NPK 50%	13.66	29	30.66	12	34.33	33.33	41.78	72.3	71.96	45.53	70.73	71.66
FYM @ 5 t ha^{-1} +VW@10% +50% NPK	12.66	29.33	30.33	13.66	36	36	35.5	63.56	70.6	46.4	72.2	70.33
VC @ 2.5 t ha^{-1} + VW@10% + 50% NPK	12.66	24.33	25.66	13.33	37	35	33.16	69.33	69.18	48.53	71.16	66.33
FYM@5tha^{-1} +VC @2.5tha^{-1} +VW@ 10% + 50% NPK	16.2	32	34	19.66	41	38	44.36	76	75.63	51.53	79.66	78.66
FYM @ 10 t ha^{-1} 50% NPK	15	30.66	29.33	17	39	34.33	39.66	73.33	70.12	50.66	76	70.33
VC @2.5tha^{-1} +50% NPK	13	26	28	15.33	39.66	35.33	37.7	69.66	69.7	44.76	72.33	73.33
VW@10% + 50% NPK	12.33	25	27	16.66	37.33	34.66	37.99	68.13	70.02	51.4	71.9	72.66
SEm (±)	2.34	1.89	1.51	1.60	2.92	1.78	2.13	3.42	2.43	42.40	2.09	2.82
CD (P=0.05)	NS	5.56	4.48	4.64	8.45	5.23	6.26	NS	NS	122.61	6.05	8.25

addition of FYM and vermicompost in soil microbial number and activity increased due to more available carbon and nutrients like, N and P to soil microorganisms which have synthesized more cellular components and provided more energy, later on the nutrients were exhausted by soil microorganisms and crop plant and reduced the microbial biomass in soil. This finding is supported by Wang Yan *et al*. (1998) who reported that soil microbial biomass increased greatly after application of organic manures at beginning of experiment and thereafter the biomass C decreased. The maximum microbial biomass carbon (Table 10.3) at both the stages was recorded with the application of FYM @ 5 t /ha + VC @ 2.5 t /ha+ VW @ 10 per cent +50 per cent NPK during both year (2006 and 2007), it might be due to the improvement in the soil physical properties like soil structure, aeration, porosity and structure, and more availability of nutrients concentration in soil to the plant. Similarly, Manna *et al*. (2001) and Ghosh *et al*. (2002) have reported that application of enriched compost significantly increased soil microbial biomass C in soil.

Combined application of FYM and vermicompost along with recommended dose of NPK maximum increased seed yield of soybean over the alone application of composts. This may be due to the improvement in soil physical and biological properties of soil. These findings corroborate with Bachhav and Sabale (1996) who conducted an field experiment in 1993-94 at Pune, Maharashtra, soybean cv. MACS 124 were given 50 kg N/ha as urea, FYM, Vermicompost, or 50 per cent urea + 50 per cent FYM, VC. Seed yield (3.29 t/ha) was highest with 50 per cent each of urea and FYM. The maximum grain yield (Table 10.3) of soybean (kg /ha) recorded with the treatment of FYM @ 5 t /ha + VC @2.5 t /ha + VW @ 10 per cent + 50 per cent NPK in both years (2006-07 and 2007-08). This may be due to the improvement in soil physical and biological properties of soil. These findings corroborate with (Thomas and Lal., 2003) who observed that application of farm compost + poultry manure or vermicompost in combination with inorganic fertilizers showed synergistic effect on the growth of the crop (Soybean-Mustered-Cowpea) and showed increased in the yield attributes of crops during 1997 to 1998. Application of different treatments did not affect the 100-seed weight of soybean.

Therefore the productivity of soybean can be increased with the use of any of the organic sources of nutrients used along with recommended NPK fertilization.

Table 10.3: Effect of Nutrient Management on Microbial Biomass C (μ g g^{-1}soil) at 50% Flowering and at Harvest and Yield of Soybean

Treatment	Year (2006-07)		Year (2007-08)		Year (2006-07)		Year (2007-08)	
	50% Flowering	At Harvest	50% Flowering	At Harvest	GY (kg ha^{-1})	100-Seed Wt. (gm)	GY (kg ha^{-1})	100-Seed Wt. (gm)
NPK 100%	255.5	245.5	256.3	262.9	2716.0	9.9	2213.0	10.6
NPK 50%	283.8	278.1	267.2	263.2	2870.3	10.1	2938.1	10.5
FYM @ 10 t ha^{-1}	289.2	279.4	274.4	275.5	2839.5	10.1	2868.0	10.7
VC @ 5 t ha^{-1}	282.9	271.6	265.7	261.8	2962.9	10.1	2757.6	10.5
VW @ 10% (Two sprays at 30 and 45 DAS)	281.3	270.6	268.9	268.5	2406.1	10.1	2878.3	11.0
FYM @ 5 t ha^{-1} ÷ VC @ 2.5 t ha^{-1}	308.1	298.3	271.5	270.3	2870.3	10.4	2810.6	10.7
FYM @ %t ha^{-1} +VW @10%	278.1	270.3	278.2	264.1	2641.9	10.0	2572.3	11.0
VC @2.5t ha^{-1} +VW @10%	304.0	269.7	283.3	260.0	2993.8	9.9	2533.2	11.3
FYM @ 5 t ha^{-1} + VC @ 2.5 t ha^{-1} + VW @ 10%	303.5	297.5	282.9	266.7	2832.0	10.1	3127.3	11.5
FYM @ 5 t ha^{-1} + VC @ 2.5 t ha^{-1} + NPK 50%	323.0	280.6	274.6	274.1	3024.6	10.5	2931.2	10.5
FYM @ 5 t ha^{-1} +VW@10% +50% NPK	305.6	296.6	261.5	266.1	2637.0	10.7	2912.1	11.0
VC @ 2.5 t ha^{-1} + VW@10% + 50% NPK	280.6	270.2	273.0	267.4	3024.6	10.3	2748.1	10.9
FYM@5tha^{-1} +VC @2.5tha^{-1} +VW@ 10% + 50% NPK	308.2	302.5	292.0	277.6	3209.8	10.5	3230.8	11.5
FYM @ 10 t ha^{-1} 50% NPK	305.4	298.2	273.2	268.6	2746.9	10.2	2815.1	8.2
VC @2.5tha^{-1} +50% NPK	283.5	275.1	273.5	265.9	2962.9	10.1	2859.2	8.4
VW@10% + 50% NPK	291.4	282.1	265.2	264.6	2685.1	10.1	2858.4	11.3
SEm (±)	7.54	2.61	7.93	5.33	167.2	0.29	165.9	0.86
CD (P=0.05)	22.9	7.6	22.9	15.3	470.7	0.8	486.3	2.5

REFERENCES

Bachhav, P. R. and Sabale, R.N. 1996. Effect of Different Sources of Nitrogen on Growth Parameters, Yield and Quality of Soybean. *Maharashtra Agric.* Uni. 21(2): 244-247.

Chandel, A.S.; Pandey, K.N. and Saxena, S.C. 1989. Symbiotic Nitrogen Benefits by Nodulated Soybean (*Glycine max* (L.) Merrill.) to Interplanted Crops in Northern India. Trop. Agric., 66(1): 73-77.

Ghosh, P.K.; Manna, M.C.; Chaudhry, R.S. and Acharaya, C. L. 2002. Effectiveness of Application of Phosphocompost on Groundnut in Vertisol of Central India. *Internatational Arachis Newsletter*. 21: 51-53.

Gracia, R. and Hanway, J.J. 1976. Foliar Fertilization of Soybean during the Seed Filling Period. *Agronomy* J. 68: 653-657.

Khutate, N.G.; Mendhe, S.N.; Dongarkar, K. P.; Gudadhe, N. N. and Gavande, V.H. 2005. Effect on Nutrient Management Treatments on Growth and Yield of Soybean. *J. Soils* and *Crop*. 15(2): 411-414.

Manna, M.C.; Hajara, J.N. and Singh, A. B. 2001. Comparative Effectiveness of Enriched Phosphor-compost and Chemical Fertilizer on Crop Yields and Soil Biological Activity in Alluvial Soil. Indian J. Agric. Sci.35 (4): 247- 250.

Matho, T.P and Yadav, R.P. 2005. Effect of Vermicompost Alone and in Combination with Chemical Fertilizer on Stem Fly Incidence and Yield Attributes in Vegetable Peas Under Bihar Conditions. *J. Applied Zoological Res*. 16(1): 70-72.

Nelson, W.L. 1989. Determining Soybean Fertility Needs. *Soybean World Research Conference*. 4(1): 615-620.

Smith, Allan, K. and Circle, Sidnay, J. 1972. Soybean: Chemistry and Technology, V-1 (Proteins), pp. 93-143.

Thomas, A. and Lal, R. B. 2003. Stratagies for INM Technology in Sustainable Edapho Cultivar Management for a Legume Based Cropping System for the Inceptisols in the NEPZ. *Crop Res. Hissar* 26(1): 33-41.

Vance, E.D.; Brookes, P. C. and Jenkinson, D. S. 1987. An Extraction Method for Measuring Soil Microbial Biomass Carbon. *Soils Biol. Biochem*. 19: 678-680.

Wang-Yan.; Shen, O.; Shi-Rwhi.; Wang, Y.; Shne, Q. R and Shi, R. H. 1998. Change in Soil Microbial Biomass, Carbon, Nitrogen and Phosphorous and the Nitrogen Transformation after Application of Organic and Inorganic Fertilizers. *Acta- Pedologica-Sinica*. 35(2): 227-234.

11

Metals and Organochlorine Insecticides (HCH, DDT) Pollution in Water of Lake Nainital (Uttarakhand), India

Rashmi Yadav, *India*

ABSTRACT

The aim of this study is to assess the extent of organochlorine insecticides and heavy metal contamination of lake water of Naini lake. Samples of water for heavy metals and insecticides have been analysed for five heavy metals, viz. Fe, Zn, Cu, Mn and Cd using atomic absorption spectrophotometry. The results show the presence of some of the heavy metals in lake water surface in higher concentrations.

Keywords: Heavy metals, lake water, insecticides, water pollution.

Introduction

Nainital district is situated at southern extremity of lesser Himalayan zone in Kumaun region of Uttaranchal state, India. Lake Nainital is a natural kidney shaped; it is the heart of city Nainital. The lake Nainital is warm monomictic type situated at 39°22′49″ N latitude & 79°32′79″ E longitude in lesser Kumaun Himalayan region. The maximum and minimum depths of the lake are 26 and 18 m respectively, and their catchments areas comprise a large population of about 50,000 inhabitants with an additional load of 5000 tourists per day.

Heavy metals today have a great ecological significance due to their toxicity and accumulation. These elements, contrary to most pollutants, are not biodegradable and undergo a global eco-biological cycle in which natural waters are the main pathways. (Nurnberge, 1984).

Lakes are used as sources of drinking water for the local people. Industrial effluents, burning fossil fuels, animal and human excretions and geologic weathering and domestic waste contribute metal pollution load in to the water bodies (Moore and Ramana Moorthy, 1984; Adnano, 1986). Scavenging of pollutants from water and aquatic sediments is extremely costly and technically challenging (International Joint Commission) as the concentration and variety of persistence toxins is serious and escalating. In accordance with that water management plan have recently initiated to focus on preventing pollutants from entering the aquatic bodies rather than on cleanup technologies (International Joint Commission).

The extensive use of organochlorine insecticides has led to human health hazard as well as to deteriorate in environment quality. Several studies were conducted on organochlorine insecticides contaminated in lakes and water reservoirs from different part of the world (Kucklick *et al*., 1994, Tanabe *et al*., 1983). Few investigation have assessed organochlorine residues in water reservoir in India e.q. drinking water in Lucknow (Kaphalia *et al*., 1988), Pond at Khuda Alisher, Chandigarh (Jindal and Singh 1989). Jal mahal Lake of Jaipur (Kumar *et al*., 1988). In Ganga water (Halder *et al*., 1989, 1990).

The water quality of lake has also been considerably changed due to toxic metal and organochlorine insecticides pollution. In the background of lake utility and its importance at national level, such study is essential which is focused on toxic metal and organochlorine insecticides pollution of the lake.

Materials and Methods

Four 500 ml water samples from lake were collected in clean glass bottles by immersing them about 35 cm below the surface of water during the months of April, August, and December 2004. All samples stored in the refrigerator at 4°C.

The extraction of DDT and HCH from samples collected from Nainital lake was carried out as reported earlier (Agarwal *et al*. 1986).

Water samples were filtered using Whatman filter paper No. 1.25 ml water was extracted three times with 50 ml n-Hexane for 10 minutes in a separating funnel and upper n- Haxane layer was pooled and concentrated to 1 ml using vortex evaporator. The concentrated extract was cleaned with anhydrous sodium sulphate- alumina column eluted with in hexane- benzene (40:60). The elunt was evaporated on a vortex evaporator and kept 4°C in refrigerator until analysis. Samples were analysed for HCH and DDT residue on Hewlett Packard 5980 gas chromatograph fitted with Ni 63 electron capture detector on fused silica capillary TM 5 column PTE Spelco Crop. U.S.A. Nitrogen was used as a carrier gas. The injector, oven and detector temperatures were set at 210, 190 and 220°C respectively all the five water samples were analyzed and their mean value was calculated for the determination of insecticides in the lake. The detection of DDT was 0.1 ng while HCH was 0.2 ng. The correlations between two variables were calculated by Carl Pearson method.

For metal analysis we took 100 ml water samples from the lake and collected in clean seven polyethylene bottles, samples were collected randomly and preserve through HNO3 and filtered using Whatman filter paper No.1. All samples stored in the refrigerator at 4°C until analysis. Five metals (Fe, Mn, Cd, Zn and Cu) were detected through Atomic Absorption Spectrophotometer (AAS 4129 model).

Result and Discussion

Residual level of HCH and DDT in Lake Nainital study given in Table 11.1 and Table 11.2. HCH residue in lake Nainital in months of April, August and December and value ranged from 2.181-4.722 μg/L, 2.87-5.395 μg/L and 3.409-4.866 μg/L respectively. August and December months were similar with slightly higher value in August 4.186μg/L. γ HCH was maximum in August and December while β HCH was maximum in April month. αHCH represented maximum in the month of August.

Table 11.1: HCH Concentration in Water from Lake Nainital

Mean Concentration ug/l				
Seasons	α-HCH	β-HCH	γ- HCH	Total HCH
April	0.633 (.0560-1.252)	0.633 (1.925-2.980)	0.356 (0.200-0.490)	3.452 (2.181-4.722)
August	1.192 (0.950-1.340)	1.133 (0.795-1.328)	1.861 (1.125-2.727)	4.186 (2.87-5.395)
December	0.447 (0.415-0.490)	1.620 (1.138-2.232)	2.027 (1.856-2.144)	4.094 (3.409-4.866)

Maximum residual level of DDT was found in lake Nainital in month of August (32.146 μg/L). ppDDE was found maximum in April (6.126μg/L). ppDDT and ppDDD were recorded maximum in August (19.154μg/L and 11.246μg/L) respectively.

Table 11.2: DDT Concentration in Water from Lake Nainital

Mean Concentration ug/l					
Seasons	pp DDE	opDDT	ppDDT	ppDDD	Total DDT
April	6.126 (5.280-6.985)	ND	1.732 (0.800-2.832)	6.231 (4.920-7.456)	14.089 (11.000-17.273)
August	1.746 (1.280-2.240)	ND	19.154 (15.100-23.218)	11.246 (9.560-13.207)	32.146 (25.84-38.665)
December	3.863 (3.527-4.220)	ND	7.155 (7.850-10.456)	2.708 (1.890-3.485)	13.726 (13.267-18.161)

Contamination of organochloride insecticide was found in the samples collected during the month of August while minimum level was recorded for the samples of April. Nainital lake are surrounded by small agricultural farms in hills and illegal use of DDT is quite common in agricultural farming thereby resulting in very high DDT contamination in the lake. Kumar *et al.* (1988) have found higher concentrations of organochlorine insecticides residues during Sepetember/October and slighter lower concentrations during March in the two lakes of Jaipur.

Result of present study indicates a moderate level of contamination of the lake with HCH residues and moderate to high level of contamination with DDT residue. The average total HCH residues varied within a small range; seasonal variation being more dominant as the spatial distribution was rather uniform. The variation was comparatively large in case of total DDT, with both seasonal as well as spatial variations being observed. Nayak et al. (1995) have found that many water samples from Ganga river exceeded the safe limit and Bakre *et al*. (1990) reported that almost all samples in Mahala water reservoir were above the maximum permissible limit for DDT and HCH.

Table 11.3: Total Metal Analysis Depth Wise in Nainital Lake Water Samples

	Depth	Mn (mg/l)	Cd (mg/l)	Fe (mg/l)	Zn (mg/l)	Cu (mg/l)
1.	01 m	22.54	.022	1.10	0.14	0.35
2.	03 m	21.10	.018	0.71	0.12	0.29
3.	05 m	18.26	.016	0.62	0.11	0.26
4.	07 m	17.23	.014	0.58	0.09	0.25
5.	09 m	16.47	.013	0.45	0.06	0.20
6.	14 m	13.65	.013	0.32	0.06	0.18
7.	18 m	13.87	.010	0.30	0.04	0.17

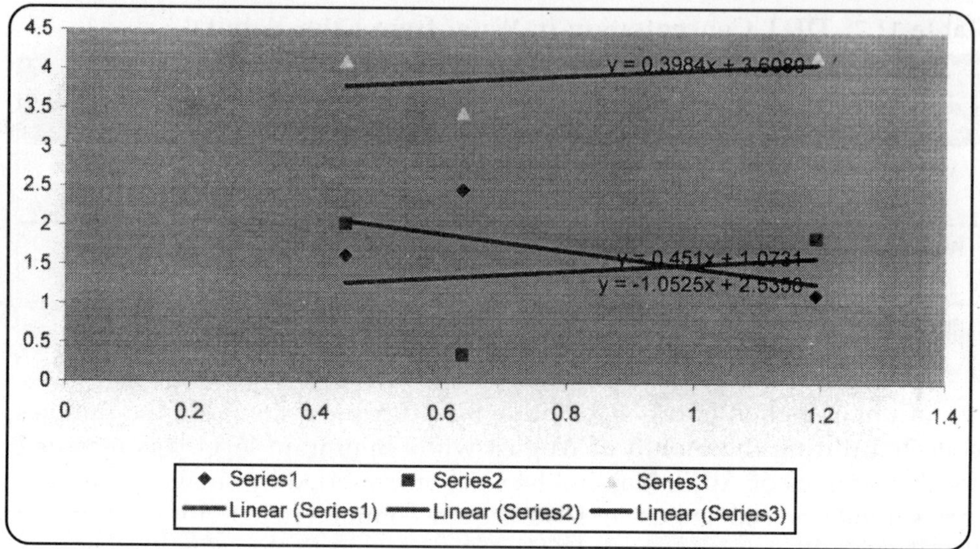

Fig. 11.1

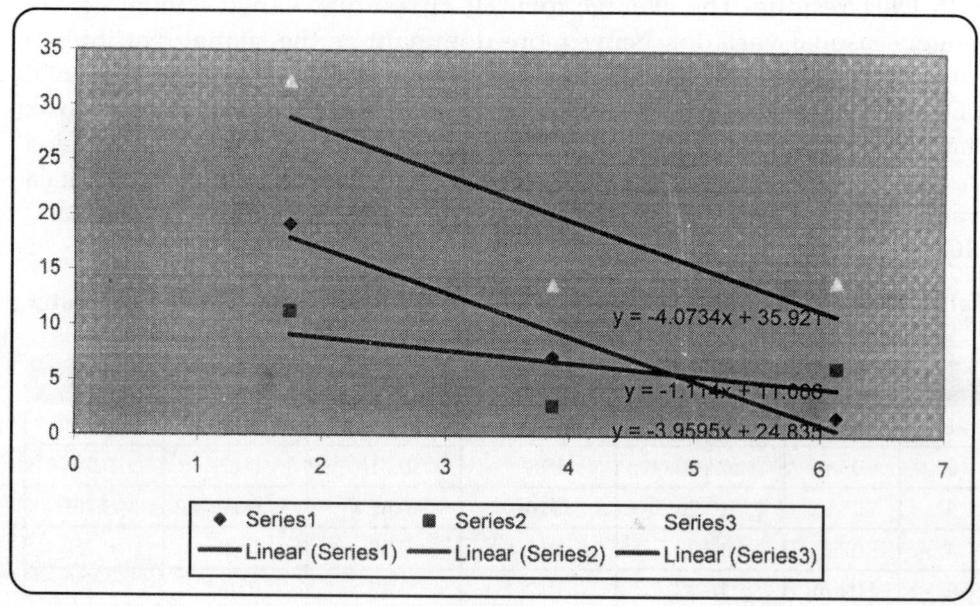

Fig. 11.2

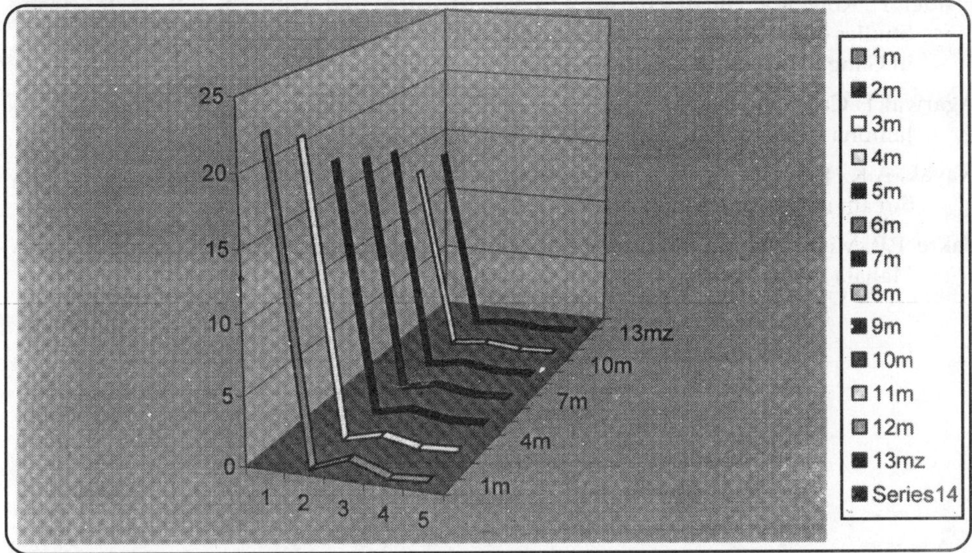

Fig. 11.3

REFERENCES

Adnano, D.C. (1986), Trace Metal in the Environment. New York: *Springer Verlag*.

Moore, J.W., Ramana Moorthy, S. (1984), Heavy metals in natural waters. New York: Springer Verlag.

Nurnberg, H.W. (1984), The Voltametric Approach in Trace Metal Chemistry of Natural Waters and Atmospheric Precipitation. *Anal Chem Acta*, 164: 1-21.

International Joint Commission (1991), Persistence Toxic Substances: Virtually Eliminating Inputs to the Great Lakes, *IJC*, Ottawa.

International Joint Commission, (1992), Sixth Biennial Report on Great Lakes Water Quality, *IJC*, Ottawa.

Kucklick JR, Bidleman TF, MeConnell LL, Walla MD, Ivanov GP (1994), Organochlorines in Water and Biota of Lake Baikal, Siberia. *Environ Sci Technol*. 28: 31-37.

Tanabe S, Hidaka H, Tatsukawa R (1983), PCBs and Chlorinated Hydrocarbon Pesticides in Antartic Atmosphere and Hydrosphere. *Chemosphere*, 12: 277-288.

Kaphalia, B.S., Bhargava, S.K., Nigam, U. and Seth, T.D.(1988), Contamination of water with organochlorine pesticides residue in Srinagar. *Ind. J. Environ. Prot*. 8: 326-329.

Jindal, A. and Singh,J. (1989), Toxicity of Pesticides to the Productivity of Fresh Water Pond. *India J. Environ. Hlth*., 31(3): 257-261.

Kumar, S.L., Lal, R. and Bhatnagar, P. (1988), Residue of Organochlorine Insecticides in Two Lakes of Jaipur, *Water, Air, Soil Pollut*. 42: 57-65.

Halder, P., Raha, P., Bhattacharya, P., Chowdhary, A. and Adityachaudhary, N. (1989), Studies on the Residues of DDT and Endosulfan Occurring in Ganga Water. *Indian J. Environ. Hlth*. 31 (2): 156-161.

Halder, P., Kole, R.K., Bhattacharya, A., Chowdhary, A. and Adityachaudhary, N. (1990), Studies on the Residues of BHC Isomers (alpha-, beta-, Gamma- and delta-) Occurring in Ganga Water. *Poll. Res*. 9: 51-56.

Agarwal, H.C., Mittal, P.K., Menon, K.B. and Pillai, M.K.K. (1986), DDT Residue in the River Jamuna in Delhi, India. *Water Air Soil Pollut*. 28: 89-104.

Nayak, A.K., Raha, R. and Das, A.K. (1995), Organochlorine Pesticide Residue in Middle Stream of Ganga River, India. *Bull. Environ. Contam. Toxicol*. 54: 68-75.

Bakre, P.P., Mishra, V. and Bhatnagar, P. (1990), Organochlorine Residues in Water from the Mahala Water Reservoir, Jaipur India. *Environ. Pollut*. 63: 275-281.

12

Rhizobacteria
A Boon to Environmental Concern

Shailesh Joshi, ***India***
A. Bohra, ***India***
Amir Khan, ***India***

ABSTRACT

Extensive application of chemical fertilizers and pesticides have overwhelmed our aquatic bodies and pushed many species to the verge of extinction. Moreover many eco-friendly efforts have been put forward to resolve this issue, including the use of microorganisms for degradation of xenobiotic pesticides and as biofertilizers. Rhizospheric organisms are best suited to be used as biofertilizers as they are native to the niche. Rhizospheric bacteria that augment the plant growth are referred as Plant Growth Promoting Rhizobacteria or PGPR, are sought as one of the best means to reduce the flooding of chemicals to aquatic bodies. Phosphate solubilizing microorganisms (PSMs) are also a part of rhizobacterial population that can solubilize the insoluble forms of phosphate and make them available for plant uptake, thereby reducing the application of phosphate fertilizers. Another category of rhizobacteria can fix environmental nitrogen reducing the need of nitrogen fertilizers. Some of the PGPRs are also able to function as biocontroling agents, which could be a potential means of reducing application of pesticides. Rhizospheric population has an excellent potential to save the mother earth.

Key words: Xenobiotic, Rhizobacteria, PGPR, PSM

Introduction

India is the seventh largest country in the world, with a total land area of 3,287,263 sq. km. (1,269,219 sq. miles). A change in land use pattern implies variation in the proportion of area under different land uses at a point in two or more time periods. Over the past fifty years, while India's total population increased by about three times, the total area of land under cultivation increased by only 20.2 per cent (from 118.75 Mha. in 1951 to 141.89 Mha. in 2005-06). Most of this expansion has taken place at the expense of forest and grazing land. Despite fast expansion of the area under cultivation, less agricultural land is available on per capita basis. Direct consequences of agricultural development on the environment arise from intensive farming activities, which contribute to soil erosion, land salination and loss of nutrients. The introduction of Green Revolution in the country has been accompanied by over-exploitation of land and water resources and excessive usage of fertilizers and pesticides. (MOEF, 2009).

Moreover Intensive agriculture is an inevitable menace around the globe that have generated various negative side effects on the agro-ecosystem and the environment such as pollution and soil degradation. Various nations all around the world framed policies and laws to ensure sustainable agriculture and better environment. The policies aim to sustain productivity and conserve environmental quality of soil and water, reduce pollution and other environmentally harmful effects, recycle organic resources, and produce safe foods. Rhizospheric bacteria can play an important role in proper implementation of eco-friendly policies of various nations.

Plant growth promoting rhizobacteria or PGPR benefit plants through different mechanisms of action including production of secondary metabolites such as antibiotic, cyanide and hormone like substance, production of siderophores, antagonism to soil born root pathogens, phosphate solubilizaion and dinitrogen fixation (Dubeikovsky *et al.*, 1993; Leong, 1986) among them anagonistic attributes could be exploited to develop biocontroling agent and direct plant growth promotion attributes could be used for developing fertilizers. Moreover many efferots have been made to develop biocontroling agents and biofertilizers however need of better performers is always there.

Need of Enhancing Nitrogen Bioavailability

Molecular nitrogen (N_2) is the major component (approximately 80%) of the earth's atmosphere. The element nitrogen is an essential part of many of the chemical compounds, such as proteins and nucleic acids, which are the basis of all life forms. However, N_2 cannot be used directly by biological systems to build the chemicals required for growth and reproduction. Before its incorporation into a living system, N_2 must first be combined with the element hydrogen. This process of reduction of N_2, commonly referred to as "nitrogen fixation" (N-fixation) may be accomplished chemically or biologically. (Hubbell and Kidder; 2003)

It is estimated that BNF on a global scale may reach a value of 175 million metric tons of nitrogen fixed per year. The amount of nitrogen fixed in any given situation would depend upon the environmental conditions and the nature of biological system(s) present which are capable of nitrogen fixation. (Zaharan, 1999) For particular situations, nitrogen fixation rates may vary from barely detectable to several hundred kilograms per hectare per year. The significance of the contribution of any BNF system to the nitrogen economy in any situation is a function of the supply and demand of the biological community for nitrogen. (Hubbell and Kidder; 2003)

Along with BNF the Synthetic N fertilizer input into global agricultural systems increased by approximately 430 per cent (~19 to ~82 Tg N) from 1965 to 1998. (Mosier, 2002). The forecast for world nitrogen fertilizer demand to increase at an annual rate of about 1.4 per cent until 2011/2012, which is an overall increase of 7.3 million tonnes. About 69 per cent tonnes of this growth will take place in Asia. (Hubbell and Kidder; 2003).

Moreover Fertilizer N use efficiency remains relatively low. Globally fertilizer N use efficiency was approximately 50 per cent in 1996. Since fertilizer N is not used efficiently in most parts of the world, N use in excess of crop potential utilization leads to losses to the environment through volatilization and leaching. These N losses result in N fertilization of pristine terrestrial and aquatic systems through NHx and NO_y deposition and contribute to global greenhouse gases through N_2O production and local elevated ozone concentrations due to NOx emission. Inefficient use of N and energy is exacerbated by the global inequity of use distribution. (Mosier, 2002)

The world's largest consumers of nitrogen are East Asia, South Asia, North America and West Europe. While their share of global consumption is modest, it is forecast that the relative contribution of Latin America and East Europe and Central Asia (EECA) to change in nitrogen use will be 10.4 per cent and 5 per cent respectively. The relative contribution to change in world nitrogen consumption by East Asia and South Asia is expected to be about 65 per cent.(Hubbell and Kidder; 2003)

Which will make the scenario worst for environment in south Asian countries including India, thus it became imperative for countries like us to employ biofertilizers to save natural environment of world.

Need of Enhancing Phosphorus Bioavailability

Phosphorus (P) is the second most important plant nutrient after nitrogen. However, most Phosphorus in soil (up to 95-99%) is part of insoluble compounds, which makes P unavailable for plant nutrition (Corona et al.; 1996). In order to increase crop yields, mineral phosphate fertilizers are regularly incorporated into the soil. However, immediately after fertilizer application is done, most of the applied phosphorus transforms into an insoluble form (Pundarikakshudu,, 1989). As a result, most P in the soil is found in poorly soluble, highly stable forms with limited availability to plants. Only 5 per cent or less of the total amount of P in soil is available for plant nutrition (Boronin, 1998). The vicious cycle continues as such low bioavailability of P requires regular application of phosphate-based fertilizers (Omar, 1998). According to assessments made by the experts from the U.S. Geological Survey and the International Association of Fertilizer Producers, the demand for fertilizers over the next 5 years will increase by 2.5-3 per cent annually (Gilbert, 2009). At such rate of phosphate consumption, all global phosphate resources would be exhausted within 100-125 years (Gilbert, 2009). Taking into account the long-term increase in demand for P and phosphate production, peaking in 20 years, the importance of partial P recycling continues to grow. Recovering phosphates from livestock waste is one of the examples of reusing P for agriculture (Gilbert, 2009). Other ways to control the wastage of phosphate resources include reducing P run-off into the oceans.

Considering the anticipated food production crisis as it relates to phosphate deficit in the future, efforts to study and apply microbiological phosphate solubilization processes are well justified. Phosphate solubilizing Microorganisms (PSM) play an important role in plant nutrition and growth promotion, especially when phosphate fertilizers are used extensively for long periods of time. It has been proven that agricultural application of PSM boosts crop yields (Khan *et al.*; 2007). On the other hand, soil activity depends on the activity of phosphate solubilizing bacteria. P solubilization mechanisms include acid formation, chelating metal ions and exchange reactions. The most active among PSM are genera: *Aspergillus, Penicillium, Curvularia*, and phosphate-solubilizing yeast, which is more active in solubilizing phosphates than bacteria.

In soil with low P bioavailability, free-living phosphate-solubilizing bacteria may release phosphate ions from sparingly soluble inorganic and organic P compounds in soil (Kucey, et al.; 1989), and thereby contribute with an increased soil phosphate pool (Smith & Read, 1997). The inorganic form of P may be held firmly in crystal lattices of largely insoluble forms, and may also be chemically bonded to the surface of clay minerals and unavailable to plants. Organic P is also largely unavailable to plants until it is converted to an inorganic form, by phosphate-solubilizing bacteria. Soluble P entering the soil after mineralization by such bacteria results in localized and short-term increases in the concentration of phosphate ions in the soil solution, which AM fungal hyphae and subsequently plants may benefit from. Organic P may be mineralized by bacteria that secrete phosphatases whereas inorganic P may be released by bacteria that excrete organic acids (Smith & Read, 1997).

Conclusion

The ever increasing demand for fertilizers is a manifestation of the increasing poplation and its demand. The indiscriminate use of fertilizers is needed to be reduced with increasing use of biofertilizers. Research toward exploring or creating better bioinoculant needed to be accelerated.

REFERENCES

Arvin R. Mosier, 2002. Environmental Challenges Associated with Needed Increases in Global Nitrogen Fixation. *Nutrient Cycling in Agroecosystems* 63,(2-3), 101-116, DOI: 10.1023/A:1021101423341

Boronin, A.M. (1998) Rhizosphere Bacteria of the Genus Pseudomonas Enabling Plant Growth and Development. *Sorovsky Educational Magazine*, 10, 25-31.

Corona, M.E.P., Klundert, I.V.D. and Verhoeven, J.T.A. (1996) Availability of Organic and Inorganic Phosphorus Compounds as Phosphorus Sources for Carex Species. New *Phytologist*, 133(2), 225-231.

Dubeikovsky, A. N.; Mordukhova, E. A.; V. V. Kochetkov, F. Y.; Polikarpova, and A. M. Boronin. 1993. Growth Promotion of Blackeurrant Softwood Cuttings by Recombinant Strain *Pseudomonas fluorescens* BSP53a Synthesizing in Increased Amount of Indole-3-acetic Acid. Soil. Biol. Biochem. 25: 1277-1281.

Gilbert, N. (2009) Environment: The disappearing nutrient. *Nature*, 461(7265), 716-718.

Hubbell, D.H.and Kidder, Gerald, 2003. Biological Nitrogen Fixation, Series of Fact Sheets of the Soil and Water Science Department, Florida Cooperative Extension Service, Institute of Food and Agricultural Sciences, University of Florida.

Khan, M.S., Zaidi, A. and Wani, P.A. (2007) Role of Phosphate-solubilizing Microorganisms in Sustainable Agriculture—A Review. *Agronomy for Sustainable Development*, 27(1), 29-43.

Kucey, R.M.N., Janzen, H.H. & Leggett, M.E. 1989. Microbiologically Mediated Increases in Plant-available Phosphorus. In *Advances in Agronomy*, Edited by N.C. Brady. New York: Academic Press. pp. 199-228.

Leong, J. 1986. Siderophores: Their Biochemistry and Possible Role in the Biocontrol of Plant Pathogens. Annu. Rev. Phytopathol. 24: 187-209.

Omar, S.A. (1998) The Role of Rock-phosphate-solubilizing Fungi and Vesicular-arbusular-mycorrhiza (VAM) in Growth of Wheat Plants Fertilized with Rock Phosphate. *World Journal of Microbiology and Biotechnology*, 14(2), 211-218.

Pundarikakshudu, R. (1989) Studies of the Phosphate Dynamics in a Vertisol in Relation to the Yield and Nutrient Uptake of Rainfed Cotton. *Experimental Agriculture*, 25(4), 39-45.

Smith, S.E. & Read, D.J. 1997. *Mycorrhizal Symbiosis*. Academic Press. San Diego.

State Trends of the Environment in State of Environment Report India, 2009 Environmental Information System (ENVIS) Ministry of Environment & Forests Government of India, 10-19.

Zahran, Hamdi Hussein, 1999. *Rhizobium*-legume Symbiosis and Nitrogen Fixation Under Severe Conditions and in An Arid Climate. Microbiology and Molecular Biology Reviews, 63 (4), 968-989.

13

Biocontrol of Soil Borne Plant Pathogens and Boosting Plant Growth Using Microbial Fungicide *Trichoderma*

K.K. Sharma, *India*
U.S. Singh, *India*
Pankaj Sharma, *India*
K.K. Mishra, *India*
Ashish Kumar, *India*
Lalan Sharma, *India*

ABSTRACT

Species of Trichoderma are being widely used in agriculture as agent of plant disease control and as a biofertilizer for boosting plant growth. Morphologically and molecularly characterized thirty rhizospheric isolates of Trichoderma (T. harzianum and T. virens) were evaluated for their antagonistic potential against Rhizoctonia, Sclerotium and Fusarium via dual culture technique as well as sclerotial parasitization. The plant growth promotion activity on rice, tomato and mustard was evaluated via pot experiment under glass house condition. All the isolates exhibited the antagonistic effect against these phytopathogens under dual culture and hyphal growth of phytopathogens was inhibited at the zone of contact with the hyphae of the antagonist. Isolates PB 2, PB 19 and PB 15 were recorded most aggressive to inhibit hyphal growth of R. solani, S. rolfsii and F. oxysporum respectively. Out of 30 isolates excluding T. virens, 14 isolates showed mycoparasitic ability by coiling around the hyphae of R. solani. Isolate PB 28 was most aggressive sclerotia colonizer for against R. solani and PB 16 against both pathogens. Maximum root length was recorded with isolate PB 15 (80.3%), PB 6 & 30 (60%) and PB 2 & 4 (59.7%) in rice, tomato and mustard respectively.

Maximum shoot length was achieved with Isolate PB 8 (38.5%) in rice whereas PB16 promoted maximum shoot growth in both tomato and mustard by 32.1 per cent and 28.7 per cent.

Key words: Antagonism, growth promotion, *Trichoderma*, sclerotia,

Introduction

The use of microorganisms that antagonize plant pathogens (biological control) is risk-free when it results in enhancement of resident antagonists. Ninety percent of such applications have been carried out with different strains of the *Trichoderma* which have long been recognized as agents for the control of plant disease and for their ability to increase plant growth and development. Due to their antifungal properties many *Trichoderma* spp. like *T. asperellum, T. atroviride, T. harzianum, T. hamatum, T. koningii, T. virens* and *T. viride* are used widely for biocontrol of plant diseases incited by fungal pathogens (Mukhopadhyay and Mukherjee, 1996; Harman and Bjorkmann, 1998; Hjeljord and Tronsmo, 1998; Singh *et al.*, 2006). Besides of different mode of perpetuation, soil borne fungi like *R.solani, S.rolfsii* and *Sclerotinia* spp. (broad host range) have the ability to survive for decades in soil by 'sclerotia' play important role in disease cycle of the pathogen and are highly resistant to degradation by microbial attack or fungicides (Metcalf *et al.* 2004). Dipon and Salinas (1991), Paningbaton (1994), Palomar *et al*, (1999), Cuevas *et al.* (2001), Phillips (1989) and Wu (1991) reported that sclerotia of *Rhizoctonia solani* and *S. rolfsii* are colonized by *Trichoderma,* completely rotted and do not germinate if parasitized by *Trichoderma*. The root colonization by *Trichoderma* increases the growth of roots and of the entire plant, thereby increasing plant productivity. In both academic research and commercial practice, strain T-22 has been well established for its effectivity to increase root development in maize and numerous other crop plants (Harman, 2000; Harman *et. al.*, 2004). The lot of work has been done regarding mycoparasitism and plant growth promotion activity with *Trichoderma,* however, very few studies have actually concentrated on the ability of *Trichoderma* species to colonize and kill pathogen sclerotia of soil borne pathogens. The present study was carried out to know the potential isolates of *Trichoderma* obtained from rhizhospheric soil samples of different crop plants and locations of Uttarakhand for their hyphal (against *Rhizoctonia solani, Sclerotium rolfsii* and *Fusarium oxysporum*) as well as sclerotia parasitization (against *Rhizoctonia solani* and *Sclerotium rolfsii*) efficacy in addition with boosting plant growth (on rice, tomato and mustard) as a biofungicide and biofertilzer in ecofriendly management of phytopathogens.

Materials and Methods

Experimental materials, three phytopathogens used in the present study were isolated from agricultural fields of district Udham Singh Nagar and thirty *Trichoderma* strains were isolated from rhizospheric soils of different crops and locations of Uttarakhand (Table 13.1). The seeds of paddy (Pant Dhan-4), tomato (Pant t-3) and mustard (Varuna) were obtained from SPC, VRC and oil seed pathology lab- G.B.P.U.A. & T. Pantnagar respectively. All the 30 *Trichoderma* isolates were evaluated for their mycoparastic ability against *Rhizoctonia solani*, *Sclerotium rolfsii* and *Fusarium oxysporum* following dual culture technique (Dennis and Webster, 1971) on poured PDA medium plates. The Petri dishes were incubated at 25 ± 2°C. These plates were regularly observed for growth of antagonist, its ability to colonize the pathogen was recorded at regular intervals. Per cent reduction in hyphal growth of pathogen was calculated by using following formula:

$$I = \frac{(C-T)}{(C)} \times 100$$

(Where, I = Per cent inhibition in mycelial growth, C = Growth of pathogen in control plate, T = Growth of pathogen in dual culture plate). Co-culture studies were done to study the interaction between the *Trichoderma* isolates and the pathogen. After the fungal hyphae of *R. solani* and *Trichoderma* met after 24 to 48 h, a small mat of mycelium was picked up from the zone of interaction between the two and placed on a slide in drop of fluorescent dye. The mycelium was observed under reflected fluorescent microscope (Nikon E1000) and presence or absence of coiling of *Trichoderma* around the host hyphae was recorded. Experiment was carried out in triplicates and the results were expressed as average.

Table 131: Soil Samples Collected from Different Locations

Sl. No.	Sample Code	Crop	Location	Isolate Code
1	2	3	4	5
1.	R1KG	Rice	Kathgodam-Haldwani	PB1
2.	R3H	Rice	Halduchaur-Haldwani	PB2
3.	R2LCb	Rice	Lamachaur-Haldwani	PB3
4.	R1Da	Rice	Kherna-Almora	PB4
5.	R1Db	Rice	Kherna-Almora	PB5
6.	R2Da	Rice	Kherna-Almora	PB6
7.	R2Db	Rice	Kherna-Almora	PB7
8.	SPC1	Rice	SPC-Pantnagar	PB8
9.	SPC2	Rice	SPC-Pantnagar	PB9
10.	1a	Rice	Rudrapur-U.S. Nagar	PB10
11.	1ab	Rice	Rudrapur-U.S. Nagar	PB11

(Contd...)

1	2	3	4	5
12.	1bc	Rice	Rudrapur-U.S. Nagar	PB12
13.	3	Rice	Rudrapur-U.S. Nagar	PB13
14.	5	Rice	Rudrapur-U.S. Nagar	PB14
15.	AM	Apple	Mukteshwar-Almora	PB15
16.	BM	Broccoli	Mukteshwar-Almora	PB16
17.	PM1	Pea	Mukteshwar-Almora	PB17
18.	PM2	Pea	Mukteshwar-Almora	PB18
19.	SM	Strawberry	Mukteshwar-Almora	PB19
20.	WM	Walnut	Mukteshwar-Almora	PB20
21.	RP1	Rice	Premnagar-Dehradun	PB21
22.	TR1	Mustard	Premnagar-Dehradun	PB22
23.	A	Maize	Dhalwala-Rishikesh	PB23
24.	B	Maize	Bhaniawala-Dehradun	PB24
25.	B1	Rice	Bhaniawala-Dehradun	PB25
26.	C1	Rice	Mazra-Ranipokhri	PB26
27.	D	Maize	Geetanagar Rishikesh	PB27
28.	D1	Rice	Raipur-Dehradun	PB28
29.	F1	Rice	Raiwala-Hardwar	PB29
30.	G1	Rice	Nagani, Tehri Garhwal	PB30

Isolates were also studied for their ability to parasitize the sclerotia of the pathogens *Rhizoctonia solani* and *Sclerotium rolfsii in-vitro* using a novel methodology. Pre inoculated PDA plates after covered with the growth of *Trichoderma* (incubation at 26±2°C for approximately 72 hrs) were removed from the incubator and 15 g of sterilized sandy soil (pH 6.8, 25% moisture) was then spread evenly over the surface growth of *Trichoderma* in the petri plates. Four sclerotia of the test pathogen (*R. solani, S. rolfsii*) were then placed at equal distance from each other with three replicates for each *Trichoderma* isolate and again incubated at 26±2 °C for 5 days. After 5 days, observations were recorded on the number of sclerotia colonized in each replication and per cent colonization was calculated.

To study growth promotion efficacy surface sterilized seeds of rice, tomato and mustard were treated with powdered formulation of *Trichoderma* isolate (@ 10g/kg seed (cfu=10^9/g powder) except for control. Ten seeds were sown per pot (5 kg capacity) having autoclaved soil (at 20 lbs psi for 2 hrs). Pot were then incubated under continuous illumination and thinned to six plants per pot 5 days after germination. Three replications were maintained for each treatment including control. Pots were irrigated on alternate days with sterilized water. Three plants were uprooted after four weeks of sowing from each pot. Observations were recorded for root and shoot length, fresh and dry weight and compared with control.

Results and Discussion

Antagonistic potential of different isolates of *Trichoderma* against hyphae (mycoparasitism)

Results of the mycoparasitism of *Trichoderma* against *Rhizoctonia*, *Sclerotium* and *Fusarium* are summarized in Tables 13.2 & 13.3 & plate 13.1. All thirty isolates were effectively suppressed the hyphal growth of *R. solani in-vitro* which was ranged from 37.2 per cent to 58.9 per cent. Maximum reduction in hyphal growth was recorded with isolate PB 2 (58.9%) followed by PB3 (53.4%) while isolate PB 17 resulted in minimum reduction of hyphal growth. Only six isolates viz. PB 2, 3, 9, 18, 22 & 23 inhibited more than 50 percent hyphal growth of the pathogen *in-vitro*. Isolates PB 3, 9, 18 & 23; PB 5 & 11; PB 15, 16 & 25; PB 8, 10, 19, 27 & 29; PB 14, 20 & 24; PB 4 & 26; PB6, 12 & 13 were at par. Against *S. rolfsii* reduction in hyphal growth was in the range from 2.0 to 23.5 percent. Maximum reduction in hyphal growth was recorded with isolate PB 19 (23.5%) followed by PB 16 (22.7%) while the isolate PB 12 resulted in only 2.0 per cent reduction in hyphal growth after *in-vitro*. Only eight isolates viz. PB 1, 2, 8, 15, 16, 19, 28 & 30 were found to inhibit more than 20 per cent hyphal growth. Isolates PB 8 & 11; PB 1 & 15; PB 1, 2 & 28; PB 9, 10 & 21; PB 3, 14, 25 & 27; PB 18 & 22 were at par. Percent reduction in hyphal growth of *Fusarium oxysporum* was ranged from 9.0 per cent to 49.6 per cent. Maximum reduction in hyphal growth was recorded with PB 15 (49.6%) followed by PB 23 (36.0 while PB21 resulted in minimum reduction in hyphal growth (9.0%). PB 15 was only one isolate resulted in near about 50 per cent reduction in hyphal growth. Isolates PB 4 & 7; PB 27 & 29; PB 1, 3 & 25; PB 5 & 9; PB 13, 19, 20, 24 & 26; PB 6, 10 & 28; PB 8, 17 & 18 were at par.

Significant difference was observed among the 30 isolates with respect to their antagonistic potential against the three pathogens. The range of inhibition provided by the same set of isolates also varied in different pathogens. Isolate PB 2 inhibited maximum hyphal growth of *Rhizoctonia* & *Sclerotium*. Maximum bioefficacy against *Rhizoctonia* & *Fusarium* was recorded with isolate PB 15 and this isolate also showed maximum bioefficacy against *Sclerotium* & *Fusarium*. Isolate PB-12 which was practically ineffective against *Sclerotium*, exhibited inhibition in range of 34.02-36.62 per cent against the remaining two pathogens. The time taken by the *Trichoderma* isolates to overgrow the pathogens did not vary much among the isolates but their ability to overgrow the various hosts was different. Seven isolates of *T. harzianum* (PB 6, 11, 14, 20, 21, 29 & 30) did not overgrow *S. rolfsii* while three isolate of *T. harzianum* (PB 14, 20 & 30) did not overgrow *Fusarium oxysporum*. Presence or absence of coiling of host hyphae by the different isolates of *Trichoderma* is presented in Table 13.3. Among the 30 isolates of *Trichoderma,* 14 isolates showed mycoparasitic ability by coiling around the hyphae of *R. solani*. None of the *T. virens* isolates showed coiling around *R. solani* hyphae.

Table 13.2: Per cent Reduction in Hyphal Growth of Different Pathogens

Isolate code	Percent Inhibition After 48 Hours			Mean
	Rhizoctonia	*Sclerotium*	*Fusarium*	
PB1	46.02	21.19	29.00	32.07
PB2	58.90	20.68	17.31	32.30
PB3	53.45	15.86	28.97	32.76
PB4	39.62	17.93	31.97	29.84
PB5	48.50	8.29	26.98	27.92
PB6	36.63	19.98	23.98	26.86
PB7	47.01	18.61	32.00	32.54
PB8	47.03	22.08	22.96	30.69
PB9	52.97	16.55	26.98	32.17
PB10	47.01	16.55	24.00	29.19
PB11	48.51	18.61	20.97	29.37
PB12	36.62	2.05	34.02	24.23
PB13	36.63	15.16	26.00	25.93
PB14	44.06	15.86	20.97	26.96
PB15	47.52	21.36	49.97	39.62
PB16	47.52	22.75	17.97	29.41
PB17	32.17	13.11	22.99	22.76
PB18	52.96	14.48	22.99	30.14
PB19	47.03	23.46	25.97	32.15
PB20	44.06	11.72	25.97	27.25
PB21	34.66	16.55	9.00	20.07
PB22	51.98	14.47	19.96	28.80
PB23	52.97	13.79	36.01	34.26
PB24	44.04	12.41	25.97	27.47
PB25	47.52	15.84	28.97	30.78
PB26	39.11	11.72	25.97	25.60
PB27	47.03	15.86	29.98	30.95
PB28	41.07	20.68	23.98	28.57
PB29	47.50	10.35	30.01	29.29
PB30	43.06	22.05	12.00	25.71
Mean	45.44	16.33	25.79	29.19
CD (p = 0.05)	CD1 = 0.52	CD2 = 1.63	CD3 = 2.83	

Table 13.3: Hyphal Interaction of *Trichoderma* with Different Pathogens

Isolate No.	Coiling of *R. solani* Hyphae	*Rhizoctonia solani*		*Sclerotium rolfsii*		*Fusarium*	
		IZ*	Time for OG**	IZ*	Time for OG**	IZ	Time for OG
PBAT-1	+	–	4	+	8	–	6
PBAT-2	+	–	5	+	7	+	6
PBAT-3	–	–	4	+	7	–	5
PBAT-4	–	–	5	+	9	–	7
PBAT-5	+	–	5	+	8	–	6
PBAT-6	–	–	5	+	–	–	5
PBAT-7	+	–	5	+	8	–	6
PBAT-8	+	–	5	+	8	–	6
PBAT-9	+	–	5	+	8	–	7
PBAT-10	–	–	5	+	–	–	7
PBAT-11	–	–	5	+	–	+	7
PBAT-12	–	–	5	+	8	–	7
PBAT-13	–	–	5	+	8	+	6
PBAT-14	+	–	5	+	–	+	-
PBAT-15	+	–	5	+	8	–	7
PBAT-16	–	–	4	+	7	+	6
PBAT-17	+	–	5	+	7	–	6
PBAT-18	+	–	4	+	8	–	6
PBAT-19	+	–	4	+	7	–	5
PBAT-20	–	+	8	–	–	+	–
PBAT-21	–	–	6	–	–	+	7
PBAT-22	+	–	5	+	8	–	6
PBAT-23	–	–	5	+	8	–	4
PBAT-24	+	–	5	+	8	–	5
PBAT-25	+	–	5	+	8	–	4
PBAT-26	–	–	5	+	7	+	5
PBAT-27	–	–	4	+	–	–	4
PBAT-28	–	–	5	–	8	–	4
PBAT-29	–	–	5	+	–	–	4
PBAT-30	–	–	6	+	–	+	–

* IZ=Inhibition Zone, ** OG= Overgrowth

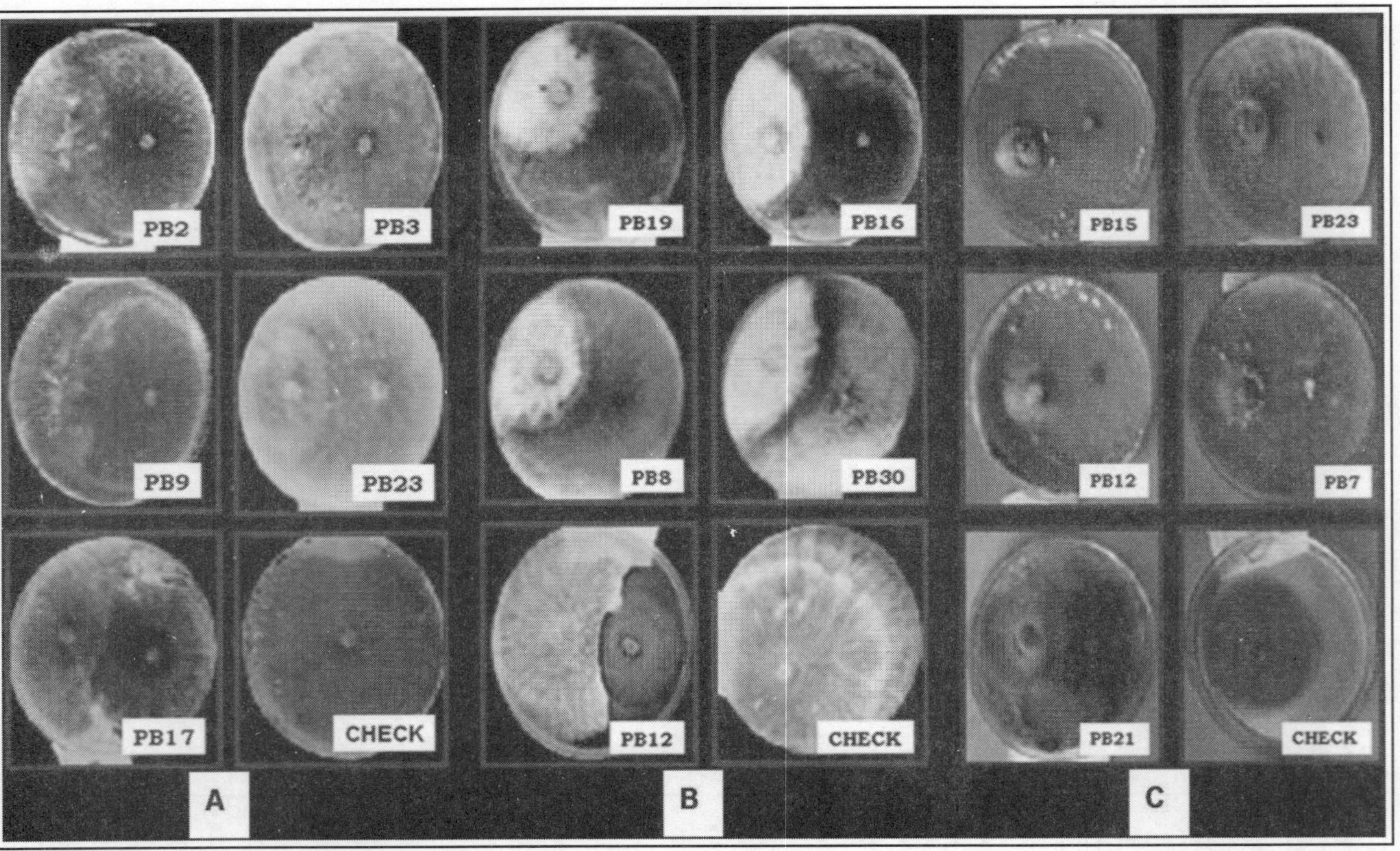

Plate 13.1: Antagonistic Potential of Selected *Trichoderma* Isolates Against (A) *R. solani* (B) *S. rolfsii* (C) *F. oxysporum*

Studies involving antagonistic activity of different isolates of *Trichoderma* against hyphal growth of three fungal pathogens revealed some important observations: *(i)* in general most of the isolates exhibited high (40% and above) antagonistic potential against *R. solani*, medium (20-30%) against *Fusarium oxysporum* and low (10-20%) *S. rolfsii*; *(ii)* two isolates (PB15 and PB 23) consistently exhibited a high level of antagonistic potential (>36%) against *R. solani* and *F. oxysporum*; *(iii)* some isolates varied significantly in respect to antagonistic activity against the 3 pathogens and PB 1, 3, 5, 9, 19, 25, 27 and 29 were observed to exhibit high level of antagonistic potential against *R. solani* (>45%), medium against *F. oxysporum* (25-30%). Similarly isolates PB 2, 16 and 22 showed high antagonistic activity (>45%) against *R. solani* but showed low inhibition activity against *F. oxysporum* (<20%). According to Punja and Utkhede (2003) *Trichoderma* spp. are the most widely studied mycoparasitic fungi. Variability for antagonistic potential among isolates of *Trichoderma* spp. was also observed by Deb and Dutta (1991) as they found a clear inhibition zone between *Trichoderma viride* and *Sclerotium rolfsii* while there was overgrowth of *Trichoderma harzianum* and *Trichoderma koningii* on test pathogen. Similarly Li *et al.* (2001) studied eighteen isolates of *Trichoderma* spp., of the isolates, TR13 showed greatest antagonistic effect against *Rhizoctonia solani*. A lot of work has been done to elaborate Mycoparasitism (Benhamou and Chet, 1993; Benitez, *et al.*, 2004; Howell, 2003; Elad, 2000) shown by *Trichoderma* sp. and its host specificity (Benhamou, *et al.*, 1999) which improved our understanding of Mycoparasitism.

Against Sclerotia (Sclerotial Parasitization)

Twenty one out of 30 isolates of *Trichoderma* parasitized the sclerotia of at least one pathogen. Nineteen isolates colonized the sclerotia of only *R. solani* and seven isolates colonized the sclerotia of only *S. rolfsii* while five isolates (PB 1, 3, 8, 16 and 27) colonized the sclerotia of both pathogens. Nine isolates PB 2, 4, 6, 10, 13, 20, 22, 24 and PB 26 did not colonize the sclerotia of any pathogen (Table 13.4). Sclerotial parasitization ranged from 20-93.3 per cent against *Rhizoctonia solani*. Out of these 19 isolates, 14 isolates exhibited more than 50 per cent colonization and maximum (93.%) and minimum sclerotial (20%) colonization was recorded with isolates PB 16 & 28 3 (Plate 13.2-A & B) and PB 14 respectively against *Rhizoctonia solani*. Against *Sclerotium rolfsii* sclerotial parasitization recorded with seven (PB 1, 3, 8, 11, 16, 27 & 30) isolates ranged from 20-53.3 per cent and only one isolate, PB 16 (Plate 13.2-C & E) resulted in more than 50 per cent colonization and minimum with isolate PB 27 (20%) among the sclerotia colonizing isolates. Out of these 21 sclerotia colonizing isolates, 18 belonged to *T. harzianum* and 3 were *T. virens*. Among the *T harzianum* isolates,. Twelve isolates (PB 5, 7, 9, 12, 14, 15, 17, 18, 19, 21, 25 and 29) of *T. harzianum* were selective for *R. solani* and two isolates (PB 11 and 30) for *S. rolfsii* while four isolates (PB 1, 3, 8 and 16) colonized the sclerotia of both pathogens. Among *T. virens* isolates, PB 23 & 28 showed selectivity for *R. solani* sclerotia while PB 27 colonized the sclerotia of both pathogens. The isolates Isolate PB 28 was observed as a very efficient sclerotia colonizer of *R. solani* (93.3%). PB 16 which was found most aggressive sclerotial colonizer against both the pathogens viz. *R. solani* (93.3%) *S. rolfsii* (53.3%). In their ability to colonize the sclerotia of major pathogens also, the isolates showed considerable variability. In the present investigation *T. harzianum* isolates colonized the sclerotia besides of *T. virens* (general sclerotia colonizer).Two isolates amounting 6.67 per cent of the total isolates parasitized sclerotia by 80 per cent and above and 11 isolates amounting 36.67 per cent of total isolates did not parasitized sclerotia of *R. solani*. Similarly, the isolates differed significantly as far as parasitizing sclerotia of *S. rolfsii* indicating specificity and revealed that only one isolate amounting 3.33 per cent of the total isolates parasitized sclerotia of *S. rolfsii* by above 50 per cent and 23 isolates amounting 76.67 per cent of the total isolates did not parasitized the sclerotia of *S. rolfsii*. The present findings of sclerotial parasitization are accordance with Coley-Smith *et al*. (1974) and Henis *et al*. (1982). Jones and Stewart (2000).

Table 13.4: Sclerotial Colonization by Different *Trichoderma* Isolates

Isolate code	Colonization of Sclerotia (%)		Mean
	R. solani	*S. rolfsii*	
1	2	3	4
PB1	60.0	40.0	40.0
PB2	0	0.0	0.0
PB3	40.0	26.7	31.7
PB4	0	0.0	0.0
PB5	60.0	0.0	0.0
PB6	0	0.0	0.0
PB7	53.3	0.0	0.0
PB8	60.0	33.3	28.3
PB9	66.7	0.0	0.0
PB10	0	0.0	0.0
PB11	0.0	46.7	51.7
PB12	40.0	0.0	0.0
PB13	0.0	0.0	0.0
PB14	20.0	0.0	0.0
PB15	60.0	0.0	0.0

(Contd...)

1	2	3	4
PB16	93.3	53.3	48.3
PB17	60.0	0.0	0.0
PB18	53.3	0.0	0.0
PB19	73.3	0.0	0.0
PB20	0.0	0.0	0.0
PB21	40.0	0.0	0.0
PB22	0.0	0.0	0.0
PB23	53.3	0.0	0.0
PB24	0.0	0.0	0.0
PB25	40.0	0.0	0.0
PB26	0.0	0.0	0.0
PB27	53.3	20.0	20.0
PB28	93.3	0.0	0.0
PB29	60.0	0.0	0.0
PB30	0.0	40.0	40.0
Mean	36.0	8.7	8.7
CD (p = 0.05)	CD1 =1.70	CD 2=6.60	CD 3 =9.33

Plant Growth Promotion

Results of growth promotion on paddy revealed that all isolates except PB 1 resulted in higher root length as compare to check (Table 13.5, Plate 13.3). Maximum root length was recorded with isolate PB 15 (31.5cm) followed by PB 18 (17.2cm) and PB 7 (16.2cm whereas minimum root length was recorded with isolate PB 13 (6.5cm). All the thirty isolates exhibited higher shoot length as compared to check. Isolate PB 8 resulted in maximum shoot length (57.1 cm) followed by PB 7 (56.4cm) and PB 23 (56.1cm) whereas minimum shoot length was recorded with isolate PB 3 & PB 14 (37.3cm). Maximum fresh and dry weight was recorded with isolates PB 18 (10.2g) and PB 23 (2.0393g) respectively. In tomato, significantly higher root length was recorded with twenty three isolates as compare to check (Table 13.6, Plate 13.4). Maximum root length was recorded with isolate PB 6 and 30 (5 cm) followed by PB 11 (4.5cm) and PB 23 (4.2cm) whereas PB 12 resulted in minimum root length (2.1 cm). Maximum shoot length in tomato was recorded with isolate PB 16 (13.4cm) followed by PB 23 (12.9cm) and PB 18 (12.2cm) while Minimum shoot length (9.2cm) was recorded with isolate PB 9. All the thirty isolates except PB 11 and PB 20 resulted in significantly higher fresh and dry weight respectively as compare to check. Maximum fresh weight and dry weight of tomato plants was recorded with isolates PB13 (0.89g) and PB 29 (0.1496g) respectively.

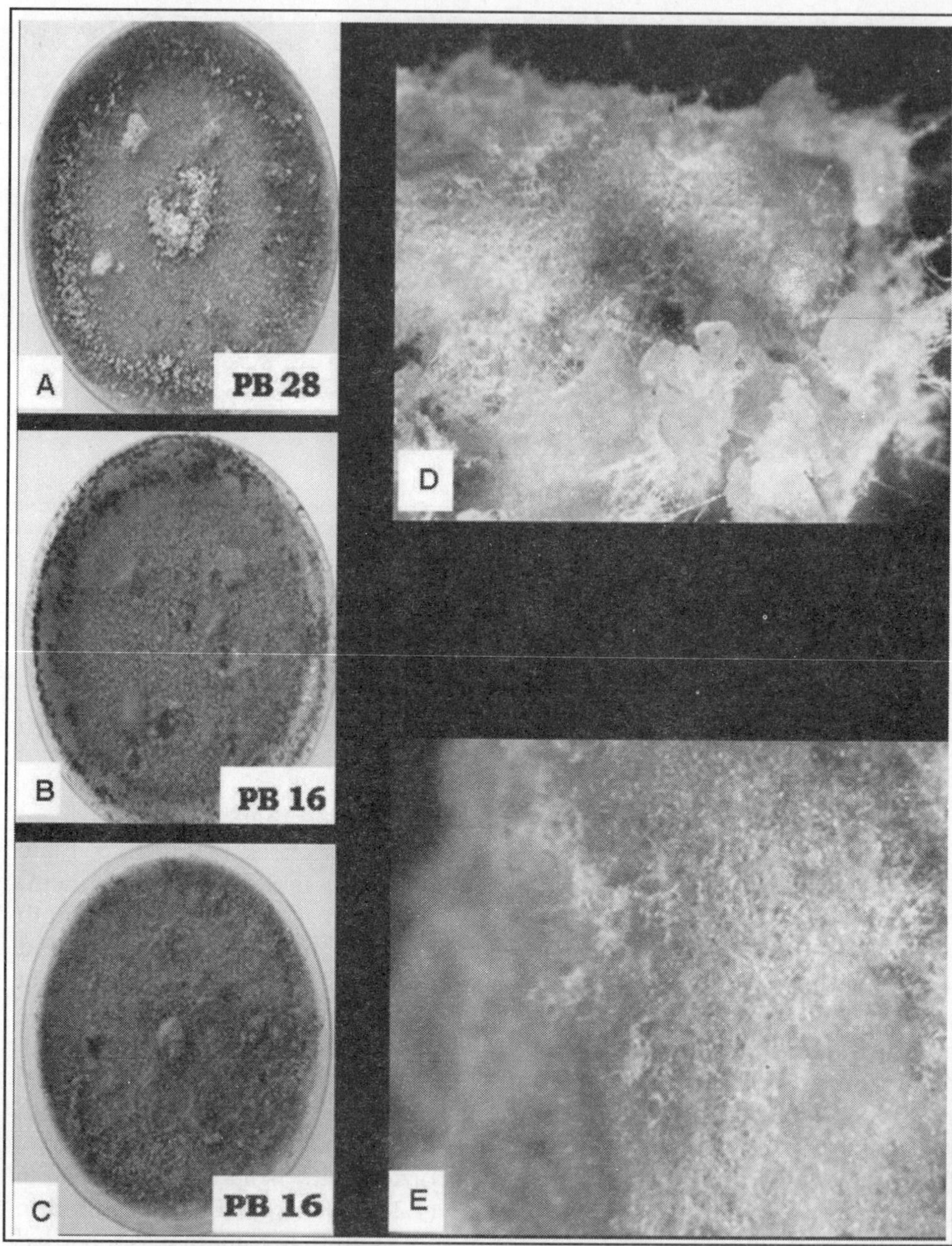

Plate 13.2: Sclerotia of *Rhizoctonia solani* Colonized by *Trichoderma* Isolate PB 28 (A) and PB 16 (B), Sclerotia of *Sclerotium rolfsii* Colonized by *Trichoderma* Isolate PB 16 (C), Stereobinocular Microscopic View of Colonized Sclerotia of *R. solani* by *Trichoderma* Isolates PB 28 (D), Stereobinocular Microscopic View of Colonized Sclerotia of *S. rolfsii* by *Trichoderma* Isolate PB 16(E)

Table 13.5: Growth Promontory Effect of *Trichoderma* Isolates on Rice

Isolate No.	Root Length (cm) 21 DAT	Shoot Length (cm) 21 DAT	Fresh Weight (g) 21 DAT	Dry Weight (g) 21 DAT
PB1	6.1	40.0	1.97	0.4534
PB2	7.5	39.4	1.21	0.2261
PB3	7.4	37.3	1.51	0.3167
PB4	13.7	52.4	3.42	1.6576
PB5	12.7	46.1	6.31	1.0259
PB6	9.2	42.1	2.77	0.9676
PB7	16.2	56.4	9.36	1.5222
PB8	14.2	57.1	3.91	1.6375
PB9	8.2	38.2	3.55	0.6975
PB10	14.1	54.1	5.94	1.3182
PB11	7.2	39.3	1.81	0.3981
PB12	10.1	39.1	5.41	1.0346
PB13	6.5	48.8	0.98	0.1188
PB14	8.8	37.3	1.33	0.1941
PB15	31.5	51.1	3.44	0.6361
PB16	14.1	51.3	6.56	1.2391
PB17	13.3	50.8	3.52	0.6113
PB18	17.2	51.3	10.23	1.8846
PB19	10.0	38.2	2.01	0.3819
PB20	7.1	40.2	1.94	0.3143
PB21	6.7	42.2	3.22	0.5536
PB22	7.4	44.9	3.75	0.7269
PB23	10.6	56.1	9.76	2.0393
PB24	7.8	48.4	3.25	0.5404
PB25	11.3	37.6	4.03	0.6582
PB26	9.4	39.0	1.20	0.2286
PB27	14.0	46.2	5.66	1.0595
PB28	7.1	45.5	2.95	0.4175
PB29	12.1	53.7	6.91	0.9489
PB30	11.9	53.2	5.41	1.3351
Control	6.2	35.1	1.03	0.2195
CD (p = 0.05)	CD =12.05	CD =0.20	CD =0.05	CD =0.0012

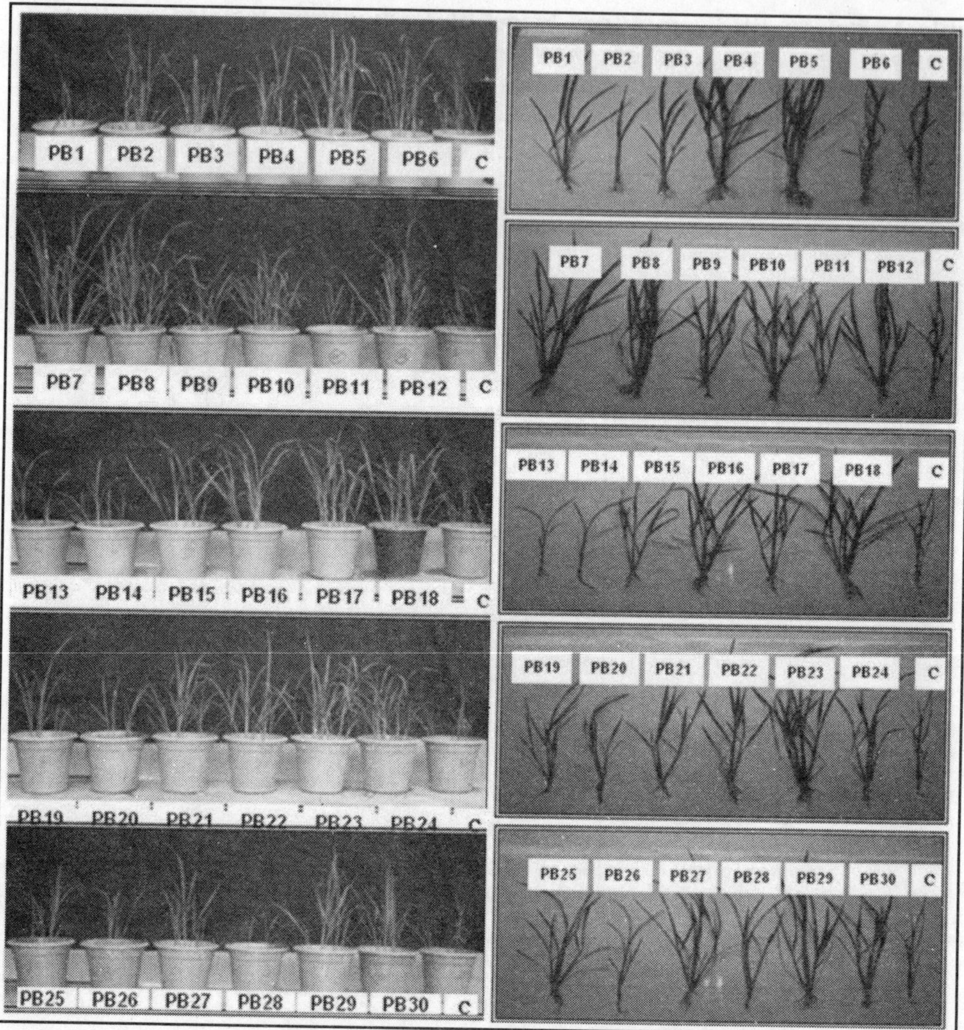

Plate 13.3: **Growth Promontory Effect of *Trichoderma* Isolates on Rice**

All the isolates of *Trichoderma* resulted in significantly higher root length of mustard seedlings except PB 9 & 21 as compare to check while all the thirty isolates resulted in higher shoot length of mustard seedlings, however, differences were statistically non-significant (Table 13.7, Plate 13.5). Maximum root length of mustard seedling was recorded with PB 2 (15.9 cm) followed by PB 20 (15.5 cm) and PB 30 (15.4 cm) whereas maximum shoot length was recorded with isolate PB 16 (19.5 cm) followed by PB 7 (19 cm), PB 29 & 30 (18.6 cm). Maximum fresh (7.65 g) and dry weight (0.6482 g) of mustard seedling was recorded with PB 5.

Table 13.6: Growth Promontory Effect of *Trichoderma* Isolates on Tomato

Isolate No.	Root Length (cm) 21 DAS	Shoot Length (cm) 21 DAS	Fresh Weight (g) 21 DAS	Dry Weight (g) 21 DAS
PB1	2.6	10.3	0.3354	0.0536
PB2	3.2	10.0	0.3145	0.0399
PB3	1.7	10.1	0.2976	0.0413
PB4	3.1	9.7	0.3280	0.0419
PB5	3.7	10.0	0.3414	0.0486
PB6	5.0	12.0	0.5310	0.0747
PB7	4.1	9.9	0.3969	0.0446
PB8	2.9	11.5	0.5644	0.0872
PB9	1.9	9.2	0.5052	0.0587
PB10	3.1	10.0	0.2362	0.0385
PB11	4.5	12.0	0.1831	0.0294
PB12	2.1	9.8	0.3877	0.0481
PB13	2.0	9.0	0.2405	0.0437
PB14	2.2	9.9	0.3681	0.0420
PB15	2.2	10.2	0.4353	0.0651
PB16	4.1	13.4	0.5943	0.0708
PB17	2.3	9.9	0.3471	0.0518
PB18	3.5	12.2	0.5733	0.0677
PB19	2.0	10.0	0.2303	0.0334
PB20	2.1	9.1	0.2556	0.0239
PB21	2.3	9.1	0.2514	0.0334
PB22	3.5	10.5	0.3769	0.0528
PB23	4.2	12.9	0.7685	0.0342
PB24	1.9	11.7	0.2762	0.0418
PB25	1.8	9.5	0.2221	0.0325
PB26	2.0	9.6	0.2200	0.0791
PB27	4.1	11.0	0.5304	0.0696
PB28	2.6	10.9	0.5193	0.0448
PB29	3.4	11.9	0.4605	0.1496
PB30	5.0	12.0	0.8953	0.0945
Control	2.0	9.1	0.1840	0.0239
CD (p = 0.05)	CD =0.16	CD =0.15	CD =0.0035	CD =0.0036

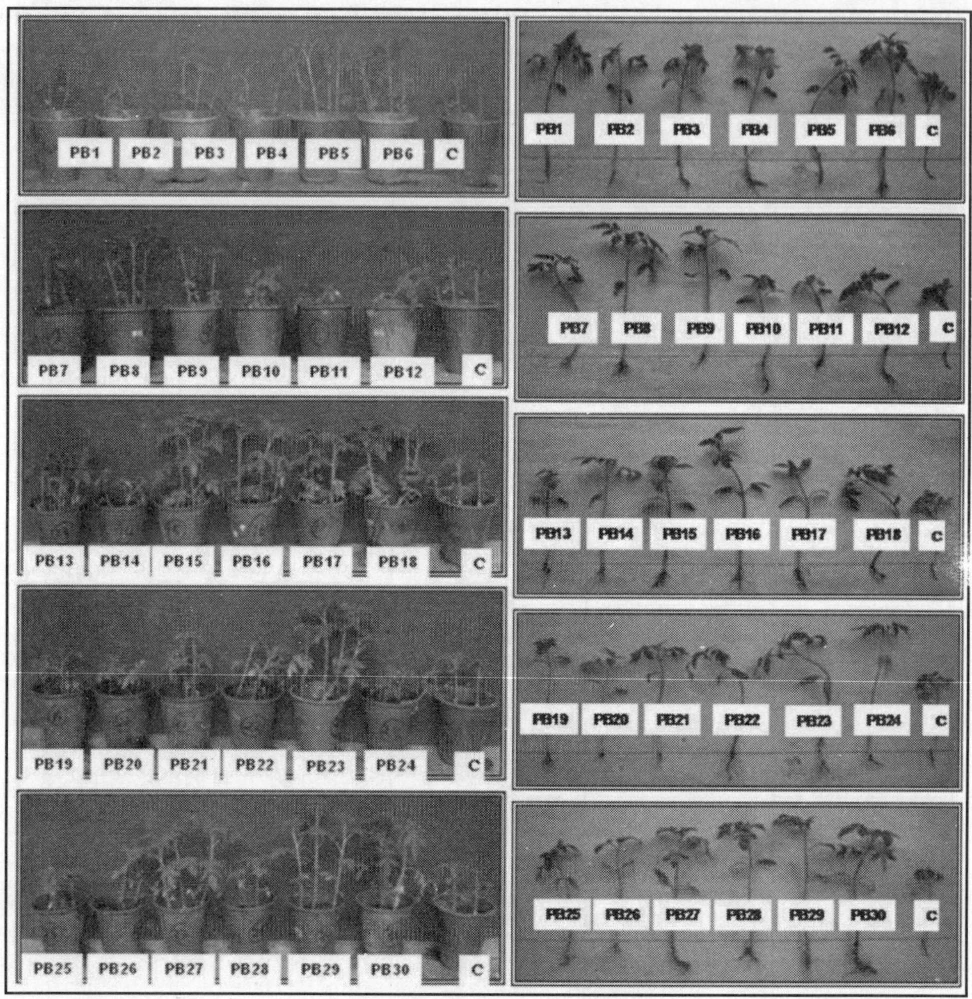

Plate 13.4: **Growth Promotary Effect of *Trichoderma* on Tomato**

Our studies revealed the significance of *Trichoderma* as growth promoter of rice, tomato and mustard. Some of the isolates either were good root growth promoting or shoot growth promoting or both. Glass house experiments revealed the difference in growth promoting effect of *Trichoderma* among the crop which also varied within the isolates. Three isolates (PB 7, 15 and 18) were found highly efficient root growth promoting isolates in rice among tested three crops as they incremented 60-80 per cent root length followed by 40-60 per cent root length increment was achieved by 11 and 13 isolates in tomato and mustard. Out of thirty isolates, 11 isolates incremented 30-40 per cent shoot length in rice. In case of tomato 20-35 per cent increment in shoot length was recorded with nine isolates whereas 11 isolates promoted shoot length by 20-30 per cent in mustard. As far as fresh weight is concerned more than 80 per cent and 60-80 per cent increment in fresh was achieved by 10 isolates in rice and tomato respectively but in case of mustard only 5 isolates incremented maximum fresh weight by 40-60 per cent. More than 80 per cent increment in dry weight was recorded in rice and tomato with 8 and one isolates respectively whereas none of the isolate came in this category in case of mustard. The above results are in accordance with Dubey (1998 & 2002) where he reported the increased seed germination of horse gram & french bean, Yossen *et al.* (2003) reported increased weight and height of lettuce seedlings and Yehia *et al.* (1985) reported increased fresh and dry weight of shoots, roots and nodules of broad bean when seeds treated with *Trichoderma*. The results are also supported with the findings of Chet *et al.* (1997), Barea *et al.* (2002) and Mariola *et al.* (2007) where they reported seeds germinated more synchronously, plant sizes were more homogeneous, and the root system grew more profusely and considerable yield increase in fields and green house conditions when plant seeds were previously treated with spores from *Trichoderma*.

Table 13.7: Growth Promontory Effect of *Trichoderma* Isolates on Mustard

Isolate No.	Root Length (cm) 21 DAS	Shoot Length (cm) 21 DAS	Fresh Weight (g) 21 DAS	Dry Weight (g) 21 DAS
1	2	3	4	5
PB1	7.2	15.3	4.33	0.4270
PB2	15.9	16.1	5.12	0.3421
PB3	7.0	14.2	3.38	0.4412
PB4	15.9	17.9	4.59	0.4940
PB5	10.4	17.4	7.65	0.6482
PB6	12.9	17.2	4.21	0.3449
PB7	9.8	19.0	6.28	0.6161
PB8	8.6	18.1	4.56	0.3846
PB9	5.7	14.4	3.13	0.3745
PB10	9.4	15.4	4.71	0.3222
PB11	13.3	16.7	5.74	0.4940
PB12	10.0	14.6	4.63	0.3739
PB13	7.2	16.0	3.75	0.3249
PB14	8.0	15.9	3.14	0.2796
PB15	12.4	16.3	3.57	0.3291
PB16	12.9	19.5	5.81	0.3368
PB17	14.2	16.8	5.90	0.4766
PE18	13.1	19.0	4.87	0.4405
PB19	8.3	15.4	5.50	0.4529
PB20	15.5	16.1	3.55	0.2858
PB21	6.3	14.5	5.36	0.4931

(Contd...)

1	2	3	4	5
PB22	11.7	17.4	4.48	0.3920
PB23	12.6	16.1	3.47	0.3924
PB24	9.6	17.6	4.99	0.4721
PB25	10.5	14.2	5.03	0.4558
PB26	9.5	15.7	4.63	0.3967
PB27	9.3	16.8	3.68	0.3513
PB28	8.2	17.4	4.45	0.3620
PB29	14.6	18.6	4.58	0.3921
PB30	15.4	18.6	3.79	0.3409
Control	6.4	13.9	3.32	0.3055
CD (p = 0.05)	CD =0.37	CD =8.98	CD =0.08	CD =0.0023

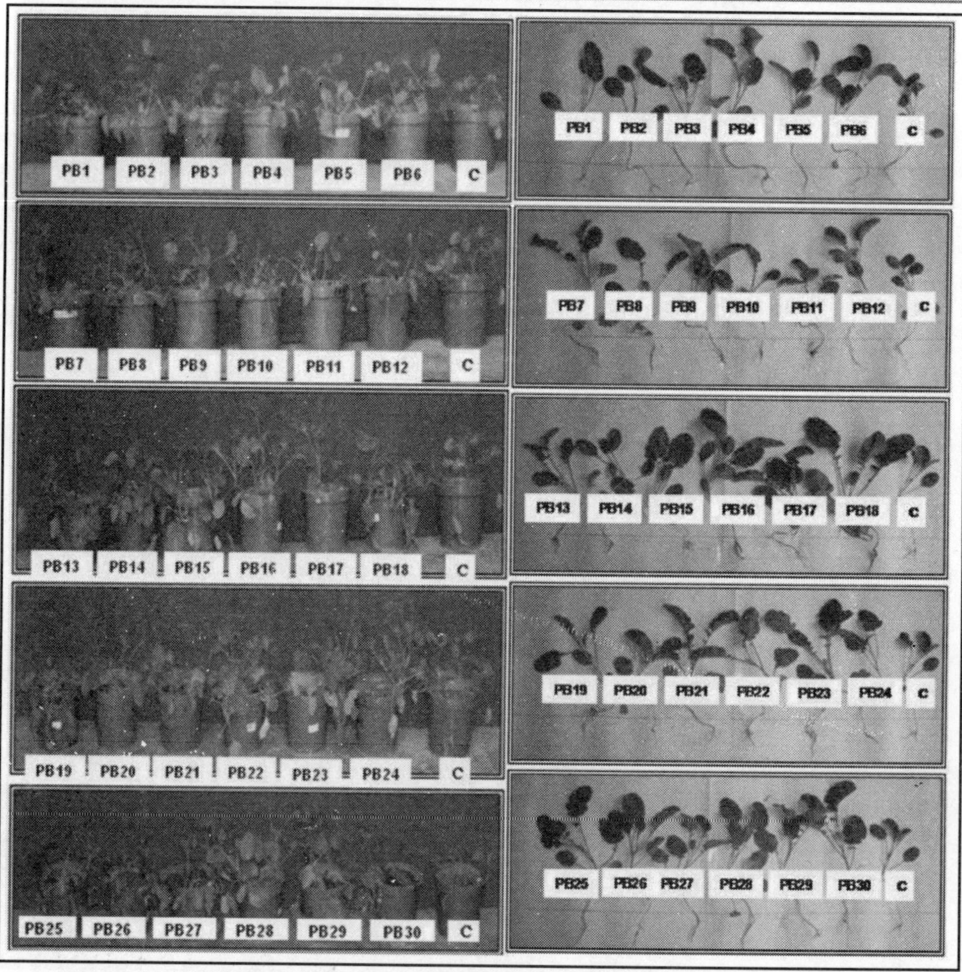

Plate 13.5: **Growth Promotary Effect of *Trichoderma* on Mustard**

REFERENCES

Barea, J.M., Azcón, R. and Azcón-Aguilar, C. (2002). Mycorrhizosphere Interactions to Improve Plant Fitness and Soil Quality. *Ant. Leeuw*. 81: 343-35.

Benhamou, N., Rey, P., Picard, K. and Tirilly, Y. (1999). Ultrastructural and Cytochemical Aspects of the Interaction Between the Mycoparasite *Pythium oligandrum*, and Soil Borne Plant Pathogens, *Phytopathology* 89: 506-517.

Benhamou, N. and Chet, I. (1993). Hyphal Interactions Between *Trichoderma harzianum* and *Rhizoctonia solani*: Ultrastructure and Gold Cytochemistry of the Mycoparasitic Process, *Phytopathology* 83: 1062-1071.

Benitez, T., Rincón, A.M., Limón, M.C. and Codón A.C. (2004). Biocontrol Mechanisms of *Trichoderma* Strains, *Int. Microbiol*. 7: 249-260.

Chet, I. (1979). *Trichoderma*: Application, Mode of Action and Potential of As a Biocontrol Agent of Soil Borne Plant Pathogenic Fungi. *In*: Innovative Approaches to Plant Disease Control (I. Chet, ed.). John Wiley and Sons, New York. pp. 137-160.

Chet I, Inbar J, Hadar I. (1997). Fungal Antagonists Andmycoparasites. In: Wicklow DT, Söderström B (eds) The Mycota IV: Environmental and Microbial Relationships. Springer-Verlag, Berlin, pp: 165-184.

Coley-Smith, J.R., Ghaffar, A. and Javed, Z.U.R. (1974). The Effect of Dry Conditions on Subsequent Leakage and Rotting of Fungal Sclerotia, *Soil Biol. Biochem*., 6: 307-312.

Cuevas, V.C., Sinohin, A.M. and Arro, E.A. Jr. (2001). Efficacy of *Trichoderma* spp. as Biological Control Agent of *Sclerotium rolfsii* Sacc. *Philip. Agr. Sci*., 84 (1): 35-42.

Deb, P.R. and Dutta, B.K. (1991). Studies on Biological Control of Foot Rot Disease of Soybean Caused by *Sclerotium rolfsii* Sacc. *Zeitschrif fuer Pflanzenkrankheiten und Pflanzenschutz*, 98 (5): 539-546.

Dipon, P.N. and Salinas, M. (1991). Evaluation of *Trichoderma* spp. for the Control of Damping-off of Tobacco. *Manila*. p. 1.

Dubey, S.C. (1998). Evaluation of Fungal Antagonists of *Thanatephorus cucumeris* Causing Web Blight of Horsegram. *J. Mycol. Plant Pathol*., 28 (1): 15-17.

Dubey, S.C. (2002). Bioagent Based Integrated Management of Collar Rot of French Bean. *Indian Phytopathol*., 55 (2): 230-231.

Elad, Y. (2000). Biological Control of Foliar Pathogens by means of *Trichoderma harzianum* and Potential Modes of Action, *Crop Prot*. 19: 709-714.

Harman, G.E., Howell, C.R., Viterbo, A., Chet, I. and Lorito, M. (2004). *Trichoderma* Species—Opportunistic, Avirulent Plant Symbionts, *Nat. Rev. Microbiol*. 2: 43-56.

Harman, G.E. (2000). Myths and Dogmas of Biocontrol. Changes in Perceptions Derived from Research on Trichoderma Harzianum T22. *Plant Dis*. 84: 377-393.

Harman, G.E. and Bjorkmann, T. (1998). Potential and Existing Uses of *Trichoderma* and *Gliocladium* for Plant Disease Control and Plant Hrowth Enhancement. Edited by G. E. Harman and C. P. Kubicek. London: Taylor and Francis. *Trichoderma* and *Gliocladium*, Vol. 2. Enzymes, Biological Control and Commercial Applications, pp. 229-265.

Henis, Y., Adams, P.B., Papavizas, G.C. and J.A. Lewis (1982). Penetration of Sclerotia of *Sclerotium rolfsii* by *Trichoderma* spp., *Phytophathology*, 72: 70-74.

Hjeljord, L. and Tronsmo, A. (1998). *Trichoderma* and *Gliocladium* in Biological Control: An Overview. In *Trichoderma* and *Gliocladium*, Vol. 2. Enzymes, Biological Control and Commercial Applications, Edited by G. E. Harman and C. P. Kubicek. London: Taylor and Francis. pp: 129-155.

Howell, C.R. (2003). Mechanisms Employed by *Trichoderma* Species in the Biological Control of Plant Diseases: The History and Evolution of Current Concepts. Plant Disease 87: 4-10.

Hyakumachi, M., Kubota, M. and Arora, D.K. (2004). Fungi As Plant Growth Promoter and Disease Suppressor. *Fungal Biotech. Agri. Food Env. Appli.*, New York, Marcel Dekker, pp. 101-110.

Kleifeld and Chet. I. (1992). *Trichoderma harzianum* Interaction with Plants and Effect on Growth Response. *Plant and Soil*, 144: 267-272.

Li, M.Y., Wang, G., Li, T.F. and Liu, K. (2001). Selection for *Trichoderma* Isolates Applicable in Biocontrol of Major Fungal Diseases of Tobacco. *J. Southwest Agri. Univ.*, 23 (1): 10-12.

Mariola, R. Chacón, Olga Rodríguez-Galán, Tahía Benítez, Sonia Sousa, Manuel Rey, Antonio Llobell and Jesús Delgado-Jarana1. (2007). Microscopic and Transcriptome Analyses of Early Colonization of Tomato Roots by T. Harzianum. International Microbiology, 10: 19-27.

Metcalf, D.A., Dennis, J.J.C. and Wilson, C.R. (2004). Effect of Inoculum Density of *Sclerotium cepivorum* on the Ability of *Trichoderma koningii* to Suppress White Rot of Onion. Plant Disease, 88: 287-291.

Morton, D.J. and Stroube, W.H. (1955). Antagonistic and Stimulating Effects of Soil Micro-organism on Sclerotium. *Phytopathology*, 45: 417-420.

Mukhopadhyay, A.N. and Mukherjee, P.K. (1996). Fungi as Fungicides. *Int J Trop Plant Dis*. 14: 1-17.

Ousley, M.A., Lynch, J.M. and Whipps, J.M. (1993). Effect of *Trichoderma* on Plant Growth: A Balance Between Inhibition and Growth Promotion. *Microb. Ecol.*, 26 (3): 277-285.

Palomar, M.K., Salamat, E., Palermo, V. and Edwise, G. **(1999).** *In vivo*, Screening of Promising Antagonists Against Postharvest Pathogen of Sweetpotato and Yam. *Philip. Phytopathol.*, 33 (2): 138.

Paningbatan, R.A. (1994). *Trichoderma* sp. for the Biocontrol of Stem Rot of Sweet Pepper. *In*: Integrated Pest Management: Learning from Experience. College, Laguna, Philippines. PMCP, p. 68.

Phillips, A.J.L. **(1989).** Fungi Associated with Sclerotia of *Sclerotinia sclerotiorum* in South Africa and Their Effects on the Pathogen. *Phytophylactica*, 21 (2): 135-139.

Punja, Z.K. and Utkhede, R.S. (2003). Using Fungi and Yeasts to Manage Vegetable Crop Diseases. Trends Biotechnol., 21: 400-407.

Singh, U.S., Zaidi, N.W., Joshi, D., Varshney, S. and Khan, T. (2006). Current Status of *Trichoderma* As a Biocontrol Agent. In: Ramanujam B, Rabindra RJ (eds) Current Status of Biological Control of Plant Diseases using Antagonistic Organisms in India, Project Directorate of Biological Control, Bangalore.

Whipps, J.M. and Lumsden, R.D. (2001). Commercial Use of Fungi as Plant Disease Biological Control Agents: Status and Prospects, in: T. Butt, C. Jackson, N. Magan (Eds.), Fungal Biocontrol Agents: Progress, Problems and Potential, CABI Publishing, Wallingford, 2001, pp. 9-22.

Wu, T., Kabir, Z. and Koide, R.T. (2005). A Possible Role for Saprotrophic Microfungi in the N Nutrition of Ectomycorrhizal *Pinus resinosa, Soil Biol. Biochem.* 37: 965-975.

Wu, W.S. (1991). Control of Sclerotinia Rot of Sunflower and *chrysanthemum*. *Plant Prot. Bulle. Taipei*, 33 (1): 45-55.

Yehia, A.H., El-Hassan, S.A. and El-Bahadli, A.H. (1985). Biological Seed Treatment to Control *Fusarium* Root Rot of Broad Bean. *Egyptian J. Phytopathol.*, 14: 59-66.

Yossen, V., Vargas, G.S., del-P-Diaz, M. and Olmos, C. (2003). Composts and *Trichoderma harzianum* as Suppressors of *Rhizoctonia solani* and Promoters of Lettuce Growth. *Manejo Integrado de Plagas y Agroecologia*, 68: 19-25.

Index

P

R

S